Building Data Integration Solutions

Unifying Data for Enhanced Decision Making

Jay Borthen

O'REILLY®

Building Data Integration Solutions

by Jay Borthen

Published by O'Reilly Media, Inc., 141 Stony Circle, Suite 195, Santa Rosa, CA 95401.

O'Reilly books may be purchased for educational, business, or sales promotional use. Online editions are also available for most titles (*https://oreilly.com*). For more information, contact our corporate/institutional sales department: 800-998-9938 or *corporate@oreilly.com*.

Acquisitions Editor: Andy Kwan	**Indexer:** nSight, Inc.
Development Editor: Jeff Bleiel	**Cover Designer:** Susan Brown
Production Editor: Elizabeth Faerm	**Cover Illustrator:** José Marzan Jr.
Copyeditor: Vanessa Moore	**Interior Designer:** David Futato
Proofreader: Arthur Johnson	**Interior Illustrator:** Kate Dullea

November 2025:   First Edition

Revision History for the First Edition

2025-10-28:   First Release

See *http://oreilly.com/catalog/errata.csp?isbn=9781098173067* for release details.

978-1-098-17306-7

[LSI]

Table of Contents

Part II. Tools, Technologies, and Frameworks

Preface

This book presents a pragmatic, hands-on approach to data integration by first baselining the reader's knowledge with important terminology and concepts and eventually walking through the building of a plausible, real-life data integration solution, step by step. For the hands-on parts in the later chapters of the book, familiarity with Linux,[1] Python, Structured Query Language (SQL), and Amazon Web Services (AWS) would be beneficial, but I'll attempt to explain what takes place at each step in simple terms.

The combinations of tools and techniques that are described in this book are almost surely not "the best" for your specific use case. There are far too many variables and trade-offs to consider for an adequate presentation of all possible solutions. However, many of the technologies that are discussed are considered dominant players by some of the leading advisory and consultancy firms and have a significant presence within the US federal government. In this book, I prioritize the tools and technologies that meet current government mandates such as HIPAA and FedRAMP (see "Security and Compliance" on page 85 for a more in-depth discussion regarding government regulations).

It should be noted that containerization is not utilized in the hands-on sections of this book. However, it may be prudent for the practitioner to use containers (e.g., Docker (*https://docker.com*)) and perhaps even a distributed container management tool like Kubernetes for large, enterprise data integration initiatives.

Also, while the book focuses on aspects directly related to data integration, because of inherent complexity within data engineering and data management, topic tangents and parallel subject matter discussions are inevitable. There are also many concepts included in the book that live within the blurred lines between data engineering and software development.

---

1 O'Reilly Media has some great resources to explore Linux, particularly its *Linux Sandbox.*

Further, my intention is not to delve too deeply into any single concept but rather to brush the surface enough to understand where the concepts are applicable within a data integration solution and to assist with the hands-on integrations in later chapters.

Overview of the Book Structure and What Readers Can Expect to Learn

In the first part of the book, readers will explore the foundational principles of data integration and its role in modern data management. I explain the importance of data integration methods in unifying and organizing diverse data sources to ensure data accuracy, accessibility, and consistency. Part I, "Foundations of Data Integration", focuses on key concepts and processes involved in data integration and its connection to related subjects such as data analytics and data governance.

It also covers essential topics and terminology helpful for data engineers including data properties, structures, types, and encodings. It emphasizes the classification of data into structured, unstructured, and semistructured categories and the significance of understanding these classifications for effective implementation of data integration solutions.

The second half of Part I delves into the challenges and limitations of data integration, particularly the difficulties in incorporating data from legacy systems and adapting to diverse, rapidly changing data sources. It also examines organizational issues, including the impact of policies and data governance and management practices.

Part I lays a solid foundation for understanding the critical aspects of data integration, setting the stage for exploring tools, technologies, and practical implementation strategies in subsequent parts of the book.

Part II, "Tools, Technologies, and Frameworks", gives an in-depth examination of various data integration software tools and technologies. It starts by describing many of the options available in regards to the different tools and technologies, such as open source versus commercial tools.

There is also a hardware aspect to data integration, but that is not the focus of this book.

Open source solutions are praised for being cost-effective, flexible, and supported by active communities, making them ideal for organizations with skilled technical staff and limited budgets. Conversely, commercial tools are noted for their user-friendliness, dedicated customer support, and advanced features such as low-code and no-code interfaces, as well as typically strong security measures, which help minimize operational risks and ensure compliance.

The section then delves into the growing popularity of low-code and no-code platforms. These platforms enable nontechnical users to perform data integration tasks through intuitive interfaces and prebuilt connectors, significantly speeding up integration processes and reducing reliance on technical teams. The book outlines how these platforms can democratize data access and simplify complex data work-flows, making data integration more accessible to a broader range of users within organizations.

A detailed comparison of cloud and on-premises integration solutions follows, discussing their respective advantages and drawbacks. Cloud integration solutions are recognized for their scalability, flexibility, and cost-effectiveness, but they also raise concerns regarding data security, compliance, and vendor lock-in. On-premises solutions, while offering enhanced control and compliance, are criticized for being less scalable and more expensive to maintain.

The book further explores the capabilities of major cloud service providers such as AWS and Microsoft Azure. It evaluates their unique strengths and ideal use cases, such as the extensive ecosystem and global reach offered by AWS, and Azure's seam-less integration with Microsoft products. This comparative analysis helps readers understand which cloud services might best suit their specific data integration needs.

Part II provides readers with a balanced understanding of various data integration tools and technologies, along with their benefits, limitations, and best use cases. By exploring both traditional and modern solutions, the section equips readers with the knowledge to make informed decisions on the right tools and platforms for their organizational requirements. This knowledge is invaluable for those looking to navigate the complex landscape of data integration technology.

Part III, "Introducing the Example Data Integration Solution", presents a comprehensive guide to setting up a data integration solution, providing a practical example infrastructure that highlights key components, configurations, and tools necessary for seamless dataflow across various systems. It starts with the foundational elements of infrastructure setup for data integration projects, including database selection, cloud services, and network considerations, emphasizing scalability and maintainability. The section introduces publicly available datasets from the International Energy Agency (IEA) and the US Energy Information Administration (EIA). These datasets are used in the example integration solution.

The architecture employs an Amazon EC2 instance, hosting Qlik Replicate, and showcases a hybrid deployment using both Linux and Windows Server environments. Security is mentioned as an essential aspect, though the primary focus remains on the technical components and configuration of data integration technologies. The part delves into practical implementation with AWS, Confluent Kafka, Databricks, and Qlik. It provides step-by-step instructions for setting up Qlik tools alongside an integration of Databricks for unified data analytics. Confluent Kafka is introduced for streamlining event-driven data pipelines, with examples of configurations on Ubuntu Linux.

This part serves as a practical resource for setting up a robust, scalable data integration infrastructure, enabling organizations to unify and optimize their data pipelines for better analytics and decision making. It balances technical detail with actionable insights, offering a blueprint adaptable to various organizational needs.

Conventions Used in This Book

The following typographical conventions are used in this book:

Italic
> Indicates new terms, URLs, email addresses, filenames, and file extensions.

`Constant width`
> Used for program listings, as well as within paragraphs to refer to program elements such as variable or function names, databases, data types, environment variables, statements, and keywords.

`Constant width bold`
> Shows commands or other text that should be typed literally by the user.

`Constant width italic`
> Shows text that should be replaced with user-supplied values or by values determined by context.

> This element signifies a tip or suggestion.

> This element signifies a general note.

> This element indicates a warning or caution.

Using Code Examples

Supplemental material (code examples, exercises, etc.) is available for download at *https://github.com/jlb226/building_data_integration_solutions*.

If you have a technical question or a problem using the code examples, please send email to *support@oreilly.com*.

This book is here to help you get your job done. In general, if example code is offered with this book, you may use it in your programs and documentation. You do not need to contact us for permission unless you're reproducing a significant portion of the code. For example, writing a program that uses several chunks of code from this book does not require permission. Selling or distributing examples from O'Reilly books does require permission. Answering a question by citing this book and quoting example code does not require permission. Incorporating a significant amount of example code from this book into your product's documentation does require permission.

We appreciate, but generally do not require, attribution. An attribution usually includes the title, author, publisher, and ISBN. For example: "*Building Data Integration Solutions* by Jay Borthen (O'Reilly). Copyright 2026 Jay Borthen, 978-1-098-17306-7."

If you feel your use of code examples falls outside fair use or the permission given above, feel free to contact us at *permissions@oreilly.com*.

O'Reilly Online Learning

O'REILLY®   For more than 40 years, *O'Reilly Media* has provided technology and business training, knowledge, and insight to help companies succeed.

Our unique network of experts and innovators share their knowledge and expertise through books, articles, and our online learning platform. O'Reilly's online learning platform gives you on-demand access to live training courses, in-depth learning paths, interactive coding environments, and a vast collection of text and video from O'Reilly and 200+ other publishers. For more information, visit *https://oreilly.com*.

How to Contact Us

Please address comments and questions concerning this book to the publisher:

O'Reilly Media, Inc.
141 Stony Circle, Suite 195
Santa Rosa, CA 95401
800-889-8969 (in the United States or Canada)
707-827-7019 (international or local)
707-829-0104 (fax)
support@oreilly.com
https://oreilly.com/about/contact.html

We have a web page for this book, where we list errata and any additional information. You can access this page at *https://oreil.ly/building-data-integration-solutions*.

For news and information about our books and courses, visit *https://oreilly.com*.

Find us on LinkedIn: *https://linkedin.com/company/oreilly-media*.

Watch us on YouTube: *https://youtube.com/oreillymedia*.

Acknowledgments

I owe a special debt to Sean Applegate, Bharath Chandra Memmadisetty, Aarohi Tripathi, and Mark Zalubus for their clear-eyed reviews, technical depth, and practical advice.

To Cara, my wife—thank you for the patience and perspective that made the writing possible.

My sincere thanks to the O'Reilly editorial and production team for their guidance from concept to copyedit. Your clarity, rigor, and craftsmanship raised the quality of this book at every step.

## PART I

Foundations of Data Integration

Chapter 1, "Introduction to Data Integration", delves into the fundamentals of data integration, exploring its critical functions within the data life cycle and its alignment with broader organizational goals. By unifying and organizing diverse data sources, data integration ensures that data is accurate, accessible, and consistent, ultimately enhancing decision-making processes. The chapter outlines key concepts and processes involved in data integration and illustrates its importance in transforming raw data into valuable insights and driving business efficiency. Additionally, it provides an overview of related fields, such as data analytics and data governance, and emphasizes the interconnected nature of these disciplines within a robust data management framework.

Chapter 2, "Key Concepts in Data Integration", introduces key concepts of data integration that form the foundation of effective data management strategies and encompasses a variety of terms and practices essential for data engineers. The chapter highlights the importance of understanding and correctly applying terms related to data properties, data structures, data types, and encodings. The chapter covers the classification of data into structured, unstructured, and semistructured categories and explains their unique characteristics and relevance in the data ecosystem. Additionally, Chapter 2 covers data file formats, metadata, and the context of data usage and how these elements play critical roles in data integration processes. Establishing a clear understanding of these fundamental concepts will help data engineers better architect and implement durable data integration solutions tailored to organizational needs.

Chapter 3, "Data Integration Challenges", addresses the common obstacles and limitations that organizations face when attempting to integrate data from multiple sources. We will examine technical, data, and organizational challenges and provide insights into why data integration can be a complex and resource-intensive process. The chapter explores strategies for overcoming these barriers to ensure successful data integration projects.

The chapter also addresses the technical complexities associated with various data formats, protocols, and standards alongside the challenges posed by ensuring data quality, consistency, and scalability. By identifying and understanding these challenges, organizations can better navigate the intricate landscape of data integration to maximize the value derived from their data assets.

Chapter 4, "Models, Architectures, Methods, and Patterns", aims to clarify data integration concepts by exploring foundational elements including models, architectures, methods, and patterns. Each of these components plays a crucial role in shaping how data flows between systems and how efficiency, consistency, and scalability are maintained.

Together, the chapters in Part I of this book provide a solid foundation for understanding important aspects of data integration and set the stage for exploring the tools, technologies, frameworks, and practical implementation strategies covered in Parts II and III.

## CHAPTER 1

Introduction to Data Integration

This chapter provides an overview of what data integration actually is, what role it plays in the overall data life cycle, and how it relates to an organization's data strategy. It aims to equip you with the basic understanding necessary to effectively implement a data integration solution and align the solution to broader organizational objectives.

Data Integration and Data Management

Data life cycle management encompasses all the disciplines related to obtaining and maintaining value from data. Effective data management ensures that data is accurate, available, and accessible and is a primary component in the decision-making process. You may have heard the term *DataOps*, which is a style of data management that focuses on collaboration between stakeholders throughout the data life cycle, much the same way that *DevOps* is centered around collaboration between software development teams. DataOps emphasizes automation, quality, and continuous delivery in data processes, similar to DevOps in software development.

I prefer to partition the management of the data life cycle into three segments. As you can see in Figure 1-1, the segments include *data integration*, *data analytics*, and *data governance*. Each has distinct objectives and consists of lower-level processes that combine to form data pipelines.[1] The lower-level processes sometime live in the gray area between the components.

Data analytics and data governance are no less important than data integration is to the overall data life cycle. Let's begin with brief descriptions of data analytics and data governance.

---

1 See "Pipelines" on page 42 for a discussion on data pipelines.

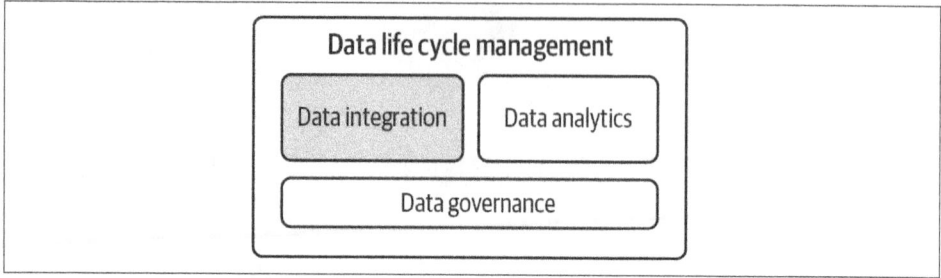

Figure 1-1. Components of data life cycle management

Data analytics consists of all the tasks you would expect a typical data scientist or data analyst to perform, from creating data visualizations[2] to developing *machine learning* (ML) models. You could consider analytics to be the frontend of data management. It is the component of data life cycle management that is typically most familiar to the end users and decision makers.

> Like a web browser is to the internet, data analytics (and, in particular, data visualization) is to data life cycle management.

Data governance, on the other hand, refers to the policies, standards, and practices that ensure data is handled properly throughout the data life cycle while simultaneously aligning with organizational objectives and risk management strategies. It involves all activities related to enforcing data integrity, privacy, compliance with regulations, and maintaining authority and control over the management of data assets. For example, the US Department of Defense (DOD) published seven data governance goals they must achieve to become data-centric. The data must be visible, accessible, understandable, linked, trustworthy, interoperable, and secure. These goals are collectively known as VAULTIS, and, although they do not speak to specific laws or regulations, they are designed to ensure that the data is suitable to literally, and figuratively, represent the DOD.

> In the parlance of data, *life cycle* does not necessarily imply a cycle.

---

2 I generally consider data visualization and business intelligence (BI) to be elements within data analytics, but I sometimes see them grouped with components of data integration.

Defining Data Integration

Digital data exists in the *cloud* (i.e., in remote datacenters), in on-premises computing environments, in external hard drives, on thumb drives, and in edge devices that can include active and passive sensors, smart phones, and other systems that interface with the real world. Data integration is the process of unifying and organizing the data and its infrastructure. It involves activities related to discovering, profiling, collecting, consolidating, combining, cleaning, sorting, moving, migrating, replicating, masking, filtering, mapping, syncing, and automating data.[3]

Data integration solutions are typically created using a combination of software tools that often include data quality management capabilities and data governance features. The best integration tools will also automate many of the processes involved and will help identify and connect data sources, map data elements between source and target systems, and implement transformation rules to ensure consistency and accuracy. We'll go over many of the specific tools in Part II.

A typical data integration process involves several key steps to ensure data from various sources is accurately and effectively combined for analysis and reporting. We'll cover many of these steps in detail in later chapters, but it starts with identifying the data sources such as databases, spreadsheets, cloud services, and APIs. Then, data extraction is performed to retrieve data from the identified sources, often using a variety of tools and methods. Data mapping then occurs where *schemas* are created to align data elements from different systems and ensure consistency in field names and structures.

To check for errors and inconsistencies, data validation and quality assurance are carried out. In the data transformation phase, extracted data is converted into a common format via conditioning, enriching, and normalizing. After transformation, the data loading step involves transferring the converted data into a data store, like a data warehouse, or using the data immediately for further processing or analysis, either in batches or in streams.

To keep the integrated data current, data synchronization is employed that periodically, or in near real time, updates a dataset as the data becomes available. Ensuring compliance with regulations and safeguarding data integrity and security then becomes paramount, especially when handling sensitive data.[4]

The discoverability and usability of integrated data is enhanced by metadata that provides contextual information about its source and meaning. These integrated

---

3 This is not an exhaustive list, nor is it a mutually exclusive one.

4 Regulations are discussed in Chapters 3 and 5.

datasets are made available and accessible for analysis using BI and analytics tools to derive insights that inform decision making and business strategies.

In summary, data integration involves a combination of technical processes, tools, and strategies to ensure that the data from potentially diverse sources is harmonized, accurate, and available for meaningful analysis and decision making. We'll delve further into these processes in the coming chapters.

Why Data Integration Is Important

The primary factors that drive the need for data integration solutions include:

- Significant growth of the volume of data
- Increasingly diverse types of data
- Proliferating expectation for near-real-time[5] processing
- Increasing adoption of cloud services
- Changing regulatory environments
- Continuous evolution of technologies

> According to Precedence Research, the "global data integration market size was evaluated at USD 13.6 billion in 2023 and is expected to hit around USD 43.38 billion by 2033, growing at a CAGR of 12.32%." I don't know what percentage of that is related to government procurement, but from what I continue to witness in my current role (as head of Data Science and Engineering), the number of government agency requests (RFIs, RFPs, etc.) related to data integration, as a rough percentage of overall requests, continues to increase. Given the current generative AI craze that relies on huge training sets of data, I would imagine the need for effective data integration solutions won't be going anywhere any time soon.

As Martin Kleppmann states in *Designing Data-Intensive Applications* (O'Reilly), the need for data integration "often only becomes apparent if you zoom out and consider the dataflows across an entire organization." This has been occurring in the federal government as an increasing number of senior officials embrace a data-centric culture. And with the establishment of the Federal CDO Council and the DOD's

---

5 I prefer not to use the term *real time* because nothing is truly *real time* (except, supposedly, quantum entanglement). However, some people equate *near real time* with minutes and *real time* with seconds (or even shorter time intervals). The terms are relative and somewhat subjective and will also depend on the use case to some degree. Regardless, I almost always just use the term *near real time*.

Chief Digital and Artificial Intelligence Office (CDAO), the US government has been making a concerted effort to become data driven.

Some of the main benefits of effective data integration include:

- Increased data utilization
- Better data quality and integrity
- Increased consistency, accuracy, and trust
- Reduced number of data silos and increased collaborative decision making
- Broader and more advanced insights
- Improved management efficiency
- More easily scalable data infrastructure

The Evolution of Data Integration

The primary focus of data integration is, and has been, ensuring that data from various sources can be successfully consolidated and organized to support business/ mission decision-making processes and operational objectives. However, technological advancements and changing data landscapes have created perceptible stints of innovation in the field, and the evolution of data integration practices reflects broader technological, organizational, and methodological shifts in information technology (IT) and data management.

Initially, data integration tasks were performed exclusively via custom code, which was typically time-consuming to create, error-prone, and difficult to scale. They were also largely confined to homogenous environments, where the data sources and data sinks were often from the same vendor or technology stack.

The late 1990s saw the emergence of commercial tools that automated many of the manual processes involved in data integration, significantly reducing the time and complexity of data integration initiatives. The '90s also witnessed the rise of data warehousing, which necessitated robust data integration solutions to aggregate and harmonize data from various operational systems for analytical purposes.

The explosion of web and cloud services in the 2000s introduced a plethora of new kinds of data and data sources, requiring more flexible and scalable data integration solutions. APIs and web services became instrumental in enabling more dynamic and near-real-time data integration across disparate systems and platforms.

The adoption of big-data technologies in the 2010s, such as Hadoop and NoSQL databases, required data integration solutions to scale horizontally and handle huge volumes of data. And the demand for near-real-time analytics led to the development of streaming data integration technologies capable of processing data-in-motion and delivering insights with minimal latency.

More recently, concepts like data fabric and data mesh have gained traction with an emphasis on a more decentralized approach to data integration and data management, where integration logic is embedded within the data ecosystem. We'll discuss this in further detail in Chapter 4, but for now keep in mind that decentralization generally enables more agile and scalable architectures.

Currently, AI and ML capabilities are being incorporated into data integration tools at ludicrous speed, mainly to automate complex integration tasks such as data labeling, data mapping, and transformations; this is significantly improving efficiency and accuracy. Additional flexibility, scalability, and cost-efficiency have also been gained from the shift toward cloud native applications and serverless computing.

Also, as data is increasingly generated and processed at the edge by the Internet of Things (IoT),[6] the importance of edge integration has been significantly increasing. Rather than transmitting large volumes of raw data to central repositories, processing and integration occurs (or at least starts) nearer to the data source, which can help decrease latency downstream and mitigate some data transfer challenges.

Most recently, large language models (LLMs) and agentic AI have dominated the data and technology landscape, and these AI tools have helped accelerate and, in some instances, even fully automate the integration of data. For instance, Amazon Q gives its users the ability to leverage natural language processing (NLP) to create extract, transform, load (ETL) jobs and operations. AI tools can also already accurately discern different data formats and merge them without human intervention. However, there are still some significant downsides to fully confiding in AIs. This will be discussed in Chapter 3.

The evolution of data integration is a testament to the ever-changing landscape of data management and the continuous need for organizations to adapt their data integration strategies to harness the value of their data assets. From manual processes to AI-driven automation, data integration continues to rapidly evolve but will continue to be consistently in demand.

Data Integration Use Cases and Case Studies

Data integration is somewhat inherent in the management of data, and it is utilized across various industries to address numerous business needs and challenges. Some of the most common use cases include:

---

6 IoT devices include sensors, microprocessors, and other things such as smart phones and smart TVs. IoT is generally associated with devices "at the edge."

Data warehouses

Data integration plays a crucial role in constructing data warehouses that serve as centralized data repositories for analytics and reporting.

Data lakes

In big-data environments, data integration methods are used for transferring structured, unstructured, and semistructured data from siloed on-premises platforms into flexible, centralized storage.

BI and reporting

Data integration is crucial for developing comprehensive BI reports and dashboards that provide insights into various business performance aspects, including sales, marketing, finance, and operations.

Processing IoT data

Integrating data from IoT devices enables organizations to monitor and manage connected equipment, analyze sensor data, and often automate processes based on near-real-time information.

To underscore the transformative power of integrating data across administrative boundaries, three brief case studies with which I have either been directly involved or have secondhand knowledge of are included next to round out this chapter.[7]

Healthcare

In healthcare, integrating data from electronic health records (EHRs), laboratory systems, and medical imaging allows providers to leverage robust, consolidated reports of a patient's medical history for more accurate diagnoses and more effective treatment planning. Integrated data systems can alert doctors to potential drug interactions and provide insights into patient trends, all of which enhances care.

The Healthcare Information and Management Systems Society (HIMSS) outlines three types of exchange network architecture used to coordinate the exchange of health information:[8]

Centralized

Patient data is collected and curated in a centralized repository such as a data warehouse or data lake.

Federated

Interconnected but independent databases facilitate data sharing and exchange.

---

7 None of the information in this book is confidential, controlled, or classified.

8 Healthcare Information and Management Systems Society, Inc. (HIMSS). n.d. "Interoperability in Healthcare." Healthcare Information and Management Systems Society, Inc. (HIMSS). Accessed May 2024. *https://www.himss.org/resources/interoperability-healthcare*.

Hybrid

This incorporates variations of both types (i.e., federated and centralized) to harness the advantages of both.

Tax Administration

The US Internal Revenue Service (IRS) integrates data from multiple sources to improve tax compliance and enforcement. By combining data from tax returns, financial institutions, and other federal agencies, the IRS can detect discrepancies and anomalies that help it identify underreported income, fraudulent claims, and other compliance issues, ultimately enhancing revenue collection.

The IRS has also relatively recently moved data from on-premises mainframe data stores to Amazon Web Services (AWS) GovCloud,[9] where the data is organized as a *data mart* in user-friendly formats that make it easier for querying and reporting.

Immigration and Border Control

The US Department of Homeland Security (DHS) utilizes data integration to improve immigration and border control operations. By integrating data from various sources, such as visa applications, passenger manifests, and biometric systems, DHS can better identify potential security threats. This integrated approach helps prevent illegal immigration, enhances national security, and facilitates legitimate travel and trade. The well-organized data integration pipeline that supports processing nonimmigrant visa applications at the US State Department's Bureau of Consular Affairs integrates with Customs and Border Control's (CBP's) National Vetting Center (NVC), which is credited with significantly reducing the backlog of visa applicants waiting for administrative processing.

Conclusion

This chapter provided an introduction to the field of data integration and highlighted its significance within the broader context of data management and organizational data strategy. By delineating the distinctions and connections between data integration, data analytics, and data governance, we have established a foundational understanding of how these components interact to create a cohesive data ecosystem. Data integration, as discussed, is critical for unifying diverse data sources, ensuring data accuracy and consistency, and facilitating near-real-time data processing and decision making.

---

9 Amazon Web Services (AWS) GovCloud is a set of AWS Regions that are physically isolated and have logical network isolation from all other AWS Regions. AWS is covered in more detail in Part II.

The dynamic landscape of data integration continues to evolve with technological advancements and changing data needs. From custom-coded solutions to the current trends of AI-driven automation and cloud native applications, the evolution of data integration reflects the ever-increasing complexity and scale of data management challenges. As vast amounts of data continue to be generated, the need for robust, scalable, and flexible data integration solutions will almost certainly continue to grow.

The subsequent chapters in Part I will delve deeper into the specific nomenclature, concepts, and methodologies used in implementing effective data integration solutions.

## CHAPTER 2

Key Concepts in Data Integration

There are a plethora of labels and terms within the ontology of data integration. Some of the terms are synonymous and are used interchangeably. The majority, however, describe concepts that serve unique purposes within the broader data ecosystem. It is beneficial for data engineers to understand the distinct roles various concepts play and how they relate to one another in order to effectively architect and implement data integration strategies and solutions.

 To precisely communicate these topics necessitates a clear understanding of terms, many of which are often—for whatever reason—intentionally left vague. Therefore, in this chapter, for the more ubiquitous terms and certain terms often burdened with multiple interpretations, I attempt to clarify what I mean when I use them.

The first group of concepts involves characteristics of data and datasets, including data types, structure types, metadata, data orientations, file formats, and character encodings. The second group of concepts relates to static data and storage. The third group includes concepts related to data movement and transformations. Finally, the fourth group includes a handful of data integration management topics.

Data Properties

There are different types of data, various data file formats and format categories, multiple character encodings that computers use to interpret and handle data internally, and a slew of other characteristics about data with which you should at least be familiar. We'll cover these characteristics in the following sections.

Data Types

Data types refer to the kind of data values that are stored and processed such as integers, floating-point numbers, strings, booleans, and others. Different software applications use different sets of data types. For example, some applications designate a specific data type to represent values of dates and times, while other applications recognize dates and times only as strings (i.e., sequences of characters).

As you may infer from that example, data types used in data science do not always map one-to-one with software data types. Boolean variables in raw datasets with values of "True" and "False" or "Yes" and "No" are often represented with zeros and ones within analytics software applications.

Data Structure Types

Data structure types include structured, unstructured, and semistructured. Structured data is highly organized and easily searchable. It adheres to a format and is typically associated with relational databases and data being stored in rows and columns. Structured data is used extensively in business applications, financial records, and other environments where data integrity and consistency are important.

Unstructured data, on the other hand, lacks a predefined organization and is therefore generally more complicated to work with and analyze. Unstructured data includes text files, emails, social media posts, images, videos, and audio recordings. And while unstructured data accounts for a significant portion of existing data, extracting meaningful insights from it commonly requires advanced analytical techniques such as NLP and object recognition algorithms.

Semistructured data contains elements of both structured and unstructured data. While it does not fit neatly into tables, it still possesses organizational properties such as tags and markers that allow the data to be logically separated. The separation typically creates some kind of hierarchy of records and fields. For example, XML and JSON files do not adhere to predefined structures but contain hierarchical elements whose relationships can be inferred.

Also, schemas are used to apply structure to data. Schemas are generally used to define the way the data is organized in a data store, and this helps identify tables, columns, and relationships when the data is accessed and queried. The schema represents the structure of the data and can include relationships, tables, fields, views, sequences, procedures, functions, indexes, directories, queues, and other elements that help define how the data is organized. Schemas can be applied *on-read* or *on-write*—the difference being a query taking seconds and a query potentially taking minutes or hours. However, there are good reasons for both kinds of schemas to exist, and these will be mentioned in a later section.

Finally, data *derived* from unstructured and semistructured data is typically structured. For example, a dataset of social media posts, which would normally be considered unstructured because of the combinatorially intractable use of words and symbols, could provide useful derived data that indicates how many posts each individual has generated or how frequently posts are created. In this sense, whether data is structured or unstructured depends on the data's intended use.

Metadata

Metadata is often described as "data about data." It provides information that helps identify and manage the underlying dataset with which it's associated and will typically include details such as where the data originated, when it was created, and contextual information such as descriptive tags. Metadata supplies the contextual details that make data lineage understandable, and the lineage uses metadata to map the flow of data, showing how it changes over time and through different processes.

The utility of metadata extends beyond integration, but metadata does play a vital role when combining data from disparate sources by helping to ensure data elements are accurately mapped. For instance, metadata can indicate that a particular data field in one system corresponds to an ambiguously named but related field in another system.

In his book *Data Integration Blueprint and Modeling: Techniques for a Scalable and Sustainable Architecture* (IBM Press Pearson), Anthony Giordano notes that there are five different types of metadata: business metadata, structural metadata, navigational metadata, analytical metadata, and operational metadata. Business metadata includes information such as subject area definitions, entity concept definitions, data quality rules, and organizational rules. Structural metadata is the "logical and technical descriptions of the permanent data structures within the Information Management infrastructure" and includes data models and data relationships. Navigational metadata consists of data formats, derived fields, business hierarchies, transformations, and source and target locations. Analytical metadata is the metadata used in reporting. Finally, operational metadata consists of items such as job statistics and data quality check results.

Data Orientation

Data orientation, also called *data representation*, refers to how data is represented in-memory or on-disk. There are two ways in which data can be oriented. The first is *row-oriented* data, where the data is organized by records or data points. This might be considered the more traditional way of working with data files. Writing to the dataset is computationally inexpensive and easy with this orientation. However, read operations can be very inefficient because reading the data requires a row-by-row search. Figure 2-1 shows a simple example of row-oriented data.

ID	Name	Rank	Time-in-grade
001	Alice	02	2.5
002	Bob	03	3.0
003	Cary	03	2.0
004	Dillon	05	3.0

Figure 2-1. Row-oriented data

The other way to orient data in a data file is via columns. *Column-oriented* data (also called *columnar-formatted* data or *field-oriented* data) can speed up storage and querying processes. Columnar storage is common in analytical databases designed for read-heavy workloads, particularly those involving large-scale data analysis. Figure 2-2 shows an example of column-oriented data.

Name	ID		Rank	ID		Time-in-grade	ID
Alice	001		02	001		2.5	001
Bob	002		03	002		3.0	002
Cary	003		03	003		2.0	003
Dillon	004		05	004		3.0	004

Figure 2-2. Column-oriented data

> Data scientists often prefer row-oriented data because it's easier to incorporate into data frames and matrices that are used to perform linear algebra operations. Many data visualization and business intelligence (BI) tools also expect row-oriented data as input.

Encodings

Encodings refer to the way data is converted into bytes for storage or transmission. An encoding maps characters to specific numeric values, ensuring that text can be consistently represented and understood across different systems and platforms. The most common character encodings by far are UTF-8 and ISO-8859-1.

In the context of data analytics, when data is gathered from diverse sources, such as databases, files, and APIs, discrepancies in character encoding can lead to misinterpretation and corruption of data. For instance, a dataset encoded in Western European encoding ISO-8859-1 might be read incorrectly by a system expecting UTF-8, resulting in garbled text or loss of information. This can have significant implications for data quality, as incorrectly interpreted data can lead to erroneous analysis and insights downstream. Figure 2-3 shows an example of lost information because of differing encodings.

```
Data_Status,MSN,StateCode,Year,Data
"2021F","ABICB","AK","1960",0
"2021F","ABICB","AK","1961",0
"2021F","ABICB","AK","1965",0
"2021F","ABICB","AK","1966",0
"2021F","ABICB","CT","2018",0
"2021F","ABICB","CT","2019" OSC
"2021F","ABICB","CT","2020",0
"2021F","ABICB","CT","2021",0
"2021F","ABICB","DC","1960",0
"2021F","ABICB","DE" OSC,1
"2021F","ABICB","DE","1990",2
"2021F","ABICB","DE","2004",109
"2021F","ABICB","FL","1964",0
"2021F","ABICB","FL","1965",0
"2021F","ABICB","FL","1966",0
"2021F","ABICB","FL","1967",0
"2021F","ABICB","GA","1962",0
"2021F","ABICB" DCS,"1963" DCS
"2021F","ABICB","HI","1971",0
"2021F","ABICB","HI","1972",0
"2021F","ABICB","HI","1973",0
"2021F","ABICB","HI","1974",0
"2021F","ABICB","IA","2011",0
"2021F","ABICB","IA","2012",0
"2021F","ABICB","IA","2013",0
```

Figure 2-3. Encoding errors within a CSV file

Proper handling of character encodings is essential for text analytics and NLP. Text data must be accurately encoded to perform tasks such as tokenization, sentiment analysis, and machine translation. Inconsistent or incorrect encodings can hinder these processes, reducing the effectiveness of analytics and potentially introducing bias or errors into the results. Therefore, understanding and managing character encodings is fundamental to maintaining data integrity and ensuring the reliability of analytical outcomes.

File Formats

A *file format* defines the syntax (e.g., permitted values) and semantics (i.e., meaning and interpretation) of the data within a file. It represents a bidirectional mapping of data into a computer's binary memory. Data file formats describe the way in which information is serialized for storage in a digital medium and tell the computer what it should expect to find inside a file. There are many different data formats, but some of the more common formats include CSV/TXT, JSON, XML, Parquet, Avro, ORC, and Protocol Buffers (or "protobuf").

CSV/TXT

Comma-separated values (CSV) files are text files that are delimited with commas. That is, the values that comprise the data points are separated by commas. CSV files are commonly used for storing data, but they were not designed to support massive amounts of data and are therefore highly inefficient when dealing with modern large integrations. For example, CSV files cannot intrinsically handle complex data types like arrays, lists, and maps. Although inefficient for large-scale data, CSVs are still widely used for data exchange because of their simplicity and human readability.

JSON

JavaScript Object Notation (JSON) is a relatively lightweight data interchange format that is easy for humans to read and write and easy for machines to parse and generate. JSON is extensively used to exchange data as text between servers and web applications. The JSON format is a collection of key-value pairs, which consist of data elements that represent associated groups. The keys are required to be strings; the values can be strings, numbers, objects, arrays, booleans, or null. The format is syntactically similar to JavaScript object literals but is language independent and supported by many different programming environments.

Figure 2-4 shows an example of the syntax for JSON. A JSON object gets enclosed in curly braces, keys and values are separated by a colon, and the key-value pairs are separated by commas. An array in JSON is an ordered list of values enclosed in square brackets, and the values are also separated by commas. JSON's simplicity and compatibility make it a popular choice for web APIs, configuration files, and data storage. The main downside to JSON is that it can be CPU-intensive because it supports nested data.

```json
{
    "first_name": "John",
    "last_name": "Smith",
    "is_alive": true,
    "age": 27,
    "address": {
      "street_address": "21 2nd Street",
      "city": "New York",
      "state": "NY",
      "postal_code": "10021-3100"
    },
    "phone_numbers": [
      {
        "type": "home",
        "number": "212 555-1234"
      },
      {
        "type": "office",
        "number": "646 555-4567"
      }
    ],
    "children": [
      "Catherine",
      "Thomas",
      "Trevor"
    ],
    "spouse": null
}
```

Figure 2-4. Example JSON file

Parquet

Apache Parquet is a columnar storage file format designed for efficient data processing and analytics. Developed as part of the Apache Hadoop ecosystem, Parquet is optimized for use with big-data frameworks such as Apache Spark, Apache Drill, and Apache Impala. The format supports highly efficient data compression and encoding schemes that significantly reduce the amount of storage space required and improve read performance. Parquet stores data for each column together, which allows for efficient querying and data retrieval for specific columns without reading the entire row. This is particularly beneficial for analytical workloads and online analytical processing (OLAP). Additionally, Parquet is designed to handle complex nested data structures, which makes it suitable for a wide range of data types and schemas.

Table 2-1, adapted from the Databricks website, illustrates the efficiency of Parquet files relative to CSV files.

Table 2-1. Efficiency comparisons of CSV versus Parquet

Dataset	Size on Amazon S3	Query run time	Data scanned	Cost
Data stored as CSV files	1 TB	236 seconds	1.15 TB	$5.75
Data stored in Apache Parquet format	130 GB	6.78 seconds	2.51 GB	$0.01
Savings for Parquet	87% less	34x faster	99% less data scanned	99.7% cheaper

Avro

Apache Avro was developed within the Apache Hadoop project and was initially released in late 2009 as an open source, row-based, language-neutral, schema-based serialization technique and object container file format. It's often used with Apache Kafka and is generally preferred when serializing data in Hadoop. The Avro format utilizes JSON schemas, but the data within the file is stored in binary format, which makes it efficient and compact. Using schemas to define the structure of the data being encoded also makes it a good choice for data serialization in a distributed environment. The Avro data format is known for its efficiency in both storage and transmission. Unlike other formats that embed the schema with the records, Avro keeps the schema separate, which significantly reduces the overhead for large datasets. This is particularly useful in systems like Hadoop, where the same schema can be reused across multiple data files.

Avro also supports schema evolution, meaning that as data structures change over time, new schemas can be introduced without breaking existing data. Another mechanism called *schema resolution* can handle differences between the writer's and reader's schemas.

Used in tandem with Apache Iceberg, Avro can provide a scalable and flexible solution for managing large, schema-evolving datasets in data lake architectures. Avro handles the row-level data serialization, while Iceberg handles the table-level organization, evolution, and querying features.

Protocol Buffers

According to Google documentation, *Protocol Buffers* are "language-neutral, platform-neutral extensible mechanisms for serializing structured data." Commonly known as "protobuf," it was developed by Google to facilitate efficient communication between computer systems. Protobuf defines data structures and the way data should be serialized using a special language called Interface Definition Language (IDL). The resulting serialized format is compact and can be easily parsed across various programming languages.

Additionally, protobuf is utilized in data storage and transfer scenarios where performance and bandwidth efficiency are crucial. It is often chosen over other formats like JSON or XML due to its smaller size and fast serialization and deserialization speeds. This makes it suitable for mobile applications, near-real-time data processing, and inter-service communication within microservice architectures.

One of the primary use cases for protobuf is in remote procedure calls (RPCs), where it enables efficient and reliable communication between different parts of a distributed system. For instance, protobuf is widely used in gRPC, a high-performance RPC framework developed by Google, which allows developers to define services and their methods using protobuf.

The popular OpenTelemetry project uses gRPC protobuf to efficiently stream application metrics, events, logs, and transaction information for IT teams to centrally analyze their observability platforms, such as Prometheus, Elasticsearch, Dynatrace, Datadog, and others.

ORC

An *optimized row columnar* (ORC) file is a specially designed data storage format where—as the name implies—the data storage format is optimized for column-oriented operations such as filtering and aggregation. ORC includes support for ACID (atomicity, consistency, isolation, durability) transactions and is often the default storage format for Hive data. It's ideal when reads significantly outnumber writes and when compression flexibility is desired.

HDF5

HDF5 is a high-performance storage format that can accommodate large amounts of data from multiple datasets in a single file. HDF5 is appropriate when you need to store large multidimensional arrays and has been used with great success processing convolutional neural networks (CNNs). It is widely used in scientific computing and machine learning for storing large datasets.

Data Context

The *context* of a dataset refers to the conditions or circumstances that affect the interpretation and use of the data. The context helps ensure that conclusions drawn from the data are valid and relevant to the specific situation. For example, three data contexts that are often employed within both government and commercial organizations are transactional, operational, and analytical:

Transactional data

Refers to the data that is generated from day-to-day business dealings such as sales orders, invoices, and payments. This type of data is generally structured and captured in near real time. It holds the essential details of each transaction, and its primary purpose is in supporting the organization's mission. Transactional data is generally stored in relational databases designed for high-speed insertions and updates. These databases are referred to as online transactional processing (OLTP) databases and typically operate in ACID-compliant environments.

Operational data

Overlaps in some respects with transactional data but encompasses a broader range of data used to support daily business operations. This includes not only transactional data but also data related to inventory levels, employee records, and customer interactions. Operational data is essential for managing and optimizing business processes, tends to be more dynamic and transient, and is often used to support short-term decision making and operational control. This data is generally stored in systems optimized for quick access and updates such as operational databases and enterprise resource planning (ERP) systems.[1]

Analytical data

As its name implies, is used for analytics. It is often derived from transactional or operational data but has been transformed and aggregated to support BI efforts. Analytical data is stored in data warehouses or data lakes where it is structured for querying and analysis. These data stores are referred to as OLAP systems.

Data Stores

There are many different kinds of data stores[2] commonly employed in modern data integration solutioning. Data storage options encompass a range of technologies and platforms designed to store and manage data efficiently. These options can be categorized into various types based on factors such as accessibility, scalability, performance, and cost. The simplest and likely the most familiar type of data store is the relational database, which we will touch on next. Newer types of data stores, those that are less often used, and data management systems are then discussed, including NoSQL databases, data warehouses, data lakes, and data lakehouses.

---

1 Oracle. 2022. "FAQs for Autonomous Database." Oracle. Last modified June 10, 2022. *https://www.oracle.com/database/technologies/datawarehouse-bigdata/adb-faqs.html*.

2 In this book, "data stores" refers to the software side of data storage (versus the hardware side).

Types of Storage

Data storage refers to the methods and technologies used to store data, regardless of how that data is organized or accessed. Let's now take a look at the types of storage available: file-based storage, block storage, object storage, in-memory storage, and virtual storage.

File-based storage

There are local filesystems and remote-access filesystems. Local filesystems, such as New Technology File System (NTFS) for Windows and Fourth Extended File System (ext4) for Linux, are designed for single-node environments. They facilitate managing raw data files, configuration files, and logs on individual machines.

Traditional network filesystem protocols like Network File System (NFS) and Server Message Block (SMB) provide remote access storage for files in a hierarchical structure and are suitable for shared storage in networked environments. However, they often lack the scalability and fault-tolerance capabilities that more modern storage systems and cloud-based services offer.

A Distributed File System (DFS) is a remote-access filesystem designed to manage and store data across multiple machines concurrently in a network. Externally, it will typically appear as a single, unified filesystem, but it provides scalable and reliable storage that can handle vast amounts of data and ensure data availability. By replicating data across multiple nodes and enabling parallel data access and processing, a DFS can significantly enhance performance and fault tolerance, even in the event of hardware failures.

In the domain of data integration, a DFS adds substantial value. By providing a robust and scalable storage solution, a DFS facilitates the consolidation of disparate data sources while supporting high throughput and low-latency data access, which is imperative for near-real-time data processing.

Block storage

Block storage, or *block-based storage*, divides files and data into equally sized chunks, or "blocks." Each block has an associated identifier that is unique and stored in a data lookup table. The lookup table is used to find the required blocks when data needs to be retrieved, and the blocks are then reassembled.

The data lookup table is like the key box where valets keep keys for all the cars. When a driver needs their car, the valet grabs the key and looks up where the car is in order to quickly retrieve it. Similarly, block storage uses unique identifiers stored in the data lookup table to rapidly find and retrieve data.[3]

Block storage is fast, and it is often preferred for applications that regularly need to load data from the backend. Common use cases for block storage include:

- Critical system data
- Database storage
- Mission-critical application data
- RAID volumes

Object storage

Not to be confused with object-oriented databases, which are discussed later, *object storage* is a way of storing digital data such as photos, videos, and documents in a highly organized and efficient manner. Unlike traditional filesystems that store data in hierarchical structures or block storage that divides data into fixed-sized chunks, object storage manages and manipulates data as objects. Each object has associated metadata that allows it to be efficiently indexed and quickly located. Object storage is particularly useful for handling large amounts of unstructured data. It is highly scalable, which pairs well with applications such as cloud storage services and data backups.

Object storage and block storage are both storage types used in the cloud. Object storage typically has higher latency for individual object retrieval compared to block storage, but it can achieve high throughput for large-scale operations. Block storage is fast but relatively expensive. Which one better fits an organization's use case depends on a number of factors. Overall, object storage is typically used for large volumes of unstructured data, while block storage is optimized for smaller amounts of data that are frequently accessed.

A big advantage of object storage is its cost. Storing data via object storage is usually less expensive than doing so with block storage. Block storage requires a fair amount of processing power in order to reassemble data, and the processes to optimize performance tend to make it more costly.

Common use cases for object storage include:

- Application assets
- Logs and analytics
- System backups

---

3 Cloudflare. n.d. "Object Storage vs. Block Storage: How Are They Different?" Cloudflare, Inc. Accessed July 2024. *https://www.cloudflare.com/learning/cloud/object-storage-vs-block-storage*.

- Video, audio, images, and other media
- Data archives
- Datasets for machine learning
- Data storage for serverless and microservices applications

Cloudflare, in its explanation of block and object storage, uses the analogy of block storage being like a small parking garage with valet parking, while object storage is like a huge public parking lot. The block storage "garage" allows drivers to quickly retrieve their cars, but it has limited space for vehicles, and expanding capacity would involve constructing a new garage and hiring more valets, which is expensive. The object storage "lot," in contrast, allows as many drivers to park as desired. However, some of the cars may end up at the far end of the parking lot, and it could take some time for their owners to reach them.[4]

Table 2-2 gives a summarized comparison of file storage, block storage, and object storage.

Table 2-2. Comparison of storage types

	File storage	Block storage	Object storage
Structure	Data is organized in a hierarchical structure and managed as discrete files.	Data is arbitrarily organized and managed in chunks.	Data is stored in a flat structure as objects.
Key strength	Store and handle data collaboratively with shared access.	Store and handle large volumes of structured data.	Store and handle large volumes of unstructured data via metadata.
Interface	Simple interface allows you to create, delete, and organize files.	Blocks can be accessed relatively easily across different operating systems.	Data is typically accessed via an API or user interface.
Main advantages	Broadly capable to store virtually anything, simple configuration, and rapid access to data.	Highly performant with low-latency access and a high degree of data integrity.	Highly scalable and advanced indexing, management, and searching capabilities.
Use cases	Document management systems, collaborative tools, data analytics, and others.	Large databases, VMs, HPC, and CDNs, among others.	IoT data management, cloud storage systems, disaster recovery, and others.

In-memory storage

An in-memory database (IMDB) primarily relies on main memory for data storage rather than traditional disk storage. The primary purpose of this type of database management system is to provide extremely fast data retrieval and processing speeds. This is achieved by keeping the entire dataset—or large chunks of it—in memory,

---

4 Cloudflare. n.d. "Object Storage vs. Block Storage: How Are They Different?" Cloudflare, Inc. Accessed July 2024. *https://www.cloudflare.com/learning/cloud/object-storage-vs-block-storage*.

which mitigates the latency associated with disk I/O operations. Also, IMDBs often employ optimized algorithms and data structures specifically designed to take full advantage of the high-speed access provided by RAM. The performance improvement is important for applications that require near-real-time data processing.

Virtual storage

Virtual storage refers to a method of abstracting physical storage resources to appear as a single, unified system for the end user. This concept allows storage systems to pool and manage physical resources—such as hard drives, SSDs, or even cloud storage—as though they are a single volume or entity, offering flexibility and scalability.

Virtual storage often employs several features to improve the efficiency and management of data:

Storage pooling
This allows multiple physical storage devices to be aggregated into one or more storage pools. These pools can be dynamically adjusted to meet the needs of applications, allowing for greater flexibility in allocating resources.

Thin provisioning
Thin provisioning allows the allocation of virtual storage capacity in a more efficient manner by allowing more capacity to be assigned to users or applications than is physically available. The system uses the physical storage only when data is actually written, optimizing space usage.

Data deduplication
Virtual storage often includes deduplication features to reduce redundant copies of data, further saving space and optimizing storage efficiency.

Snapshots and cloning
Many virtual storage systems allow snapshots, which capture the state of the system at a given time, and cloning, which creates identical copies of data. These features are useful for backup, recovery, and testing and are sometimes even automated.

Performance optimization
Techniques such as caching and tiering are used to optimize performance. Data that is frequently accessed can be stored on faster storage media (e.g., SSDs), while less frequently accessed data may reside on slower, less expensive storage.

Scalability
Virtual storage systems are designed to be highly scalable. They allow storage resources to be expanded easily by adding more physical devices without significant downtime or changes in the system architecture.

These features make virtual storage an attractive option for organizations looking to enhance storage flexibility, optimize costs, and ensure data protection and accessibility across diverse storage environments.

Data Models and Management Systems

Data models tell you how your data is structured, what operations can be performed on the data, and what constraints apply to the data. There are essentially two types of contemporary data models: the relational model and the non-relational model. The relational model has been employed the most extensively; relational databases can be operational, analytical, distributed, cloud based, in memory, or embedded.

There have also been many non-relational models developed over the past four or five decades, including network databases, hierarchical databases, object-oriented databases, time-series databases, key-value databases, document stores, column-family stores, wide-column stores, graph databases, and multimodel databases.

Figure 2-5 shows a high-level, object-oriented data model.

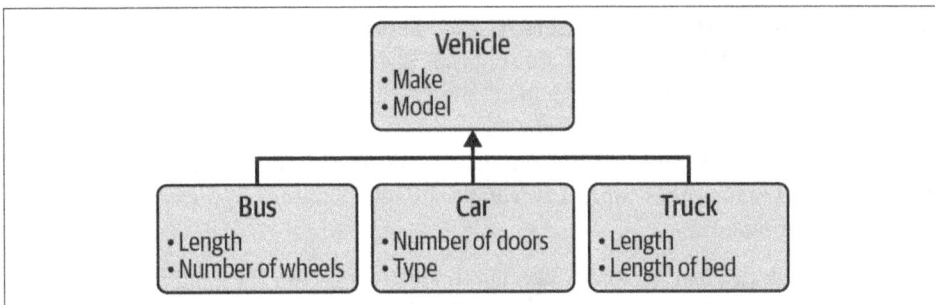

Figure 2-5. High-level, object-oriented data model

In tandem with data models, *data management systems* are software platforms designed to organize, store, manage, and retrieve data efficiently. They provide a structured environment that ensures data is easily accessible, consistent, and secure, which is essential for supporting various applications and business processes. These systems include a range of functionalities such as data storage, data retrieval, data indexing, data security, and data integrity management. By using these systems, organizations can ensure that their data is not only stored safely but also available for analysis and reporting, helping drive decision making and business strategies.

Common types of data management systems include relational database management systems (RDBMSs), NoSQL databases, data warehouses, and data lakes. Each type is suited to different types of data and use cases. For example, RDBMSs are ideal for structured data with relationships, while NoSQL databases handle unstructured or semistructured data better. Data warehouses are optimized for analytics and reporting, whereas data lakes can store vast amounts of raw data in its original format.

These systems play a crucial role in managing the life cycle of data, from creation to archival, ensuring data is a valuable asset for organizations.

Relational databases

A *relational database* organizes data into structured tables with predefined schemas. The tables have rows that correspond to individual records and columns that represent attributes. These tables are linked and related to each other through keys (e.g., primary and foreign keys) that enable complex queries and data retrieval across multiple tables. Relational databases use SQL for defining, manipulating, and querying data and can be ACID compliant. They're scalable and they can support transactions, making them suitable for a wide range of applications, from small-scale projects to large enterprise systems.

Often, someone will refer to a relational database but really mean a relational database management system. An RDBMS is the platform in which a relational database is located and, in addition to the database itself, includes utilities for data storage and management.

Using schemas allows multiple users to use the same database without interfering with one another. Relational database schemas also create manageable environments by allowing the organization of database objects into logical groups. Further, third-party applications can utilize separate schemas to avoid collisions with the names of other objects. A great book for further theory and explanations regarding relational databases (and many other topics) is *Designing Data-Intensive Applications* (O'Reilly) by Martin Kleppmann.

Relational databases can use block storage to store their data files, log files, and other necessary components, and they also commonly use file storage systems. However, traditional relational databases do not natively store their primary data files directly in object storage, as object storage typically lacks the low-latency, high IOPS (input/output operations per second) characteristics required for transactional workloads. Instead, relational databases sometimes use object storage in complementary or backup storage.

There are many popular relational database implementations, but some of the most popular include Oracle, MySQL, PostgreSQL, and Microsoft SQL.

Non-relational databases

In addition to SQL-based relational databases, there are also NoSQL databases. The term *NoSQL* is essentially synonymous with *non-relational* or *non-tabular* (i.e., it does not contain conventional linked data tables or strict schemas). In fact, *NoSQL* is somewhat of a catch-all for any databases that contain semistructured or unstructured data. Let's now take a closer look at some of the types of non-relational databases.

Column-oriented databases. *Wide-column data stores*, also known as *column-family* or *columnar databases*, are a type of NoSQL database designed to handle large amounts of sparse, semistructured data across a distributed architecture. In these databases, data is organized into tables, but unlike traditional relational databases, each row can have a different set of columns. Data is stored in column families, which are collections of rows that share the same primary key but can have varied columns. This structure allows for efficient read and write operations across vast datasets by storing data in a way that is optimized for access patterns that involve reading and writing large blocks of data.

Wide-column stores are highly scalable and are often used for applications that require high throughput and low latency, such as time-series data, recommendation engines, and large-scale data analytics. Some examples of popular implementations of wide-column stores include Apache Cassandra, HBase, and Google Bigtable.

Document stores and key-value storage. *Document stores*, also known as *document-oriented databases*, are a type of NoSQL database designed to store, retrieve, and manage document-based information. Each record, or document, is self-contained and can hold different types of data, including text, binary data, and even nested structures. Documents are typically stored in formats like JSON, BSON, or XML, making it easy to represent complex hierarchical relationships and allowing for more flexible and scalable schema designs.

Common use cases for document stores include content management systems, user profiles, and applications requiring a dynamic schema or varied data structures. Popular examples of document stores are MongoDB, CouchDB, and Elasticsearch.

Key-value storage is a simple and efficient type of database that uses a hash table structure where each unique key is associated with a specific value. This data model allows for extremely fast lookups, making it ideal for use cases where high-speed read and write operations are crucial, such as caching, session management, and near-real-time analytics. The value associated with each key can be anything from a simple string to a complex object. The simplicity of the model is its strength, as it offers quick access and ease of use for straightforward data retrievals. However, it lacks the ability to query the data by anything other than the key, which can be a limitation for more complex queries.

Key-value data stores are highly effective at scaling applications that process high-velocity, nontransactional data. Popular key-value databases include Redis, Amazon DynamoDB, Aerospike, and Riak.

Document databases store self-describing data in formats such as JSON, XML, and BSON. While they share similarities with key-value stores, the key difference lies in how values are managed—each value is a standalone document containing all the relevant data for a specific key. To enhance retrieval efficiency, frequently accessed fields within these documents can be indexed, allowing for quick searches even without knowing the key. Additionally, document structures are flexible, meaning each document within the database can follow a uniform schema or vary in structure as needed. The document-based approach generally allows for more dynamic and hierarchical data representations, which reduces the impedance mismatch sometimes encountered between relational databases and object-oriented programming models.

Graph databases. *Graph databases* are a type of NoSQL database designed to handle data whose relationships are well represented as a graph. They are particularly effective at managing complex connected data, where relationships and connections are principal aspects of the data structure. Each element in a graph database is called a *node*. The nodes represent entities such as people, organizations, or accounts. The relationships between nodes are represented by lines that join them called *edges*. Attributes can be attached to both nodes and edges.

Graph databases are optimized for querying deeply interconnected data and provide significant increases in performance over other kinds of databases for use cases such as social networks, recommendation engines, fraud detection, and network and IT operations. Many multimodal databases have graph database support as well.

Figure 2-6 shows an example of a web diagram representing a graph database.

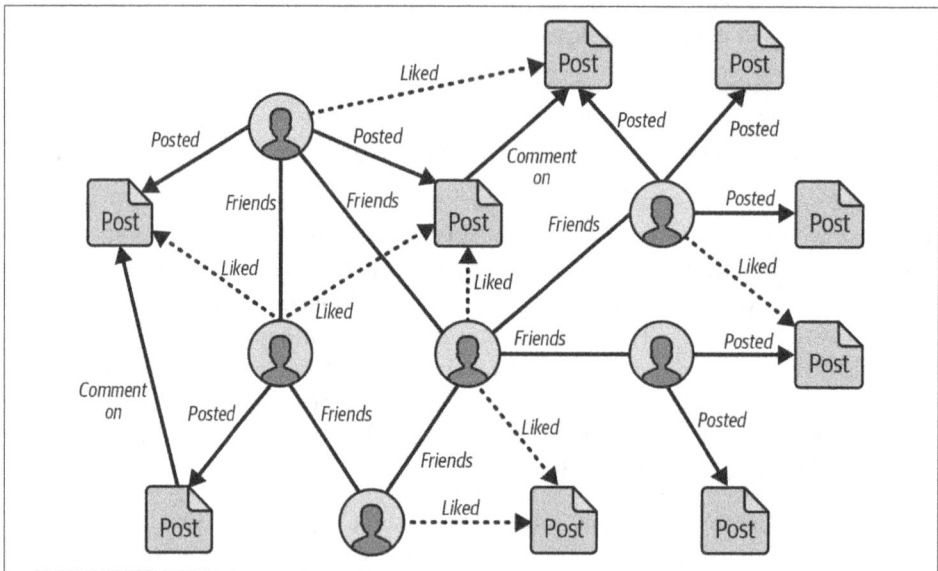

Figure 2-6. Example web diagram of hypothetical entities in a graph database

Some common graph database implementations include Neo4j, Amazon Neptune, and TigerGraph.

Object-oriented databases. *Object-oriented databases* (OODBs), or *object-oriented database management systems* (OODBMSs), are a type of database management system that integrates object-oriented programming principles with database technology. Unlike traditional relational databases, which organize data into tables with rows and columns, object-oriented databases store data as objects, similar to how data is represented in object-oriented programming languages like Java, C++, or Python. These objects can include both data, such as integers and strings, and the methods (functions) that operate on the data, encapsulating both the state and the behavior of the entity being represented.

One of the key advantages of object-oriented databases is their ability to handle complex data types and relationships more naturally than relational databases. For example, OODBs can easily model hierarchical relationships, inheritance, and polymorphism, which are common in applications requiring complex data structures such as computer-aided design (CAD), multimedia applications, and software engineering. Additionally, because the data is stored in the same way it is used in applications, object-oriented databases often reduce the impedance mismatch that can occur when mapping objects to relational tables, leading to more efficient data handling and reduced development time.

However, object-oriented databases are not without challenges. They can be more complex to design and manage compared to relational databases, particularly for those who are not familiar with object-oriented programming concepts. Furthermore, they have historically had less widespread adoption than relational databases, leading to fewer tools, resources, and support available for developers. Despite these challenges, object-oriented databases remain a powerful tool for applications that require the storage and manipulation of complex, interrelated data.

Common object-oriented databases include Object Store by MuleSoft and ObjectDB.

Vector databases. A *vector database* is designed to store and retrieve vectors generated by embedding models that encapsulate the meaning and context of data. This enables efficient similarity searches of structured and unstructured data. For example, users can perform searches for images with common elements. With the advent of generative AI models, vector databases have become increasingly prominent as reliable external knowledge bases.

Some of the downstream benefits of using vector databases include simplifying the operationalization of AI workloads and providing useful data management capabilities to address fault tolerance, security, and efficient querying.

Vector databases use vectorization for efficient search, storage, and data analysis. Figure 2-7 shows a representation of a data vectorization.

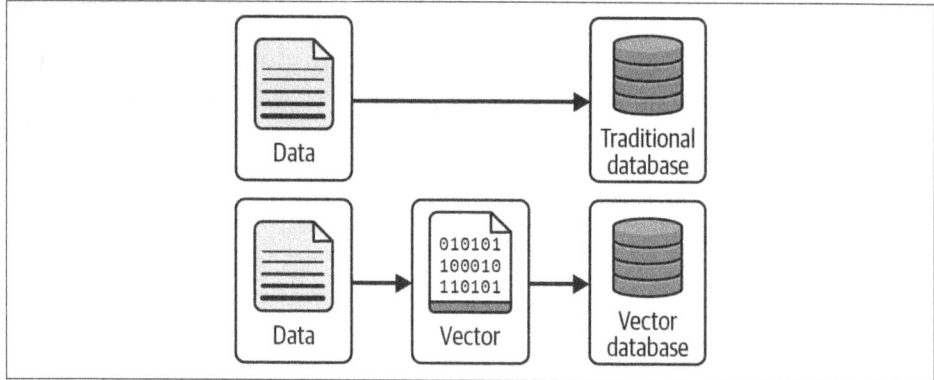

Figure 2-7. Vector database versus traditional database

Some common vector database implementations include Elasticsearch, OpenSearch, Couchbase, and Pinecone.

Multimodel databases. *Multimodel databases* are data management systems designed to support multiple data models—such as relational, document, key-value, graph, and columnar—within a single, unified backend. Unlike traditional databases that adhere strictly to one model, multimodel databases provide flexibility by allowing developers to use different data paradigms as needed for various application requirements, all while interacting with a consistent API or query interface.

This versatility helps reduce the need for multiple specialized databases and the complexity of integrating them. It enables organizations to manage diverse data types—structured, semistructured, and unstructured—more efficiently within one platform. Multimodel databases are particularly valuable in scenarios involving heterogeneous data and use cases such as content management, IoT, fraud detection, and real-time analytics, where different data models naturally coexist. Popular examples of multimodel databases include ArangoDB, OrientDB, and Microsoft Azure Cosmos DB.

Data warehouses

As implied in Table 2-3, *data warehouses*[5] typically offer analytics capabilities and support complex analytical queries. They are, therefore, considered OLAP tools and are used for storing, retrieving, and analyzing huge volumes of data. The data often comprises historical records and sometimes data derived from other data stores such as historical moving averages and standard deviations.

Table 2-3. Data warehouse versus database comparison

Characteristic	Data warehouse	Database
Purpose	Analysis	Reporting
Data processing system	OLAP (online analytical processing)	OLTP (online transactional processing)
Type of collection	Subject-oriented	Application-oriented
Query	Complex analytical queries	Simple transaction queries

Data warehouses are also used by reporting engines that operate on entire datasets at a time to generate aggregated metrics and other analytical information. In the same vein, although infrequent, data in a data warehouse is typically updated in large groups and rarely at the field or record level.

Unlike a typical database, data warehouses focus less on traditional indexes and joins, and custom query builders specific to the information architectures are often used to generate reports.

Data lakes and data lakehouses

Unlike a data warehouse that organizes stored data in a prescribed fashion for everyday operational use, *data lakes* (also called *data pools*) serve as centralized storage systems for immense volumes of structured and unstructured data in its native format and with diverse data types. A data lake will typically contain raw unstructured data that is accumulated for future transformation and use.

Data lakes are flat, meaning there are no file hierarchies. This provides consistency but also creates the opportunity for the development of a *data swamp* wherein the data in the data lake is rarely, if ever, used because it's so disorganized and unkempt.

Table 2-4 compares the characteristics of a data warehouse and a data lake.

---

5 I consider a data warehouse to be a collection of multiple structured relational databases. In reality, however, there are important differences in their architectures, technologies, and the way they're actually used.

Table 2-4. Data warehouse versus data lake comparison

Characteristic	Data warehouse	Data lake
Data	Relational from transactional systems, operational databases, and line-of-business applications	Non-relational and relational from IoT devices, websites, mobile apps, social media, and corporate applications
Schema	Designed prior to implementation (schema-on-write)	Written at the time of analysis (schema-on-read)
Cost and performance	Fastest query results using higher-cost storage	Query results getting faster using low-cost storage
Data quality	Highly curated data that serves as the central version of the truth	Any data, which may or may not be curated (e.g., raw data)
Users	Business analysts	Data scientists, data developers, and business analysts (using curated data)
Analytics	Batch reporting, BI, and visualizations	Machine learning, predictive analytics, data discovery, and profiling

Michael Armbrust and Matei Zaharia from Databricks consider a *data lakehouse* to be "a data management system based on low-cost and directly-accessible storage that also provides traditional analytical DBMS management and performance features such as ACID transactions, data versioning, auditing, indexing, caching, and query optimization."[6] Data lakehouses leverage the capabilities of both data warehouses and data lakes, and because of this, some people consider data lakehouses to be a "two-tier architecture." Regardless, the data lakehouse is intended to help increase the efficiency of administrative tasks and reduce storage costs.

Hybrid and Multicloud Storage

Solutions that combine on-premises and cloud storage or utilize multiple cloud providers offer flexibility and redundancy while maintaining data sovereignty, which allows organizations to optimize costs, performance, and compliance requirements based on their specific needs.

Data Movement and Transformation

Data movement and transformation lie at the heart of modern data systems, enabling organizations to harness the full potential of their data assets. In an era where data is continuously generated from diverse sources, its raw form often lacks the structure or context needed for actionable insights. Data movement ensures that this information

---

6 Armbrust, Michael, Ali Ghodsi, Reynold Xin, and Matei Zaharia. 2021. "Lakehouse: A New Generation of Open Platforms That Unify Data Warehousing and Advanced Analytics." *11th Annual Conference on Innovative Data Systems Research (CIDR)*. Virtual. January 11–15, 2021. *https://www.cidrdb.org/cidr2021/papers/cidr2021_paper17.pdf*.

is transported from its origins—be it databases, APIs, or event streams—to centralized storage or processing hubs. Transformation processes then refine, structure, and enrich this data, tailoring it to the specific requirements of downstream consumers such as analytical tools, machine learning pipelines, or operational systems. Data transformation mainly involves formatting data to suit an application. Together, these activities form the backbone of data engineering, bridging the gap between disparate data sources and meaningful analysis.

Connectors and Connections

A *connector* is a software layer that links applications to enable data transfer. Connectors are responsible for directing the movement of data between different components, defining the mappings between source and target data structures, and ensuring seamless interaction and efficient data exchange. Orchestrating data workflows and processes is also a key function, as it allows for the automation and coordination of complex data operations across various systems. Connectors are a vital aspect of data integration, and there are many types of connectors available to accommodate different situations and protocols:

Database connectors
> These connectors interface with relational databases and allow data extraction, query execution, and data loading into target systems, often using standard protocols such as ODBC (Open Database Connectivity) or JDBC (Java Database Connectivity).

Application connectors
> These connectors are designed for specific software applications or enterprise systems; they enable data extraction, API invocation, and synchronization between the application and other systems.

File connectors
> These connectors manage data in various file formats including CSV, XML, JSON, and Excel and facilitate the integration and exchange of file-based data between systems.

Web service connectors and APIs
> These enable communication with web services via SOAP (Simple Object Access Protocol) and REST (representational state transfer) and support data exchange and integration with systems that provide web service interfaces and third-party applications.

Messaging connectors
> These connectors are used for integrating with message-oriented middleware or enterprise messaging systems and can facilitate reliable asynchronous data and message transfer.

Cloud service connectors
> These interact with cloud platforms and services and enable integration with cloud-based storage systems, databases, messaging, and analytics services.

Legacy system connectors
> These connectors provide connectivity to older or proprietary systems such as mainframes, which may not have standard integration interfaces.

Streaming connectors
> These facilitate the integration of data from streaming sources and typically support near-real-time data ingestion, processing, and analysis.

Migration

Data migration is the part of data integration that involves transferring data between computing environments that potentially use different data types, data formats, encodings, or storage types. Data migration is a discrete, one-time (or infrequent) event with a one-way process that concludes after data is moved to its intended destination. The destination then becomes a source of data.

Data migration plays a lead role during system upgrades, in datacenter consolidations, and when legacy systems are being replaced. Moving petabytes or even exabytes of data is not unheard of. Figure 2-8 shows a Venn diagram of the relationship between data integration processes and the processes that make up data migration.

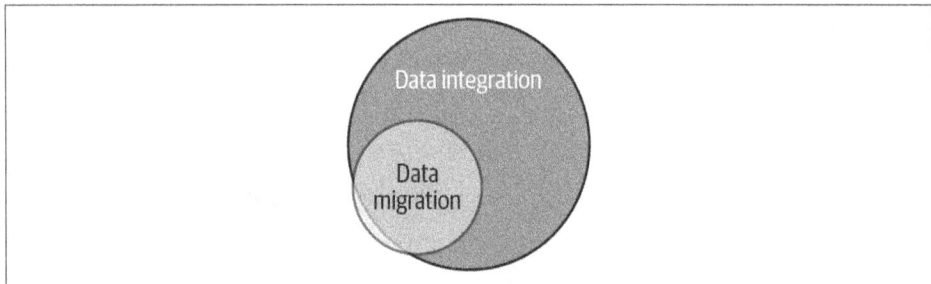

Figure 2-8. Data integration and migration Venn diagram

Data migration is often a necessary prerequisite for effective data integration, as it lays the groundwork for more complex operations. Data migration tasks require careful planning to ensure that the data remains consistent and there is no loss of fidelity. The implementation planning for a data migration usually includes establishing a transfer route and ensuring that the receiving environment can accommodate the data. Figure 2-9 shows a high-level example of a plausible data migration workflow.

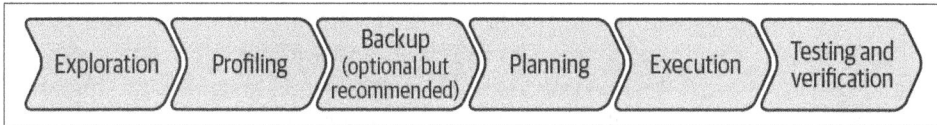

Figure 2-9. An example data migration workflow

A major benefit that migrating data to a new, centralized system can offer is easier and more comprehensive data processing. It can also help simplify additional integration processes, as data from various sources can be more easily aligned and transformed.

Ingestion

Data ingestion is a process that involves quickly and reliably importing data into a readily accessible storage environment. It also involves ensuring the data, regardless of source, enters the organizational ecosystem in a structured and manageable way.

Data ingestion is a subprocess within data integration. A single ingestion can be associated with a single dataset from a single data source, and, depending on the organization's requirements, an individual ingestion can be event driven or occur at defined time intervals.

Figure 2-10 shows a Venn diagram of data integration, data migration, and data ingestion processes.

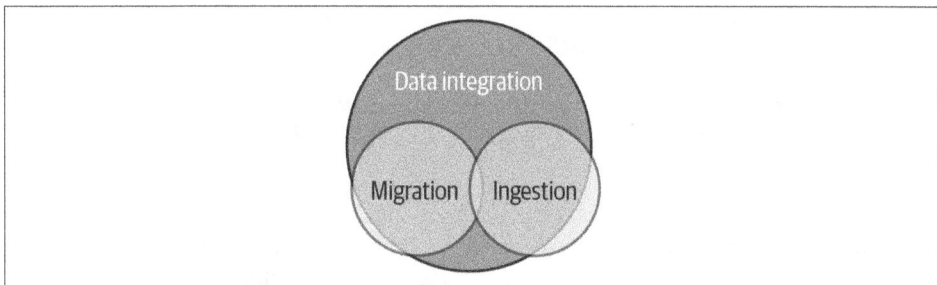

Figure 2-10. Data integration, migration, and ingestion Venn diagram

Sometimes people use the term *ingestion* in the context of importing data into an application such as an analytics platform. Where data migration might involve substantial transformation and cleaning of data as it moves to a new environment, data ingestion will typically involve only light processing, or conditioning, before the data is stored or analyzed.

Data ingestion can occur independently of data migration. The objective of an ingestion is to bring data into a system for use, while data migration is focused on moving typically large sets of data from one system to another.

Conversely, data migration cannot occur without data ingestion. Ingestion is one of the initial steps in the data migration process, and without it the data from the source system wouldn't be available to move into the target system. Data migration inherently includes data ingestion as a crucial part of the process.

Replication

Data replication, also referred to—in different contexts—as *mirroring*[7] or *propagating*, is the process of intentionally duplicating data, often to multiple locations. It can be performed in near real time (synchronous replication) or at scheduled intervals (asynchronous replication) and is routinely part of the data integration process to create backups during data migrations or to reduce latency and increase availability in distributed systems.

A good example of data replication is creating snapshots[8] of data, which generally entails duplicating data for storage or alternative consumption. In distributed storage systems, this might mean that different parts of a dataset are replicated onto different servers and potentially in different datacenters.

Similar concepts include multicasting and broadcasting data in which pieces of data are propagated to multiple endpoints in parallel. Data propagation specifically refers to using applications to copy data from a central location and distribute it to other data stores for easy access. Data propagation often uses two-way communications between the central repository and the remote data stores.

Batches, Streams, and Events

In the realm of data processing, the two primary paradigms—batch processing and stream processing—address the distinct needs of handling and analyzing data at scale.

Batch processing, the traditional approach, is characterized by the collection and processing of data in large, discrete chunks. This method is ideal for tasks that prioritize accuracy and thorough analysis, such as generating reports, performing retrospective analyses, or running predictive models.

Conversely, stream processing offers a more dynamic approach, designed for continuous dataflows where real-time or near-real-time insights and actions are critical. It enables businesses to process information as it is generated, allowing for immediate responses to changes in conditions or events.

---

7 Mirroring is a form of data replication in which a full database backup is maintained as a safety precaution.

8 A data snapshot is a copy of a dataset at a specific moment in time.

While these paradigms differ significantly in execution, they can also complement each other in hybrid systems, demonstrating the flexibility and evolution of modern data platforms to meet diverse enterprise requirements. Understanding the strengths, limitations, and use cases of these paradigms is essential for selecting the right approach for specific data-driven challenges.

Batches

Batch processing involves the handling of bulk data. It is collected, stored, and processed in large chunks, often overnight or during off-peak hours. This approach is commonly used for tasks such as data warehousing and generating reports or analytics on historical data.

Batch processing algorithms generally excel at handling large volumes of data all at once. However, batch processing may not be suitable for scenarios requiring near-real-time actions or insights because of the inherent lags within batch processing pipelines, which typically run periodically but can also be triggered by events.

Batch processing is often the best option when accuracy is essential for procedures such as:

- Data backups
- Transaction history loading
- Billing and order processing
- Data modeling
- Forecasting sales or weather
- Retrospective data analysis
- Diagnostic medical image processing

Streams

Stream processing refers to continuously flowing data that can be generated from various sources such as sensors, social media feeds, website clickstreams, network logs, and IoT devices, where information is produced and consumed in near real time. Unlike batch processing, true streaming data is processed as it's generated, allowing for immediate actions to be taken and enabling organizations to react swiftly to changing conditions and, if required, alter their plans to accommodate the most recent information available.

In "Streaming 101: The World Beyond Batch", Tyler Akidau defines stream processing as a type of data processing "designed with infinite datasets in mind." This definition includes both true streaming and microbatch implementations that process data much more frequently than traditional batch processing.

Batch processing and stream processing can theoretically be considered two sides of the same coin, and in fact, a unified approach has been suggested.[9] Stream processing can be performed on top of a batch processing engine by breaking the stream into microbatches. Batch processing can be performed on top of a stream processing engine by syphoning off data from its batches and continuously feeding it to a stream. The Apache Flink project even defines batch processing as the "processing of bounded streams."[10]

Figure 2-11 shows a representation of bounded and unbounded data streams.

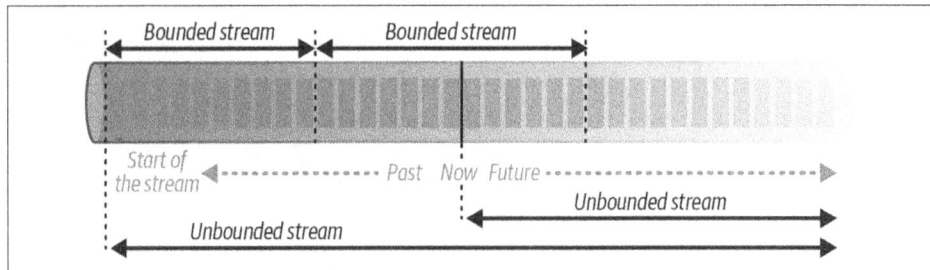

Figure 2-11. Bounded and unbounded data streams

Streams can essentially be bounded in two ways: by size and by time. *Size-bounded batches* have a predetermined fixed size that is often governed by bandwidth or available storage, but the amount of time that elapses between batches can vary. *Time-bounded batches* are based on fixed time intervals where a batch is generated or processed after each predetermined interval of time has elapsed. The batch size (i.e., amount of data) can fluctuate and may be significantly inconsistent, but time-bounded batches do maintain periodic timing that can be used to plan processes downstream.

As indicated in Figure 2-12, batch processes are usually scheduled and are generally more cost-effective than continuous stream processing. However, enterprise data platform requirements seem to be slowly shifting from a focus on historical transactional data to more near-real-time enriched organizational data.

Some common streaming data platforms include Apache Kafka, Apache Flink, Confluent, IBM Streams, and Amazon Kinesis.

---

9 Ewen, Stephan, Fabian Hueske, and Xiaowei Jiang. 2019. "Batch as a Special Case of Streaming and Alibaba's Contribution of Blink." Apache Software Foundation. February 13. *https://flink.apache.org/2019/02/13/batch-as-a-special-case-of-streaming-and-alibabas-contribution-of-blink*.

10 Apache Flink. "Use Cases." Apache Software Foundation. Accessed May 2024. *https://flink.apache.org/what-is-flink/use-cases*.

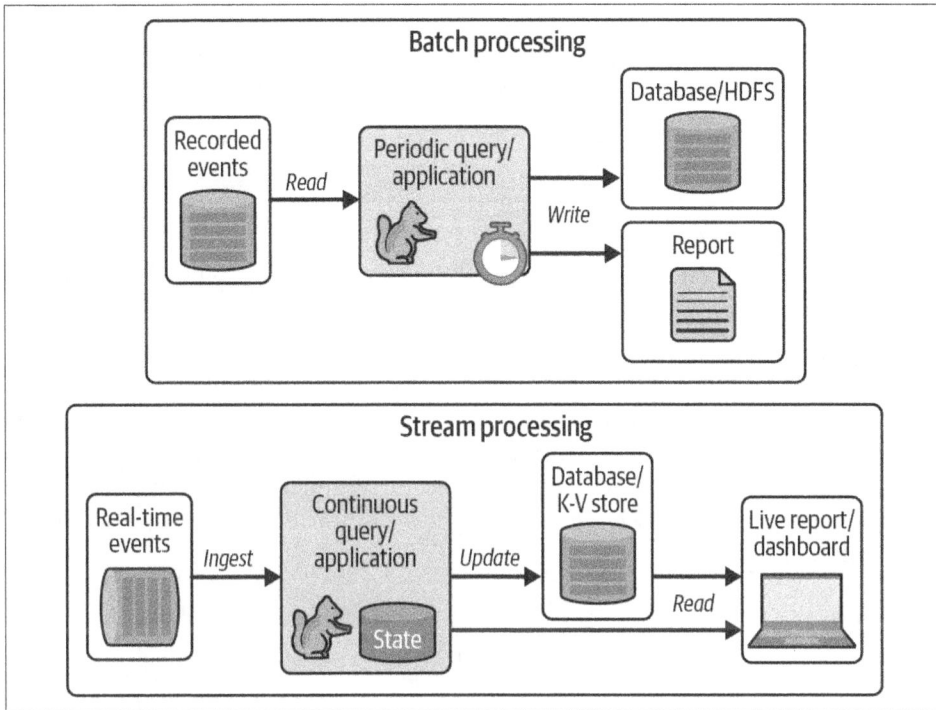

Figure 2-12. Batch versus stream processing

Enriched data refers to data with context or meaningful metadata.

Common use cases for streaming data pipelines include:

- Multimedia streams
- Social media feeds and sentiment analysis
- Fraud detection
- User behavior and advertising
- Near-real-time product pricing
- Recommender systems

Events

An *event* is a state change within a system. An event record is enriched data related to the state change. For example, consider a microcontroller (e.g., Raspberry Pi or Arduino) connected to a temperature sensor. The microcontroller may continually poll the temperature sensor, and if the temperature changes, then an event record is created with a timestamp, the new temperature value, and relevant metadata. Even just polling the temperature sensor could be considered an event. What is and is not considered an event depends on what the purpose of the data is and what is deemed important.

With stream processing, maintaining persistent information between multiple events requires a stateful component. In fact, according to the Apache Software Foundation, the definition of an event-driven application is "a stateful application that ingests events from one or more event streams and reacts to incoming events by triggering computations, state updates, or external actions." Without some kind of a storage layer, streaming data flows in and then right back out into the ether or is lost in aggregation.

Pipelines

A data *pipeline* is just a series of connected processes that move or transform data. However, a data pipeline may also encompass underlying hardware systems and architectures, depending on the situation.

The pipeline processes include things such as commands, programs, and threads and can often be clumped into separate stages that can include data extraction, ingestion, transformation, destination loading, scheduling and triggering, monitoring, and maintenance and optimization. Some processes and stages can be parallelized, but data pipelines are overall sequential. Because of this, data pipelines must be complete or else they're basically useless. This sometimes makes data pipelines awkward to design and build in an Agile manner. Figure 2-13 depicts packet flow through a data pipeline.

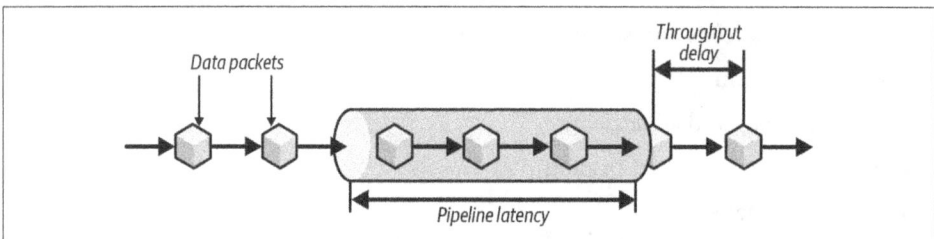

Figure 2-13. Packet flow through a pipeline

When planning and monitoring pipelines, three primary metrics that are typically considered include latency, utilization rate, and throughput.

Data latency is the amount of time between the occurrence of an event and when the data generated by that event is available for use. This delay can potentially arise at multiple stages, from data collection to storage. Each stage can contribute to the overall latency, which makes it an important factor to consider in systems requiring near-real-time data processing. For instance, in financial trading systems, low latency is essential to ensure timely decisions and actions. Conversely, high latency can lead to delays in decision making and impact performance. As discussed in Part II, Hadoop is generally not a great choice for systems that require low latency.

The data utilization rate indicates the extent that available data is actively being used for productive activities within an organization. It measures how effectively data assets are being leveraged to generate insights, support operations, and drive business outcomes. A high data utilization rate is generally a good thing and is indicative of being data-driven. A low data utilization rate suggests that much of the organization's data remains unused and potential opportunities to increase efficiency and effectiveness remain undiscovered. Maximizing data utilization involves ensuring that the data is widely accessible, relevant, and well integrated into workflows and decision-making processes.

The last metric, throughput, quantifies how much data can be fed through a data pipeline in a given period of time. Greater throughput equates to more packets of data per unit time. When throughput in the pipeline becomes irregular, the pipeline is considered to be unbalanced. Ideally, the packet throughput will be uniform across all stages, but in reality, pipelines do typically have bottlenecks of some sort and are therefore unbalanced to some degree. Load balancing consists of smoothing out packet throughput at each stage in the pipeline, and smoothing out the throughput often entails parallelization of the processes in one or more of the pipeline stages. A load-balanced pipeline will not have bottlenecks upstream and will have just-in-time data packet relays. Pipeline stages that process data packets concurrently across CPUs and GPUs makes the pipeline dynamic, or nonlinear.

Figure 2-14 depicts the potential time savings that can be realized with parallelization.

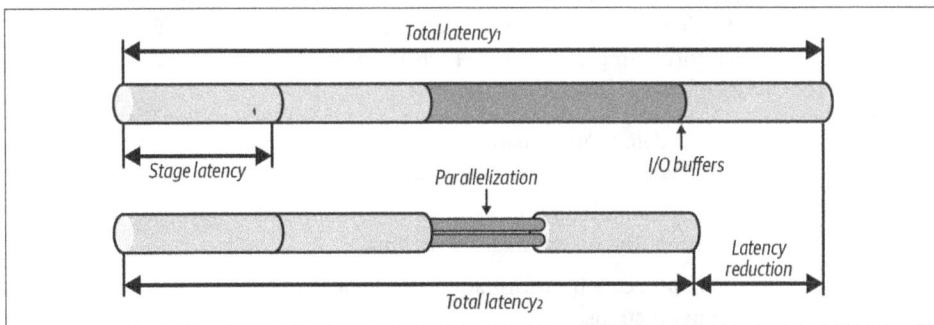

Figure 2-14. Pipeline latency

Pipeline throughput and the flow of data is largely regulated by input/output (I/O) buffers that serve as holding areas for data between different processing stages. They are also used to distribute loads across parallelized processing stages, which helps ensure efficient and balanced data handling.

Data pipelines are the backbone of data integration and are necessary in modern data-driven environments. From backing up files and facilitating migrations to providing aggregated data for analytics and reporting, data pipelines make data integration possible.

Conditioning

Data *conditioning* is an umbrella term for cleaning, organizing, munging, wrangling, and other similar tasks performed on data. The intent of data conditioning is to prepare raw data for analysis or integration by ensuring its quality, consistency, and usability.

> Using the word "conditioning" sounds better when speaking to clients who might otherwise be suspicious of phrases like "cleaning the data," which can unfortunately have a nefarious connotation sometimes.

While data conditioning generally improves the quality of data, it can significantly increase latency in a pipeline. Computing resources are required to convert values, reposition data, and perform all of the other conditioning processes. Pipeline latency only increases as additionally required processes are included.

> It's somewhat subjective where the line of distinction is, but I consider data transformation more intrusive or impactful than data conditioning. Conditioning data might include minor things such as enforcing consistent abbreviations for variable values. Transformations would include things such as creating new variables from existing ones, masking sensitive data, performing unit conversions, and reformatting a data file. Perhaps even categorizing different levels of transformation is appropriate:
>
> 1. *Basic* data transformation: Data type conversion, data format conversion, and other more basic operations.
> 2. *Intermediate* data transformation: Lookup tasks, aggregations, sorting, and deterministic searching.
> 3. *Complex* data transformation: Probabilistic searching and custom functions.

Change Data Capture

Change data capture (CDC) is a technique used to track changes such as insertions, updates, and deletions made to data in source systems, including transactional databases, ERP systems, CRM systems, data warehouses, and mainframes. The goal of CDC is to ensure that these changes are captured in near real time and propagated to other organizational systems such as data warehouses and data lakes without the need to perform a full data extraction. CDC significantly reduces the volume of data that needs to be handled during the extract phase of ETL/ELT and is particularly useful for keeping data up-to-date without overburdening source systems or reducing latency. Usually, the changes can also be retroactively applied to additional repositories or made available in a format consumable by other data integration tools.

There are at least three types of CDC: log based, query based, and event based (or trigger based). In my experience, log-based CDC has been the most prevalent type of CDC. This is where updates to datasets are identified by scanning for changes in transaction logs. This type of CDC is also one of the fastest and least disruptive because modifications to a database are not required.

When transaction logs are unavailable, query-based CDC is an option. Query-based CDC uses the actual tables in the production database to determine data changes via timestamps, version numbers, or status indicators. It has a higher production impact than log-based CDC and is sometimes used with data warehouses.

The alternative to query-based CDC when transaction logs are unavailable is event-based CDC. Event-based CDC relies on triggers from a change in the application layer and stores the changes elsewhere, such as in a secondary table.

To process captured changes from a database replication, there are several options:[11]

Transactional CDC
This is most useful when transactional consistency is more important than high performance for standard database targets. Changes are streamed on a transaction-by-transaction basis to maintain transactional integrity at any given point in time.

Batch CDC or batch-optimized CDC
This aims to accommodate high transaction rates and low latencies. Batch-optimized includes a preprocessing action that efficiently groups transactions into batches.

---

11 Qlik. n.d. Database Replication (website). QlikTech International AB. Accessed May 2024. *https://www.qlik.com/us/data-replication/database-replication*.

Ingest-merge CDC

This is similar to batch CDC but leverages performance-optimized services from the target data warehouse as the data is being delivered.

Message-encoded CDC

This involves integration with streaming systems such as Apache Kafka to ingest high volumes of data from many data sources. Source changes are automatically relayed by the message brokers through in-memory streaming.

Figure 2-15 shows a detailed example of a CDC process.

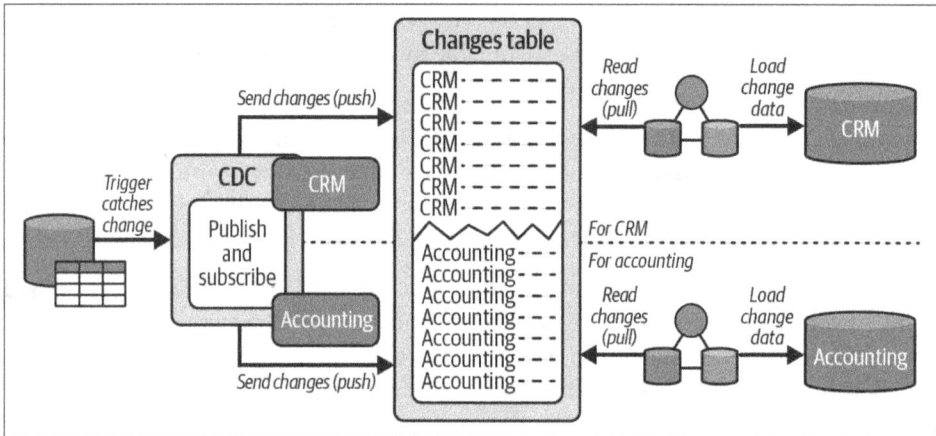

Figure 2-15. An example CDC process

CDC is an extremely useful feature, but the adoption of CDC seems to be limited because of two primary reasons. The first reason is that only a handful of commercial products do CDC well. The vendors of these software products invest heavily in understanding and adapting to the various existing database log formats, and the significant investment limits the market offerings to a few major players who charge a premium for their integration tools.

The second reason for the limited adoption of CDC, particularly in the government, is the log-level access required by these third-party CDC tools. Granting log-level access can be a huge security vulnerability. However, there are ways to mitigate the risks.

Integration Management

Integration management largely consists of data services and data orchestration, which are foundational elements in modern data integration frameworks that enable the creation of scalable, secure, and efficient systems. Data services provide the backbone for modular architectures by encapsulating data logic and management into reusable, independently deployable components. This modularity fosters consistency and flexibility in data delivery across diverse systems and stakeholders.

Complementing this, data orchestration focuses on designing, monitoring, and managing data pipelines and workflows to ensure processes are efficient, repeatable, and scalable. Closely tied to governance and automation, orchestration ensures seamless life cycle management across computing environments. Leveraging orchestration tools further enhances data operations by reducing manual intervention, improving data integrity, and enabling flexible, large-scale pipelines.

Together, these elements shape a robust, integrated approach to handling complex data ecosystems. Let's take a closer look at them next.

Data Services

Data services are an important component in modern data integration solutions. They provide the basis for modular architecture that bundles data logic and management into reusable procedures. This makes them independently deployable and, therefore, highly scalable and flexible. Modular architecture enables the integration and delivery of data in a consistent, secure, and manageable way across different systems and with various stakeholders.

Data Orchestration

Data orchestration is the process of building, monitoring, and controlling data pipelines and workflows. It involves managing the data life cycle across different computing environments to ensure data processes are efficient, repeatable, and scalable. I usually consider data orchestration and automation to be parts of data governance; however, because their processes and objectives are so interconnected with data integration, I'm including this short section on orchestration.

Figure 2-16 presents a Venn diagram that depicts the set of processes associated with data management, data governance, data orchestration, and automation. Data governance processes constitute a subset of data management processes. Data orchestration processes are a subset of data governance processes. Automation processes are not always, but can be, included in data orchestration, data governance, and data management.

Data orchestration tools streamline integrations by proactively enhancing workflow efficiency through automation and scheduling. This subsequently reduces the amount of required manual oversight, increases data integrity, and creates more flexible data pipelines that can operate at larger scales.

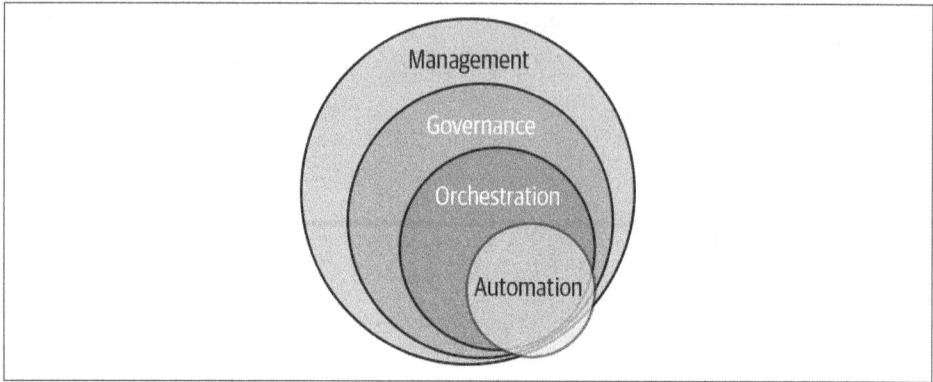

Figure 2-16. Data management, governance, orchestration, and automation Venn diagram

Conclusion

The data integration concepts outlined in this chapter, while distinct, work in concert to ensure that data flows smoothly and cohesively through different data systems, is of high quality, and aligns with business goals and regulatory requirements. We've touched on how some of these elements relate and contribute to the broader objective of effective data utilization.

In Chapter 3, we'll go over common issues and challenges that are often encountered while integrating data and data systems.

Data Integration Challenges

Data integration is a complex yet essential component of modern data management strategies, encompassing a wide range of challenges and limitations. This chapter explores these issues, particularly focusing on the difficulties of incorporating data from legacy systems and the need to adapt to diverse and rapidly changing data sources.

The issues and challenges can be organized into three main categories:

- *Organizational* issues, such as the impact of policies, the lack of skilled personnel, and the necessity of effective data governance and management practices
- *Technical* challenges associated with handling large volumes of data and various data formats and organizing smooth data pipelines
- *Security and compliance* challenges related to ensuring data quality, consistency, and accessibility

By identifying and understanding these challenges, organizations can better navigate the intricate landscape of data integration to maximize the value derived from their data assets.

Organizational Issues

Implementing a data integration solution can be significantly hindered by various factors, starting with inefficient business processes or counterproductive policies. These can create bottlenecks that slow down the flow of data and impede the smooth integration of disparate systems. For instance, outdated approval processes or over-zealous data governance policies might delay critical steps in the integration project, leading to missed deadlines and increased costs.

Creating and managing these policies and processes can be a challenge. They often take a considerable amount of time to document, implement, and enforce. Just ensuring that all stakeholders have a common understanding and agreement of the integration processes, standards, and objectives can be a taxing endeavor.

Obstructive or incompetent management is another major challenge. Leaders who fail to understand the importance of data integration, or who actively resist change due to a preference for the status quo, can prevent the project from gaining the necessary traction. This resistance can manifest in the refusal to allocate resources, failure to support key decisions, or the imposition of unnecessary barriers that complicate the integration process.

Lack of skilled personnel is a critical issue as well. Data integration projects require a range of expertise, including data engineering, database management, and data analytics. Without a sufficient number of qualified professionals, the project can suffer from delays and errors that ultimately compromise the quality and reliability of the integrated data. Table 3-1 shows four distinct data roles (in ascending order of technical expertise) for which you need skilled personnel.

Table 3-1. Skilled personnel data roles

Role	Description	Skills required	Commonly used tools
Data steward	Creates and implements data policies and strategies and facilitates internal communications	Identity management, communication, familiarity with cloud platforms	Word, PowerPoint, Azure, AWS
Data analyst, business analyst, analytics engineer	Maintains data systems, creates reports, and interprets data	Business knowledge, communication, spreadsheets, data visualization	Tableau, Qlik, SPSS, Excel, PowerPoint, HTML
Data scientist, data manager	Is able to take data science projects from conception to implementation	Math/statistics, ETL, data storage, modeling, data visualization, ML	Python, SQL, R, Databricks, Qlik, HTML/JavaScript
Data engineer, data architect, DBA	Uses computer science to implement data pipelines (often in the cloud) and develops data models	Computer programming, cloud platforms, big data, ETL, data storage	Azure, AWS, NoSQL, Hadoop, Python, Java

Financial constraints further exacerbate these challenges. Insufficient funding can limit the ability to procure essential tools, hire suitable talent, or invest in necessary training and development. This can lead to the use of subpar solutions that do not fully meet the project's needs, resulting in a system that is less efficient and more prone to failures.

Personality conflicts within the team can also be detrimental. When team members cannot collaborate effectively due to clashing personalities or competing interests, it can lead to a breakdown in communication, reduced morale, and a lack of cohesive effort. This discord can slow down progress and lead to suboptimal decision making as the team struggles to align on common goals and strategies.

Having spent almost my entire career supporting the US federal government in some capacity, I am all too familiar with how bureaucracy hinders innovation and the implementation of technology. There are some good reasons for the red tape that is so prevalent at the federal government level, the primary reasons being security and budget limitations. However, good reasons notwithstanding, there is always a trade-off that needs to be made between the benefits of adopting a technology (facilitating innovation) and risk.

A significant organizational challenge in government—and at least to some extent, presumably, in commercial organizations—is the tendency of some people to intentionally silo their data so that others, even within their organization or division,[1] cannot easily access it, if at all.

Again, sometimes there are reasonable motives for doing so. For instance, military criminal investigative services such as the Army's Criminal Investigation Division (CID), the Air Force's Office of Special Investigations (OSI), and the more publicly recognizable Naval Criminal Investigative Service (NCIS) cannot always share data internally, sometimes not even beyond a few individuals, because that data may contain evidence of a crime committed by a person or persons within that same organization.

Other times, there are more counterproductive reasons for intentionally siloing data—for instance:

- Worrying that releasing data will make jobs obsolete
- Concern that data will be altered or uncontrollably used in inappropriate ways
- Withholding data out of spite against management/coworkers

These are some of the reasons why creating a positive *data culture* is so important.

Finally, unethical behavior poses a significant risk to the integrity of data integration projects. Whether it involves misrepresenting data or engaging in favoritism during vendor selection, unethical actions can compromise the trustworthiness of the integrated system and potentially expose the organization to legal and reputational risks. Ensuring ethical conduct is, therefore, essential to maintaining the credibility and success of the data integration initiative.

---

1 *Department* and *division* are used interchangeably to describe an arbitrary organizational substructure.

Figure 3-1 shows some organizational challenges associated with data integration.

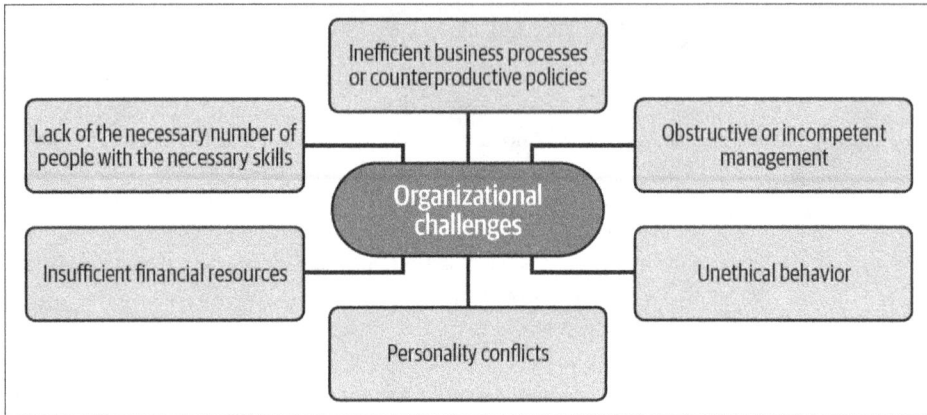

Figure 3-1. Data integration organizational challenges

Technical Challenges

With massive and continuous growth in data volume from a variety of sources such as social media, IoT devices, and enterprise applications, powerful data integration tools are a necessity to optimally extract value from the increasing velocity of information while maintaining the veracity of insights.

There are two main areas that are challenges to implementing data integration: data quality and data processing. Let's take a look at those next.

Data Quality

Several common data quality issues can significantly impact data integrations. Missing data, duplicated data, data formatting misalignments, obsolete data, and metadata inaccuracies are all common culprits of issues while handling datasets.

Missing and incomplete data can undermine the effectiveness of an integration solution. When critical data points are absent, it can lead to inaccurate analysis and insights and, ultimately, flawed decision making, because the integrated system lacks the necessary information to accurately interpolate results. In the context of machine learning, missing data can impair the training of models and result in poor predictive performance.

Unintentionally duplicated data is another common problem. It occurs when the same piece of data is repeated within a dataset. This often happens when data isn't standardized and format checking is not enforced, leading to the presence of multiple instances of the same data but just in different formats. Duplicated data can inflate the dataset size and subsequently lead to superfluous storage and increased processing time. It can also skew analysis results because the same data gets counted multiple times. Detecting and removing duplicates is important to maintain the integrity of the integrated dataset.

Obsolete data can also affect data integration efforts. Data that is outdated or no longer relevant can clutter the dataset and lead to inefficiencies and potentially misleading analyses. Relying on obsolete data can result in decisions based on outdated information. Regularly updating and cleaning data to remove obsolete entries is important to maintain an accurate and relevant integrated dataset.

Further, uninformative, missing, incorrect, or misleading metadata can complicate data integration efforts. Metadata provides context and meaning to the data and often guides its usage and interpretation. When metadata is incomplete, incorrect, or misleading, it hampers the ability to understand and utilize the data correctly. This can lead to misinterpretation and misuse of data and affect the quality of insights derived from the integration.

In summary, addressing these common data quality issues is required for the successful implementation of a data integration solution. Implementing mechanisms to detect and correct errors, as well as ensuring that data lineage is transparent and traceable, is imperative. Tackling these challenges ensures the integrated data is accurate, consistent, and reliable, which enables better decision making and more effective use of data resources.

Data Processing

Implementing a data integration solution can be significantly affected by various data processing factors that will be either hardware related or software related.

Hardware

Implementing a data integration solution can be significantly impacted by hardware and system constraints. Insufficient processing power can lead to slow data processing times, which can hamper the overall efficiency of the integration. This becomes particularly problematic when dealing with large volumes of data or complex transformations because the system may struggle to keep up with demand, resulting in delays and potentially causing time-sensitive data operations to fail.

Inadequate storage space is another critical issue. Data integration solutions often necessitate storage of vast amounts of data, including raw inputs, intermediate results, and final outputs. If the storage capacity is insufficient, it can lead to data loss, forced purges of important historical data, or the inability to capture new data, which would undermine the integrity and completeness of the data being integrated.

Similarly, an insufficient amount of memory can severely restrict the performance of data integration tasks. Memory-intensive operations such as in-memory data transformations or caching may fail or be significantly slower if there is not enough RAM available. This can cause bottlenecks in the data pipeline as processes are forced to rely on slower disk-based operations instead of faster in-memory processing, resulting in overall slower data throughput and increased latency.

Incompatible system components, such as differences in architecture (e.g., x86 versus ARM), can also complicate the implementation of a data integration solution. These incompatibilities can require additional layers of software abstraction or emulation, which can degrade performance and introduce additional points of failure. Moreover, they can limit the ability to standardize the deployment process across different environments and lead to increased complexity in managing an integration.

Each of these hardware and system constraints must be carefully evaluated and addressed to ensure that a data integration solution can perform efficiently and reliably under the expected workload.

Software

Incompatible communication protocols present a major challenge because they can prevent seamless interaction between different systems and applications (e.g., Linux and Windows). This can lead to the need for additional middleware or custom development to bridge the gaps, which increases complexity and the number of potential points of failure. Also, large variabilities in data loads and user demands require the integration solution to be highly scalable and flexible. It must be capable of handling peak loads without degrading performance, which can require sophisticated load balancing and resource management strategies.

As mentioned previously, a lack of transparency within the data pipeline is a critical issue. Without clear visibility into the dataflow, troubleshooting and optimizing the system become difficult. This can result in prolonged downtimes and inefficiencies if problems are encountered.

In terms of long-term cost-effectiveness, *vendor lock-in* poses a significant risk. When a solution is heavily dependent on a specific vendor's technology, it can limit the organization's flexibility and ability to adapt to changing requirements and potentially leverage more cost-effective options in the future. However, this often means fewer tools to learn, more turnkey integration, faster time to value, and quality support and services not available from free open source tools.

In the same vein, licensing limitations can restrict the scalability and functionality of an integration solution. If licenses are tied to specific usage metrics, such as the number of users or data volume, this can constrain growth and flexibility and require significant expenditures to make changes. Also keep in mind that with free open source options there is no licensing restriction, but you are on your own to install, integrate, operate, and patch the software.

Downtime because of maintenance, updates, and upgrades can disrupt data integration operations, leading to temporary unavailability of critical data services. This necessitates careful planning and implementation of redundancy and failover mechanisms to minimize the impact on business operations.

Each of these factors must be carefully considered and mitigated to ensure a robust and efficient data integration solution. Your team and organization will have to analyze and determine what tools and approaches work best in the various parts of your architecture.

Figure 3-2 shows many of the technical challenges involved with data integration.

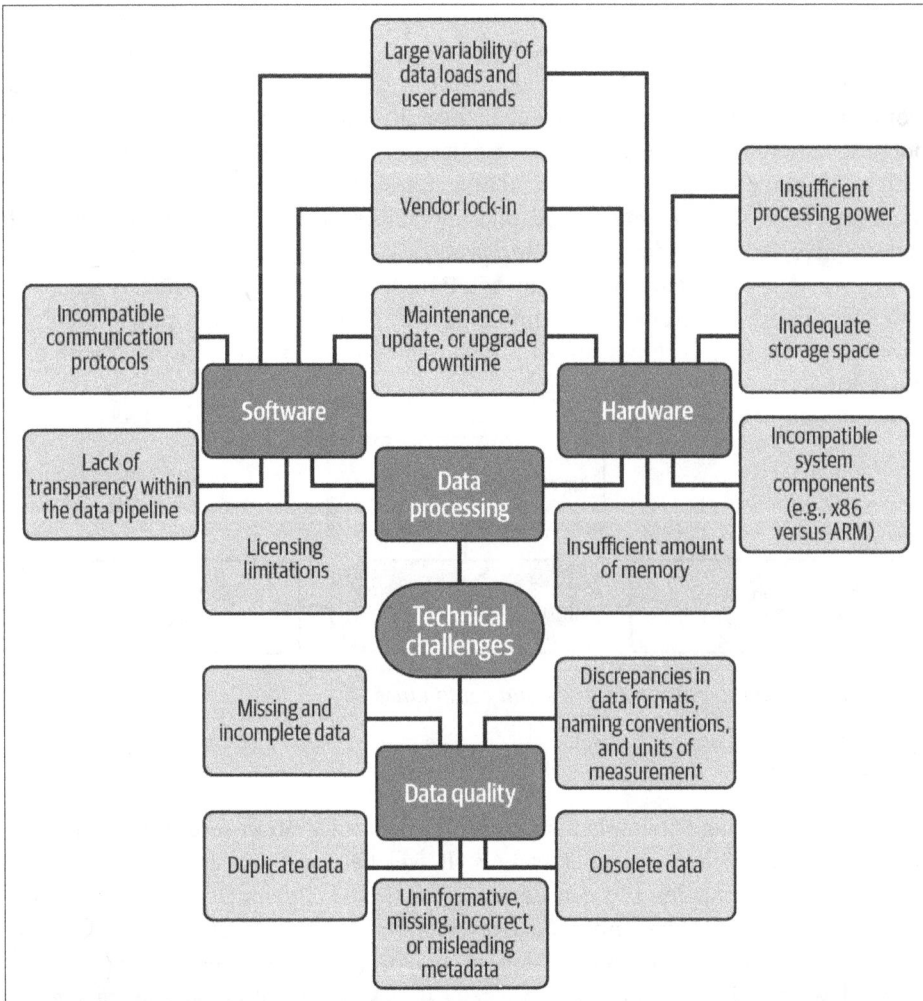

Figure 3-2. Data integration technical challenges

Security and Compliance

Regulations can sometimes impose strict requirements on how personal data is collected, processed, and stored. Organizations must ensure that their data integration processes comply with these laws, which often means implementing data governance frameworks and conducting regular audits to verify compliance. Mapping out and tracking data interactions allows security measures to be better designed to protect sensitive data and prevent unauthorized access.

When collaborating with external parties, or even across different departments, the risk of data exposure increases. Establishing clear data access controls and permissions is essential to ensure that only authorized personnel can access sensitive data. This often involves employing *role-based access control* (RBAC) and maintaining detailed logs to monitor and audit data access. The complexity of integrating data from multiple sources can lead to challenges in maintaining a consistent security posture. Different systems may have varying security protocols and levels of maturity, which can make it difficult to implement a cohesive security strategy. Organizations must strive for standardization and interoperability of security measures across all systems involved in the data integration process. As data privacy laws and regulations change, a well-built data integration solution should be able to quickly adapt to new compliance requirements. Maintaining trust, especially in the public sector, is paramount. Figure 3-3 shows some of the potential security issues involved with data integration.

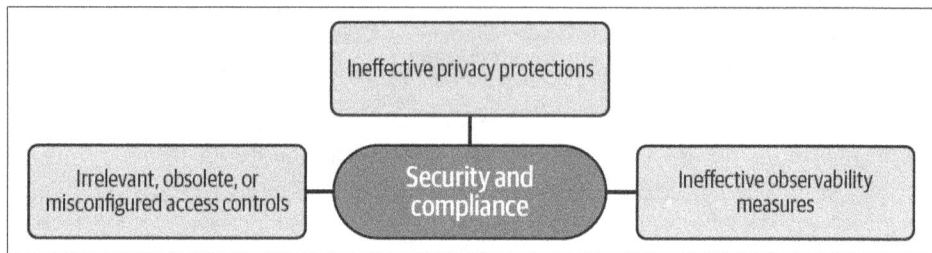

Figure 3-3. Data integration security and compliance

Conclusion

Adequately planning the implementation of a data integration solution is necessary to guarantee efficiency and effectiveness. It will help mitigate many of the issues discussed in this chapter and can decrease the need for manual intervention. Also, clear governance policies and proactive collaboration across the organization are just as important. Changes in data sources, business processes, and technologies can throw a wrench in schedules and budgets; if risks from potential change are not planned for and communication is only sporadic, the whole data integration effort can become untenable. This is especially true for large enterprise integration projects.

## CHAPTER 4

Models, Architectures, Methods, and Patterns

Unfortunately, there is not a standard, consistently used lexicon within data integration and literature involving integration topics. Some organizations and individuals will use the term *method* to indicate the implementation of certain types of data-related processes, while other organizations and individuals may use the term *technique* or *pattern* to indicate the same processes. But depending on who you ask, a method is not necessarily the same thing as a technique or pattern, and because there are so many viable pieces to the data integration puzzle, the inconsistent use of terms can be very confusing.

What I've learned from doing a rather extensive, albeit informal, survey of semantics within media on the topic of data integration is that there are many contextually overlapping meanings of the terms *model, architecture, method, pattern, technique, strategy,* and *blueprint*—among others. Also, there are subtle semantic differences between terms with similar but distinct descriptors, such as *data architecture* and *data integration architecture*. The discrepancy is not always readily apparent and is largely dependent on an individual's interpretation. Data architecture is broad and encompasses the overall management of data assets. Data integration architecture is narrower and focuses on the movement and transformation of data. Table 4-1 tabulates the differences.

Table 4-1. Differences between data architecture and data integration architecture

Aspect	Data architecture	Data integration architecture
Scope	Broad; encompasses the overall management of data assets	Narrow; focuses on the movement and transformation of data
Objective	Strategic; defines the data environment and governance	Tactical; ensures data flows efficiently between systems
Examples	Designing a data lake or defining data governance policies	Creating an ETL pipeline to sync CRM and ERP systems

So what exactly is a data integration model, a data integration architecture, a data integration method, a data integration pattern, a data integration technique, a data integration strategy, and a data integration blueprint?

If a model is a theoretical framework that represents components of a system and guides understanding of said system, then a data integration model is a framework that represents components of a data integration and guides understanding of said data integration. Specifically, a data integration model is a process model.

This definition of a model also sounds like a decent definition of what a blueprint is. So the term *model* will be assumed to be synonymous with the term *blueprint*, and the term *data integration model* will be assumed to be synonymous with the term *data integration blueprint*.

This chapter explores the foundational elements of data integration, including models, architectures, methods, and patterns. Each addresses particular combinations of source systems and their data types, the requirements of the consuming systems, and the degree of permanence of updates.

Models

Models in data integration refer to the theoretical frameworks and methodologies used to guide the integration process. They could, perhaps, be called "processing models." There are also, according to Anthony Giordano and IBM, at least three different types of models (or blueprints): conceptual, logical, and physical.[1]

Conceptual Data Integration Models

A conceptual data integration model provides a relatively abstract representation of how a data integration is expected to meet its requirements and intended objectives. It does not contain implementation details but does provide high-level information,

---

1 Giordano, Anthony David. 2011. *Data Integration Blueprint and Modeling: Techniques for a Scalable and Sustainable Architecture*. Upper Saddle River, NJ: IBM Press Pearson.

such as major conceptual processes, for project scoping. Figure 4-1 shows an example of a conceptual data integration model.

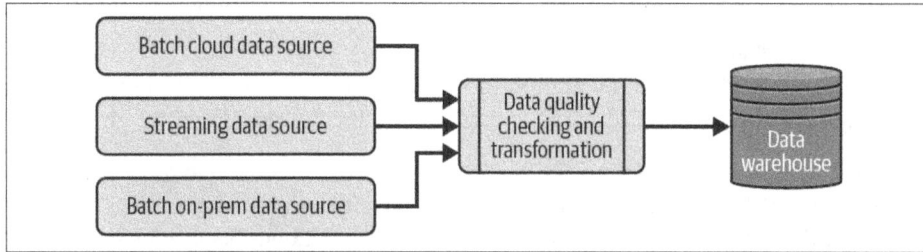

Figure 4-1. Conceptual data integration model example

Key elements of a conceptual data integration model include:

Data mapping
Specifies at a high level how data fields from source systems correspond to fields in the target system

Transformation rules
Defines how data should be cleaned, enriched, or converted to match the target format

Workflow design
Outlines the sequence of processes, including data source, ingestion, extraction, transformation, and loading (ETL, etc.)

Logical Data Integration Models

A logical data integration model displays data transformation and conditioning rules. Also, like the conceptual data integration model, it does not subscribe to specific technologies, but it does give notional representations of source and target mappings.

Logical data integration models fall into one of five subtypes:

High-level logical data integration models
High-level logical data integration models define the boundaries of the system and often include additional scoping information derived from the conceptual data integration model.

Logical-extract data integration models
Logical-extract data integration models outline the data elements that need to be extracted from the various source systems without specifying the technical details of how the extractions will occur. Connectivity to the source system should be determined and the tables or files to be transferred should be quantified.

Logical-data-quality data integration models
> Logical-data-quality data integration models specifically contain the data quality requirements, including the ability to produce reports regarding the data quality.

Logical-transform data integration models
> Logical-transform data integration models identify the transformations and conditioning steps that are required to meet the business needs downstream.

Logical-load data integration models
> The logical-load data integration model determines the load processes required to get the data into the target repositories after the data has been transformed and conditioned.

Figure 4-2 shows an example of a general logical data integration model.

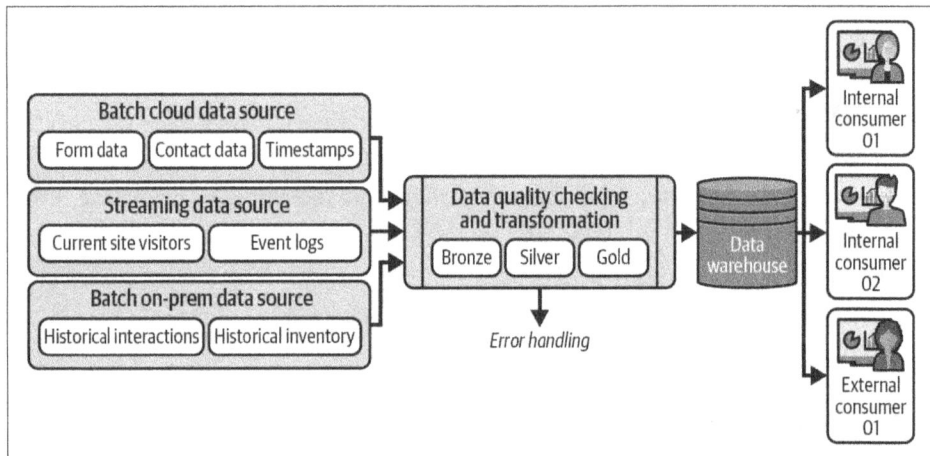

Figure 4-2. Logical data integration model example

Physical Data Integration Methods

Physical data integration models give specifications at the component level and should be at least notionally optimized in terms of dataflow through the organization's computing environment. The physical data integration model gives details on how data is getting integrated and, like the logical data integration model, is sometimes categorized into subtypes.

When working on a physical data integration model, you may find working with the server, cloud, and infrastructure teams useful. This can bring specialized domain experience to assist with system design. For example, knowing how much bandwidth is available between sites, what quality of service (QoS) will be used across a wide area network with limited capacity and latency, or what the GPU situation is for data processing can be helpful to inform the physical data integration models.

Architectures

Architectures define the structural design and organization of data systems. Data integration architectures include hub-and-spoke, point-to-point, bus, and federation. In this section, we'll describe each of them.

Hub-and-Spoke

A hub-and-spoke data integration architecture centralizes data exchange through a single hub, connecting multiple systems or applications. The connections are referred to as spokes, and the hub is sometimes referred to as a broker.

In this architecture, the hub manages all data transformations, routing, and communication between the system data sources and sinks, which eliminates the need for direct point-to-point interactions. This setup simplifies integration by reducing the number of interfaces and provides a clear, manageable structure for dataflow.

Other advantages include improved data quality and consistency and moderate scalability. With a single hub handling data transformations and validations, organizations can enforce consistent data standards across all connected systems and easily enhance overall data quality. The architecture also allows for easier scaling (to a point). New systems can be integrated by simply connecting them to the hub. That avoids the exponential growth of connections seen in point-to-point models.

In general, a single hub-and-spoke architecture is not considered scalable, mainly for two reasons. The first is because the central hub represents a critical component, and if it fails, it can disrupt communication across all connected systems. The second reason is because of the potential for performance bottlenecks. As the number of connected systems and data volume both increase, the hub's performance can drastically deteriorate if resource management does not become a priority.

Despite these challenges, the hub-and-spoke architecture remains a widely adopted model for data integration, particularly in scenarios requiring centralized control and simplified management of multiple systems.

Figure 4-3 shows a simple example of a hub-and-spoke integration architecture.

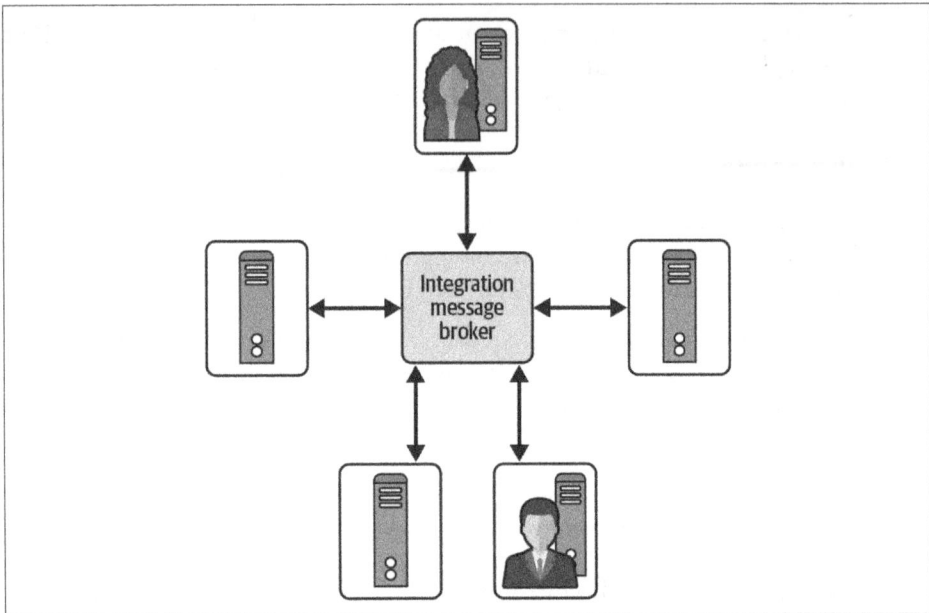

Figure 4-3. Example hub-and-spoke architecture

Point-to-Point

Point-to-point architectures are typically used for small and simple integrations. They can produce connections with low latency and are generally easy to troubleshoot and customize. However, they have some unfortunate drawbacks—specifically, for larger, more complex use cases, because they do not scale well.

For every node (e.g., data source or data target), the point-to-point architecture grows exponentially. For a fully connected point-to-point architecture with n number of nodes, there will be $n \times (n - 1) / 2$ connections. For example, with five nodes, there are ten connections, as Figure 4-4 illustrates. With six nodes, there would be fifteen connections. With seven nodes, the number of connections jumps to twenty-one.

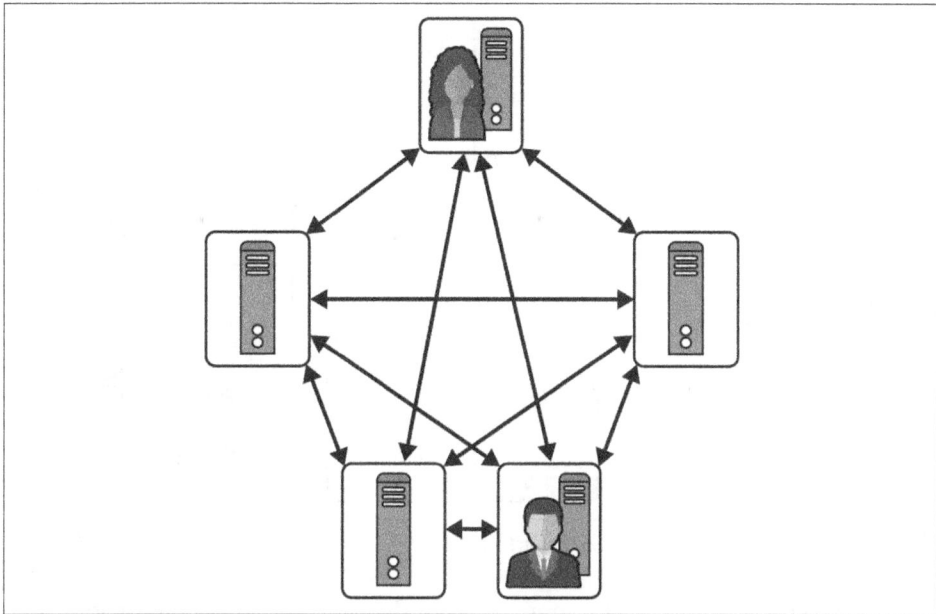

Figure 4-4. Example point-to-point architecture

Enterprise Service Bus

It seems like a significant amount of people consider a data integration bus a type of data integration architecture. Others consider it more in line with application integration. It's being included here because of the former.

Figure 4-5 shows an example Amazon ESB architecture.

In contrast to a hub-and-spoke architecture, an enterprise service bus (ESB) employs a distributed integration approach. Instead of a central hub, the ESB acts as a decentralized communication backbone, allowing data sources and sinks to interact through a common messaging bus. Each source and sink connect to the bus via adapters that handle data transformation and routing. This setup enhances scalability and flexibility, avoids a single point of failure, and can more easily accommodate the addition of new services.

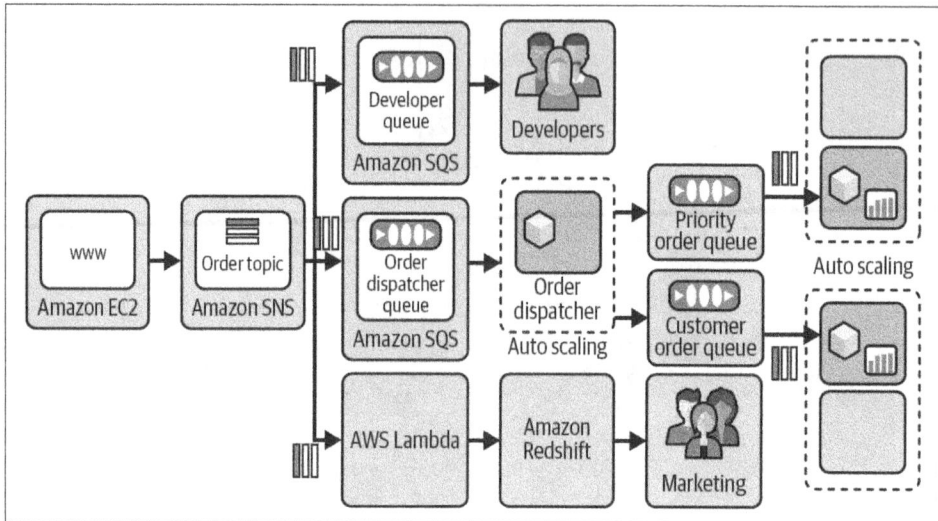

Figure 4-5. Example Amazon ESB architecture

ESB architectures are generally more scalable due to their distributed nature that allows for easier addition of new services without overloading a central hub. As stated previously, hub-and-spoke models may face performance issues as the number of connected systems increases.

Further, ESBs may be relatively more complex to set up, but they often offer better long-term flexibility and maintainability in dynamic environments.

> You may also observe the term *event-driven architecture* (EDA) used in similar context to an ESB.

Federation

Data federation is a relatively sophisticated data integration approach that allows organizations to access and query data from multiple, disparate sources as if they were a single source, without the need to replicate the data into a single repository. It typically consists of optimizing query routes from various sources such as databases, data warehouses, and data streams. Employing a federated query engine abstracts the complexity of accessing and merging data from different locations, formats, and schemas. This ensures that users and applications can access up-to-date and consistent data as if it were stored in a single location.

One of the key advantages of not needing to duplicate data across multiple repositories is that it minimizes redundancy and storage costs. Additionally, it enhances data governance and security because it simplifies the implementation of access controls and compliance requirements. In general, data federation provides a flexible, scalable, and efficient solution for organizations wanting to integrate diverse data sources while maintaining data integrity and minimizing infrastructure overhead.

Methods

Methods encompass the various techniques and approaches used to facilitate seamless dataflow and interoperability. Data integration involves various methods to combine data from different sources. Each method has its distinct approach and suitability based on organizational demands. We will now look at five common methods:

Manual integration

There is no unified view of the data in this method. Users access data directly from the source systems as needed. Although this approach is highly flexible and allows users to interact with data from multiple sources, it can be inefficient and prone to errors because it requires significant manual effort to aggregate and interpret the data, particularly in larger organizations with large diverse sets of data sources.

Application-based integration

Best suited for small teams, this method requires each application to implement its integration procedures. This approach allows for specific, tailored integrations that meet the exact needs of the application and its users. While this can be efficient for smaller setups, it can become increasingly complex and difficult to manage as the number of applications and integration points grows.

Middleware data integration

Middleware acts as a mediator that normalizes data before adding it to a main pool. This method is particularly beneficial for transferring data from legacy applications that cannot connect directly to newer systems. Using middleware, organizations can guarantee that data from different systems is standardized and can be easily integrated.

Uniform access integration

This method keeps data in the source systems but provides a unified view through several defined views. Users can access a consistent, consolidated view of data without the need to physically move the data from its source. This approach helps maintain data integrity and consistency and reduces the risk of unintentional data duplication.

Common data storage integration

This method involves creating a separate system that copies data from the primary source while also managing additional data outside of the original source. Maintaining a separate data storage system can help centralize an organization's data for more accessible analysis and reporting. This approach supports scalability and can handle large volumes of data.

Each of these methods has its pros and cons, and choosing one over another depends on factors such as the size of the team, the complexity of the data systems, and the specific needs of the organization.

Patterns

Patterns serve as reusable solutions to common problems encountered in data integration—that is, patterns in data integration refer to the most commonly recurring solutions to commonly encountered problems. Some widely used patterns include the data consolidation pattern, the data propagation pattern, the data virtualization pattern, and the event-driven integration pattern.

Ingestion Patterns

Data ingestion is a foundational process in data integration, involving the collection and transportation of data from various sources into a system for storage, processing, and analysis. Ingestion patterns define the methods and workflows used to facilitate this transfer and ensure data consistency, efficiency, and reliability. These patterns can broadly be categorized as batch ingestion, near-real-time (or streaming) ingestion, and hybrid approaches.

Batch ingestion involves transferring large volumes of data at scheduled intervals, making it suitable for scenarios where latency is not critical. Near-real-time ingestion, on the other hand, captures and processes data continuously as it's generated, which enables near-instantaneous insights and actions. This can be particularly useful for things like fraud detection or IoT monitoring. Hybrid patterns combine the strengths of both approaches and offer flexibility to accommodate diverse data sources and business needs.

Selecting the appropriate ingestion pattern depends on factors such as the velocity, volume, and variety of data, as well as the specific goals of the integration project. Next, let's look at two specific ingestion patterns that can accommodate batch, streaming, or hybrid.

Extract, transform, load

Extract, transform, load (ETL) is the "traditional" approach for moving and handling data between a data source and a data target. A target is any destination to which data gets moved or copied and can be a data sink (i.e., a storage location) or a data consumer such as an analytics platform or streaming service.

ETL is considered "traditional" because it's generally associated with batch data processing and was used extensively in on-premises data systems prior to the ubiquity of the cloud and more robust storage and processing systems.

As the name implies, data is first extracted from a source and typically placed in a staging area, also sometimes called a landing zone. The staging area can be located on the source server, on the target server, or even on both. While in the staging area, the data is curated and transformed into a useful, consolidated dataset according to business rules and conventions. The data is then loaded into storage or another application for further processing.

The book *Data Integration Blueprint and Modeling* even mentions multiple types of staging areas—namely, the clean staging area and the load-ready staging area. The clean staging area contains records that have been through data quality checks and could be thought of as a first staging area. It is the staging area before the data is enhanced or undergoes more complicated transformations.

The load-ready staging area could be considered a second staging area. If a target destination cannot take the direct output from upstream processing tools, then a load-ready staging area may be required. In a medallion refinement architecture, the load-ready staging area might be equivalent to a gold or insight layer.

To accomplish the extract phase, APIs are often used to run queries, various protocols are used to transfer the data directly from one system to another, or web pages are scraped via Python or some other scraping tool.

As touched on previously, transforming, or *wrangling*, data can include correcting errors, replacing missing values (also known as *imputing*), merging datasets, converting units, reformatting, filtering, masking, encrypting, sorting, and aggregating.

The load phase involves writing the transformed data to a target system, like a data warehouse, and making it accessible to other applications for analytics and reporting. Figure 4-6 illustrates the ETL process.

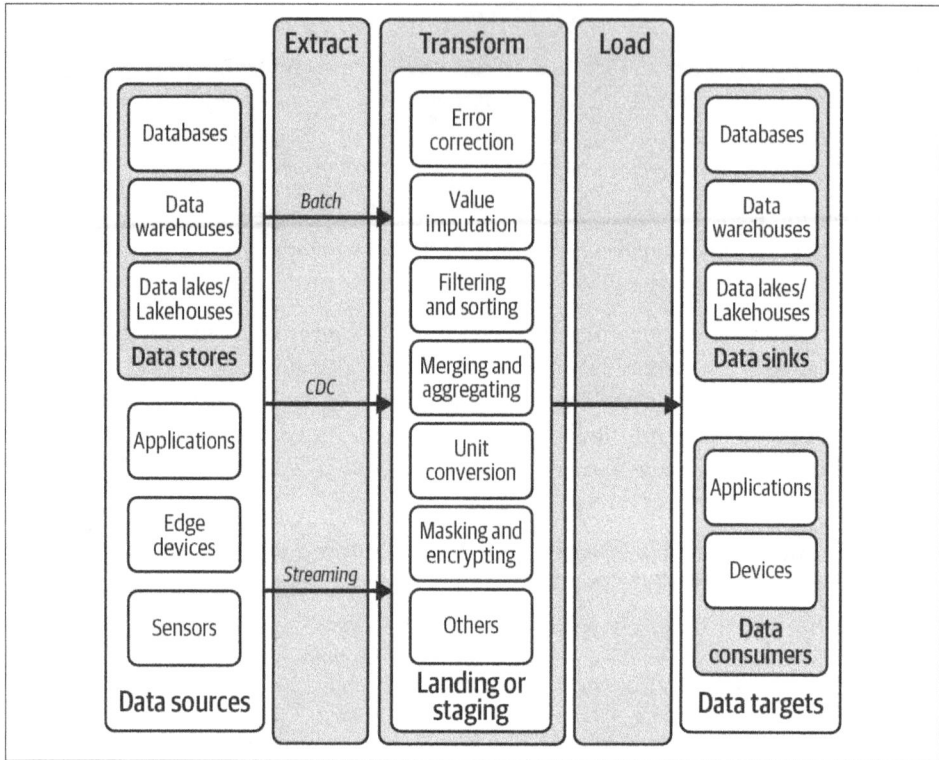

Figure 4-6. Anatomy of the ETL process

ETL is crucial in scenarios where data quality and consistency are necessary for downstream applications. A data warehouse is the typical storage type associated with the ETL process because ETL inherently accommodates structured data and data warehouses often support OLAP. The ETL process is also generally associated with smaller datasets and resources that can handle complex transformations.

Perhaps a good analogy to the ETL process is the culinary concept known as mise en place, where ingredients are prepped prior to creating an entrée. At a sandwich shop, for instance, fresh vegetables, meats, and cheeses are extracted from the refrigerator and chopped, sliced, transformed, and organized into easily accessible individual ingredients, which are then loaded onto pieces of bread to create a customized sandwich. The consumer in this analogy might represent the data analytics team at the end of the ETL process waiting for organized data so it can perform analyses, create models, and produce reports.

Reverse ETL, the poorly named concept for subsequent data movement after completing an initial ETL process, has, unfortunately, entered the data engineering lexicon. "Reverse" implies a simple inversion, which oversimplifies the complexities involved in the process of syncing data back to operational systems. The key aspect is to operationalize data, often for use in near-real-time applications, rather than merely reversing the dataflow. More descriptive terms, like "operational analytics" or "data activation," might be more appropriate.

Extract, load, transform

ELT stands for extract, load, transform, and—perhaps obviously—it differs from ETL in its sequence of stages. Unlike ETL, the ELT process prioritizes loading and leaves the data unchanged. Data transformation generally does not occur before data is loaded into the storage location, and when it does, the transformations are minimal and amount to little more than organization. Storing the raw data helps mitigate information loss, but the ELT process is also beneficial when computing resources used in transformations are unavailable or otherwise unable to keep up with the volume of data. This can also potentially result in cost savings in the cloud if the data transformations are performed during off-peak computing times.

Using the previous sandwich shop analogy, ELT is almost like taking the vegetables, meats, and condiments directly out of the refrigerator and just leaving them out on a big table for the customers to prep their own ingredients and make their own sandwiches. This works well when there aren't enough sandwich makers to individually make each customer's sandwich.

ELT is also ideal for near-real-time stream processing and rapid batch processing because the focus is on getting the data into the system quickly. ELT decouples transformation of the data from loading of the data.

You may observe ELT used in environments with big-data platforms, cloud-based data platforms, streaming platforms, or lakehouses. Key benefits are scalability, flexibility, and cost-effectiveness.

Integration projects in general seem to be shifting from ETL to a post-load transformation approach (i.e., ELT) presumably because of the large size of contemporary datasets, the increasing desire for near-real-time analytics, and the continuing adoption of data mesh and data fabric.

> A rule of thumb might be that ETL is to data warehouse as ELT is to data lake.

Data Consolidation Pattern

The data consolidation pattern in data integration focuses on combining data from multiple sources into a single, unified view. This pattern involves extracting data from various disparate systems, transforming it into a common format, and then loading it into a centralized repository such as a data warehouse or data lake. Data from various sources can be converted to common schemas, joined, and easily analyzed in these central repositories. Often a data catalog is available to help data analysts and business users explore data domains and products so they can better use the organization's data to answer complex questions. The goal of data consolidation is to provide a holistic view of the organization's data and enable more comprehensive analysis and decision making.

This pattern typically employs an ETL process. During the extraction phase, data is collected from different sources, which may include databases, applications, and external data feeds. The transformation phase involves cleaning, validating, and converting the data into a consistent format. Finally, during the loading phase, the transformed data is loaded into the central repository.

Data consolidation helps in eliminating data silos and maintaining data consistency and data quality. It also facilitates easier access to integrated data and allows for more effective data analytics and reporting. By consolidating data, some organizations can enhance operational efficiency.

Data Replication and Propagation Pattern

The data propagation pattern is used to ensure consistent and efficient data transfer between disparate systems. This pattern involves the systematic movement of data from one system to another. The data gets synchronized and updated across all involved platforms. Like the data consolidation pattern, it also typically includes processes like ETL and is particularly useful in environments where near-real-time data updates are important. Additionally, data propagation can be implemented using various mechanisms including batch processing, near-real-time streaming, and CDC. Each of these mechanisms serves different needs, from reducing latency to minimizing system load. Leveraging the data propagation pattern generally enables better data accessibility.

Data Virtualization Pattern

Creating a virtual data layer that engages data from various sources without moving or copying it is called *data virtualization*. This integration pattern can often be used to support near-real-time data access and can enhance system flexibility. Data virtualization has many similarities to data federation (discussed earlier in this chapter). Both aim to make accessing and querying distributed data easier without centralizing it.

However, while the differences are subtle, they are important. Data virtualization is often considered broader and more focused on abstraction, while data federation is focused more on query execution across systems. Table 4-2 outlines the differences between the two.

Table 4-2. Data virtualization versus data federation

Aspect	Data virtualization	Data federation
Primary focus	Abstraction of data access	Query distribution and aggregation
Data storage	Data remains in the source systems	Data remains in source systems; focuses on query aggregation
Performance dependency	Relies heavily on source system performance	Relies on query optimization across sources
Integration approach	Provides a virtual view	Provides a federated query mechanism
Use case emphasis	Near-real-time analytics and BI	Querying multiple databases as one

The appropriate use of data virtualization versus data federation ultimately comes down to the size and level of complexity of the data sources. Data virtualization uses some replication for caching purposes, and data federation optimizes queries that access sources directly, which is why data federation is included in "Architectures" on page 61 and data virtualization is included in "Patterns" on page 66. Data virtualization and data federation can complement each other. Virtualization might be used for high-level abstraction, and federation can execute distributed queries beneath that abstraction layer.

Event-Driven Integration Pattern

The event-driven integration pattern involves the use of events to trigger and communicate changes or updates across different systems or components within an architecture. This pattern hinges on the premise that systems or applications emit events whenever a significant change occurs, such as the creation, modification, or deletion of data. These events are captured and propagated to other pertinent systems in near real time.

Specifically, in this pattern, an event producer generates an event when a change happens. The event is then published to an event bus or messaging system, such as Apache Kafka or AWS SNS. The event bus acts as a central hub that distributes the event to various event consumers that have subscribed to these types of events. Each event consumer processes the event independently, which entails performing tasks like updating their own data stores, triggering additional workflows, and further propagating the event to other systems.

The event-driven integration pattern offers several advantages. It decouples the data producer and the data consumers and allows them to evolve independently. It also supports near-real-time data integration and enables systems to react promptly to changes, which helps applications requiring low latency and high responsiveness. Furthermore, systems can handle an increasing volume of events by scaling out the event bus and consumer components.

The event-driven integration pattern is a robust approach to integrating disparate systems that helps ensure that data changes are communicated swiftly and efficiently across an enterprise architecture.

Conclusion

There are detailed guidelines and best practices for implementing data integration solutions. These blueprints often include reference architectures, technology stacks, and implementation strategies. For instance, a common blueprint might outline the use of specific tools such as Apache Kafka for near-real-time data streaming, Apache Spark for data processing, and a combination of relational and NoSQL databases for storage. This helps organizations standardize their data integration efforts and safeguard consistency and reliability across different projects.

Several best practices can be followed to ensure that a data integration effort is successful, including:

Defining clear goals
> It's important to define clear goals and objectives for data integrations so processes are aligned with business needs.

Ensuring data quality
> Data quality is crucial for successful data integration, and it's important the data is accurate and up-to-date.

Ensuring data security
> Data security is an important consideration when integrating data from different sources, and it's important to implement proper security measures to protect sensitive customer data.

Using appropriate tools
> Choosing the right data integration tool is crucial for success, and it's typically necessary to consider factors such as cost, ease of use, and scalability.

Implementing incrementally
> Consider implementing the solution incrementally, beginning with data sources and then expanding from there.

Involving stakeholders
> Engage stakeholders from different departments to ensure the solution meets cross-functional needs.

Improving continuously
> Regularly assess the integration solution's performance and make improvements based on feedback and changing business requirements.

Data integration encompasses a range of models, architectures, blueprints, methods, and patterns that collectively enable organizations to unify their data from diverse sources. By leveraging the right combination of these elements, seamless data integration can be achieved, and the ability to analyze data, derive insights, and make data-driven decisions can be significantly enhanced. As discussed, the choice of models, architectures, blueprints, methods, and patterns depends on various factors that include the nature of the data, the specific requirements of the organization, and the desired outcomes of the integration process.

## PART II

Tools, Technologies, and Frameworks

There are many different data integration tools, and they include everything from freely accessible programming scripts to comprehensive proprietary platforms and à la carte cloud services. In this part, we'll discuss some of the common features and options of the technologies used in data integrations, as well as their advantages and disadvantages. Also, this part is not meant to be read end-to-end but as a reference of potential technologies to employ during the implementation of a data integration solution, so feel free to skip around.

I do not have hands-on experience with all of the individual tools and technologies discussed in this part. I have, therefore, occasionally relied on vendor websites to validate that certain capabilities exist for a given tool. I made a significant effort to include accurate information, but always do your due diligence and research a tool prior to use, especially if you're paying for it.

## CHAPTER 5

Data Integration Tool Options

When selecting tools for data integration, organizations face a variety of important decisions that can significantly impact the feasibility, efficiency, and maintainability of their data pipelines. A key consideration is the choice between open source and commercial tools. Each offers advantages in terms of cost, support, and flexibility. Additionally, the availability of low-code and no-code platforms offers simplified integration processes, but they need to be weighed against more customizable and powerful programming language–based approaches. Another critical factor is whether to opt for *software as a service* (SaaS) solutions, which offer scalability and convenience, or on-premises deployments that provide greater control. Finally, organizations must decide between distributed architectures that enable resilience and scalability across multiple nodes, and centralized solutions that may be simpler to manage but are less flexible for large-scale applications. This chapter explores these options.

> It's sometimes difficult to differentiate a "tool" from a "platform." In general, I try to designate software as a tool when it performs a relatively narrow function, such as loading a data file into object storage. I consider a platform, on the other hand, to be software that contains multiple tools in a single interface. However, the distinction is somewhat arbitrary and subjective. If you think that's confusing, you can consider the terms synonymous.

Open Source Versus Commercial Solutions

Many data engineering projects, including data integrations, can be implemented using free and open source tools. Software, like the many "flavors" of Linux and the plethora of tools maintained by the Apache Foundation, is freely available to build out top-tier data ecosystems. To compete with open source tools, commercial products aim to differentiate themselves in order to add enough value to be adopted by organizations. The value primarily comes in the form of extended capabilities and decreased risk. The government in particular benefits from commercial products because commercial solutions can often alleviate risks associated with persistent resource constraints and bureaucracy.

Now, let's take a deeper dive into some of the advantages and disadvantages of both open source and commercial options.

Advantages of Open Source Solutions

Open source data integration software offers numerous benefits for organizations aiming to streamline their data processes. One of the most obvious benefits is cost-effectiveness. The open source tools are free, which is especially advantageous for small to medium-sized organizations with limited technology budgets but technically skilled personnel.

Using open source tools can create or enhance technical skills through hands-on learning provided by easily accessible resources. Personnel are not limited by organizational licenses that can preclude them from gaining experience outside of work and subsequently leveraging that gained experience to increase their productivity on the job.

Flexibility and customization are also key advantages of open source software. Organizations can often tailor open source tools to meet their specific needs or use them as a starting point for further development by modifying source code, adding new features, or incorporating compatibility with other systems. The ability to inspect and alter the source code is what makes open source tools "transparent." The transparency ideally helps ensure the security and integrity of the end-user software. Further flexibility comes from the reduction or elimination of vendor dependency. This gives organizations the freedom to choose when, where, and how to implement software.

The more popular open source software tools often have large communities of users and developers who provide support and continuously contribute to improving the tools, almost always on a volunteer basis.

Advantages of Commercial Solutions

One of the most significant advantages of using a commercial solution is the dedicated support services that typically accompany it. Services offered can include everything from simple technical troubleshooting to hands-on training, consulting, and project management. Expert assistance can prove to be well worth the cost by minimizing downtime and maintaining productivity.

Generally, another notable benefit of commercial tools is their user-friendliness and their focus on their user interface (UI) and user experience (UX). The tools often have optimized UI/UX features, which helps shrink the learning curve and enables users to perform complex tasks through intuitive and visually appealing interfaces.

Enhanced data visualization tools offered by many of the commercial data integration and analytics platforms allow users to more easily create detailed interactive dashboards and reports. Such visualizations facilitate better data analysis and help present data in a clear and easily interpretable manner, which ultimately helps decision makers identify trends and insights quickly.

More robust security features are another advantage of commercial data integration products. Vendors invest heavily in ensuring their products comply with stringent security standards and regulations that sometimes even necessitate periodic audits. This ensures that sensitive data is protected against breaches and unauthorized access.

Finally, with commercial products, at least some of the risk associated with data integration inherently gets shifted to the original equipment manufacturer (OEM). System failures, data breaches, and compliance violations become the problem of the OEM and the integrator, particularly if the vendor has a service-level agreement (SLA). Because of this, it could be argued that commercial solutions are more reliable than their open source counterparts and can allow organizations to focus more of their time and effort on their core competencies.

Clearly, commercial data integration solutions do have their advantages that can make them a compelling option for organizations wanting to enhance the efficiency and effectiveness of their data integration and management processes.

> The contemporary commercial solutions that I mention and discuss in this part primarily include frontrunners in their industry categories per the leading advisory firms (e.g., Gartner, Forrester). However, there are many smaller OEMs and startup companies that provide great solutions that I was unable to cover in this book.

Programming Languages Versus Low-Code/ No-Code Platforms

Some commercial solutions market their applications as "low code" or "no code," which theoretically allows users with minimal technical expertise and no programming experience to build and manage data workflows. Low-code/no-code platforms attempt to democratize data integration and make it accessible to a broader range of people, reducing the reliance on data engineers and specialized IT staff.

Low-code and no-code platforms have become increasingly significant in the realm of data integration. As mentioned, these platforms allow users with little to no programming experience to move, replicate, consolidate, and organize data quickly and easily. Although the platforms are generally not quite as flexible in the nuanced capabilities that programming allows, commercial low-code/no-code products can expedite the integration of various data sources, including databases, cloud services, and APIs. Also, these platforms often come with a plethora of built-in connectors and drag-and-drop functionalities, which can make it much easier to map data fields and set up pipelines.

For technically savvy data engineers, many of the low-code/no-code commercial platforms do allow users to write code in tandem with the point-and-click features, which adds to their flexibility. Programming languages like Python, R, SQL, and JavaScript often play nicely with these flexible commercial platforms, and they subsequently offer a more robust and accommodating user experience. Moreover, prebuilt templates or code snippets are sometimes available to hasten programming efforts, and LLMs will undoubtedly provide useful code and instructions when asked. The democratization of the ability to perform these processes can significantly reduce the burden on IT departments and the more senior data engineers.

Some of the leading low-code/no-code platforms for integrating enterprise data include MuleSoft's Anypoint Platform, Boomi, Informatica's Intelligent Cloud Services, SnapLogic, Qlik's Talend Data Fabric, IBM's App Connect, TIBCO's Cloud Integration, and Adeptia Connect.

Cloud Versus On-Premises Architectures

With the rapid adoption of cloud technologies, data integration strategies have evolved significantly, differing fundamentally from traditional on-premises approaches. Understanding the distinctions between cloud and on-premises data integration is important for organizations looking to optimize their data strategies and leverage the best of both worlds.

Although the overall trend for both public and private sector organizations has been to move toward using cloud services, the majority of tools discussed in this part have the option to run on premises (i.e., to be client-managed) as well as in the cloud (SaaS, IaaS, etc.). On-premises (or "on-prem" for short) solutions are still in demand, particularly with government agencies that deal with sensitive or classified information.

Cloud platforms provide numerous advantages for data integration processes compared to traditional on-premises solutions. The first and most obvious advantage is the exceptional scalability that allows organizations to expand or contract their resources based on demand, which is especially useful for managing fluctuating workloads and large datasets. The flexibility and accessibility of cloud services can enable seamless access to data and integration tools from any location, supporting remote and hybrid work environments and facilitating integration with other cloud services and third-party tools.

The cost efficiency of the cloud's pay-as-you-go model helps organizations reduce upfront capital expenditures by paying only for the resources they use. Organizations also save money by not needing internal IT support personnel and by avoiding lost revenue or productivity from hardware and software downtime. Cloud platforms take care of hardware maintenance and system updates. They also provide robust disaster recovery and high availability options through built-in redundancy and backup solutions that enhance the resilience and reliability of data integration workflows.

While cloud platforms offer numerous advantages for data integration, they also present certain challenges. Data security and compliance can be more complex in the cloud compared to on-premises solutions because organizations must navigate stringent regulations like GDPR and HIPAA while mitigating the risk of potential data breaches. Additionally, cloud services depend heavily on stable internet connectivity, which means that any disruptions can significantly impact the performance and availability of integration processes.

Another concern is vendor lock-in, where organizations may find it difficult and costly to switch cloud providers or migrate their data integration workflows to another platform. This is especially true for government agencies, who are required to encourage vendor competition and whose affinity for multicloud architectures and CSP-independent applications is only increasing.

On-Premises Considerations

With on-premises data integration, organizations have full control over their infrastructure, data security, and workflow processes. This does allow for greater customization and adherence to specific security and operational policies. For industries with stringent data sovereignty and compliance requirements, on-premises solutions can ensure that data does not leave a specific geographic location. When data sources and integration processes are within the same physical location, on-premises integration can often offer lower latency and higher performance compared to cloud-based solutions.

On-premises infrastructure does typically require significant investment to scale, which makes it less flexible in handling dynamic workloads or rapid growth compared to cloud solutions. The initial investment in hardware, software, and skilled personnel can be substantial. Further, maintenance and upgrade costs contribute to the overall expense, as managing and maintaining on-premises systems requires a dedicated team and other resources. This can be a challenge for organizations with limited IT staff or expertise. Setting up and configuring on-premises solutions can be time-consuming, especially when dealing with complex data integration workflows and customizations.

I sometimes use the terms *on-prem*, *client-managed*, and *air-gapped* interchangeably, but there are appreciable differences. It's more accurate to consider air-gapped systems to be a subset of on-prem systems, and on-prem systems could be considered a subset of client-managed systems.

Cloud Service Providers

Now we'll look at a number of leading cloud service providers (CSPs). They each offer a comprehensive suite of services and solutions tailored to meet a myriad of business needs.

Amazon Web Services

Amazon Web Services (AWS) is arguably the most mature and most widely adopted cloud platform,[1] and this is reflected across the federal government, particularly in the DOD. AWS offers an extensive array of services including storage options, extensive networking capabilities, and effectively unlimited computing power. Its rich ecosystem of tools and integrations caters to startups, established enterprises, and governmental organizations, and its global infrastructure spans numerous regions and availability zones, which ensures high availability and reliability.

AWS gained in popularity largely through its *Simple Storage Service*, also known as *S3*. It's a highly scalable object storage service designed to store and retrieve whatever amount of data from anywhere on the web. Known for its durability, availability, and security, S3 supports various data storage classes, and at different price points. Less frequently accessed and longer-term data storage is generally less expensive than frequently accessed data, which allows users to lower their costs. S3 integrates seamlessly with other AWS services, making it a popular choice for a wide range of applications in the cloud, including data lakes, data backups and archives, and content distribution.

Google Cloud Platform

Google Cloud Platform (GCP) excels in data analytics, machine learning, and AI. Leveraging Google's expertise in big data, GCP provides powerful tools such as BigQuery, TensorFlow, and AutoML. GCP is also known for its strong emphasis on open source technologies and multicloud support, making it a preferred choice for developers and data scientists.

---

1 AWS is also the CSP with which I am currently most familiar, although my journey to the cloud began with Azure.

IBM Cloud

With its acquisition of Red Hat, IBM significantly bolstered its hybrid cloud capabilities, enabling its applications and services to run seamlessly across multiple environments. IBM Cloud also offers a robust set of AI tools through IBM Watson, which provides advanced analytics and cognitive computing capabilities. Organizations with complex regulatory and compliance requirements often choose IBM Cloud due to its strong security and governance features.

Microsoft Azure

Azure is Microsoft's cloud platform offering, and as might be expected, it integrates well with Microsoft's software ecosystem, including Windows Server, Active Directory, and Microsoft 365. Azure offers a comprehensive set of cloud services ranging from AI and machine learning to IoT and DevOps tools. Azure's hybrid cloud capabilities, which allow integration between on-premises and cloud environments, are particularly appealing to large organizations with complex IT needs.

> AWS and Azure largely offer the same services with similar features. Although the companies would likely argue otherwise, if a capability is available in one, the other almost surely has a nearly identical capability. The same is likely true for GCP, but I can't confidently attest to it.

Oracle Cloud Platform

Oracle Cloud Platform is tailored for enterprise applications and is generally the preferred choice for enterprises already heavily invested in Oracle software. It provides a suite of cloud services with a strong emphasis on databases, enterprise resource planning (ERP), and supply chain management (SCM). Oracle's Autonomous Database offering can provide significant value with "self-managing, self-securing, and self-repairing" capabilities. Oracle Cloud's infrastructure is designed to support high-performance workloads, making it suitable for large enterprises with demanding computing needs.

Distributed Versus Centralized Data Systems

Distributed storage and distributed streaming and processing are all options that can be available for implementation of a data integration solution. As mentioned in Part I, distributed storage refers to a system in which data is stored across multiple physical locations or nodes, often spread between different datacenters and even geographic regions (e.g., *availability zones*). This ensures high availability and fault tolerance. Distributed data is generally accessed and managed as if it were stored on a single system despite possibly being divvied up among many locations. Technologies like the Hadoop Distributed File System (HDFS) and cloud storage solutions like Amazon S3 exemplify this approach.

Distributed streaming involves the near-real-time processing and analysis of data that is continuously generated from various sources. In order to avoid bottlenecks in a high-throughput network, the availability of multiple paths to the same I/O buffer can help alleviate unacceptable latency. Apache Kafka is a prominent example of a distributed streaming platform that also provides the capability to publish and subscribe to streams of data so, ultimately, multiple consumers can utilize the same data source concurrently.

Distributed processing frameworks like Apache Spark can divide tasks into smaller subtasks that are then executed simultaneously on multiple threads and eventually aggregated. On the hardware side, *graphics processing units* (GPUs), like those produced by Nvidia, have facilitated highly parallelized processing. Large language models (LLMs) and other AI/ML models would not be nearly as successful if it were not for the capabilities of GPUs that allow efficient training of AI/ML models in parallel.

Distributed systems offer significant benefits in terms of scalability, fault tolerance, and resource optimization. They can handle large volumes of data and high traffic loads by delegating workloads across multiple machines. However, distributed systems can also be complicated to design and manage. They often require robust coordination mechanisms to ensure consistency and prevent data loss or corruption, which can be challenging due to the inherent latency and failure risks associated with network communication. Distributed systems can also be difficult to debug and test. Issues might reveal themselves only under specific conditions that are difficult to intentionally replicate.

In-Memory Processing

In-memory data processing refers to the practice of storing and processing data directly within a computer's main memory (i.e., RAM) rather than relying on slower storage mediums like hard drives or solid-state drives. This approach significantly improves the speed and efficiency of data operations by reducing the time spent on data retrieval and input/output operations. In-memory processing is particularly advantageous for applications requiring near-real-time data analysis such as financial analytics, online recommendation systems, and fraud detection.

Frameworks like Apache Spark and Redis have popularized in-memory processing by leveraging distributed computing to handle large datasets across clusters of machines. Keeping data in memory allows these systems to reduce latency and enable faster iterative computations that are common in machine learning, graph processing, and large-scale simulations.

However, in-memory processing does have disadvantages. The major disadvantage is the obvious RAM requirements to store and manipulate datasets. To mitigate this, modern systems often incorporate memory-efficient techniques like data compression, columnar storage formats, and intelligent caching strategies.

Security and Compliance

The level of security and compliance of a solution is another option that needs to be carefully considered. Commercial enterprise data systems are governed by a complex framework of standards and regulations designed to protect data privacy, ensure security, and maintain compliance with industry-specific requirements.

One important set of standards is the *Payment Card Industry Data Security Standard* (PCI DSS) that governs organizations that handle credit card information. PCI DSS provides a framework for securing cardholder data, including encryption, access control, and regular security assessments to prevent data breaches and fraud.

For organizations in the healthcare sector, the *Health Insurance Portability and Accountability Act* (HIPAA) sets national standards for protecting sensitive patient information with the goal to ensure that healthcare providers and their business associates implement necessary safeguards to secure health data.

Government information systems, including data integration hardware and software, are themselves subject to various laws and regulations designed to ensure data security, privacy, and the effective use of technology in public administration. In the United States, the *Federal Information Security Modernization Act* (FISMA) mandated federal agencies to develop, document, and implement information security programs to protect their data and information systems. This act also requires agencies to perform regular assessments of their security controls and report their compliance status.

Another regulation at the forefront of government IT implementation, particularly SaaS solutions, is the *Federal Risk and Authorization Management Program* (FedRAMP). FedRAMP provides a standardized approach to security assessment, authorization, and continuous monitoring for cloud products and services used by federal agencies. It ensures that cloud services and software providers meet stringent security requirements before being utilized by government entities.

The *Privacy Act of 1974* and the *E-Government Act of 2002* are also key legislation. The Privacy Act establishes guidelines for the collection, maintenance, and dissemination of personal information by federal agencies, while the E-Government Act promotes the use of the internet and other information technologies to improve citizen access to government information and services. It also includes provisions for safeguarding the privacy of individuals when agencies collect information electronically. Also, the *Federal Data Strategy* and the *Foundations for Evidence-Based*

Policymaking Act of 2018 encourage the responsible and transparent use of data in government to improve decision making and public service outcomes, emphasizing data governance, data sharing, and ethical considerations in data use.

These and other regulations and standards collectively ensure that private and public organizations operate with accountability, transparency, and robust security measures to protect both the data of individuals as well as sensitive organizational information from potential threats and legal liabilities.

Conclusion

The choice between open source and commercial data integration solutions, low-code/no-code platforms, and cloud versus on-premises architectures is fundamentally about aligning toolsets with the specific needs and constraints of an organization. Each option presents unique strengths and potential drawbacks that must be evaluated against business objectives, resource availability, and strategic goals. As data engineering evolves, it's imperative to stay attuned to the dynamic landscape of tools and platforms, ensuring that the chosen solutions not only address current needs but also support scalability, security, and potential future innovations.

## CHAPTER 6

Data Stores and Management Systems

Data storage does not necessarily need to impose structure on data. For example, a filesystem may store data as raw files with no inherent organization other than folder structure. However, throughout the majority of this book, data storage is equated with databases. And as discussed in Part I, there are two primary types of contemporary databases: relational databases and non-relational databases. For structured data that can be organized into rows and columns, relational databases are the obvious choice because of their ubiquity and efficiency. The relational databases described in this chapter include IBM Db2, Microsoft SQL Server, MySQL and MariaDB, Oracle Database, PostgreSQL, SQLite, and Sybase and SAP.

For unstructured data, such as images, videos, audio files, and text files, non-relational databases are more appropriate than relational databases. We'll go over multiple kinds of non-relational databases in this chapter, including document stores and key-value storage, graph databases, vector databases, and wide-column stores. The specific non-relational databases covered in this chapter include Amazon DynamoDB and DocumentDB, Apache Ignite, MongoDB, Redis, Amazon Neptune, Neo4j, TigerGraph, Pinecone, Apache Cassandra and HBase, AWS Keyspaces, and Google Bigtable.

Data warehouses, data lakes, and data lakehouses are also discussed in this chapter and include product offerings such as Amazon Redshift, Apache Doris, Apache Druid, Apache Hadoop, Apache Hive, Cloudera Data Warehouse (CDW), IBM Db2 Warehouse, Snowflake, and Amazon Simple Storage Service (S3).

Amazon offers a comprehensive suite of services to help organizations build and manage data lakes. It enables efficient storage and analysis of vast amounts of data, and at the core is Amazon S3, providing a durable, scalable, and secure foundation for your data lake. With AWS Lake Formation, you can expedite the creation of secure data lakes, reducing the time from months to days. AWS Glue facilitates seamless data movement between your data lake and various analytics services. This integrated ecosystem allows you to store all your data cost-effectively, foster innovation through comprehensive analytics, utilize purpose-built tools for optimal performance, and simplify management with serverless options.

This chapter underscores that effective data integration strategies must account for the diversity of storage and management systems—relational, non-relational, data warehouses, data lakes, and lakehouses—each with distinct data models, performance profiles, and scalability characteristics. Successful integration architectures need to support seamless interoperability, schema translation, and optimized data movement between these heterogeneous systems to enable unified analytics, governance, and operational efficiency.

Relational Databases

Many relational databases can operate on block storage systems provided by cloud services like AWS (e.g., Amazon EBS), Azure (e.g., Azure Managed Disks), and Google (e.g., Google Persistent Disks). In such configurations, the relational database management system (RDBMS) interacts with block storage through the underlying operating system, which handles tasks like filesystem management and block allocation.

Some of the most popular RDBMS platforms that are covered in this section, aside from those available from the three major CSPs, include IBM Db2, Microsoft SQL Server (MSSQL), MySQL, MariaDB, Oracle Database, PostgreSQL, SQLite, and Sybase, but there are many others.

IBM Db2

IBM Db2 is an RDBMS developed by IBM in the 1980s. Db2 was one of the first commercial relational databases and has since evolved into a robust, enterprise-grade database solution known for its performance, scalability, and reliability. It's used by many large organizations across various industries, particularly in environments that require high availability, strong transactional support, and the ability to manage large volumes of data.

One such organization is the US Internal Revenue Service (IRS). The IRS employs Db2 in its Customer Account Data Engine (CADE). CADE is integral to processing tax returns and managing taxpayer accounts. CADE is also designed to modernize tax processing by replacing the legacy Individual Master File (IMF) system and improve data accuracy and processing speed.

In addition to the relational model, Db2 supports a variety of file formats, including XML and JSON. It also operates on a wide range of platforms, from mainframes to distributed systems. Db2 is particularly well suited for mission-critical applications due to its advanced features, such as high availability clustering, disaster recovery solutions, and strong support for both OLTP and OLAP workloads.

Db2 includes features like advanced compression, which helps reduce storage costs, and in-memory computing for faster query performance. Db2 also offers robust security features, including encryption, access controls, and tools that facilitate auditing. It supports hybrid storage models in which cold (infrequently accessed) data can be off-loaded to object storage to save on costs, while hot (frequently accessed) data remains on faster block or file storage. Db2 also provides AI-powered query optimization and support for hybrid cloud deployments.[1]

Microsoft SQL Server

MSSQL is an RDBMS developed by Microsoft. It was first released in the late 1980s and has become one of the most robust and widely used enterprise database systems in the world. MSSQL is designed to handle a wide range of data management tasks, from small applications to large-scale enterprise solutions, and it can support both transaction processing as well as business intelligence.

MSSQL commonly uses file storage systems but can operate on block storage systems as well. MSSQL supports a variety of data types and complex queries and is known for high availability features like Always-On availability groups that ensure data is available in the event of failures.

MSSQL has advanced security features, including encryption, fine-grained access control, and compliance tools to help organizations meet regulatory requirements. Additionally, it includes built-in tools for data integration, analytics, and reporting.

It is currently available in several "editions": Enterprise, Standard, Web, Developer, and Express. The Enterprise edition is designed for large organizations and comes with high-end datacenter capabilities, unlimited virtualization, and end-to-end business intelligence, which make it somewhat of a warehousing system.

The Standard edition consists of basic data management and BI and is designed for smaller organizations to develop and run their applications on premises or in the cloud. The Standard edition is what organizations often turn to when they outgrow the Express edition. The Express edition is Microsoft's "entry-level, free database" and is meant to provide an avenue for learning and developing small, data-driven applications.[2]

---

1 IBM. n.d. IBM Db2 (website). IBM. Accessed August 2024. *https://www.ibm.com/db2*.

2 Microsoft. 2024. "Editions and Supported Features of SQL Server 2022." Microsoft. Last modified May 19, 2025. *https://learn.microsoft.com/en-us/sql/sql-server/editions-and-components-of-sql-server-2022*.

US federal agencies employ SQL Server to handle large datasets and provide robust data storage, retrieval, and analysis. For instance, the Department of Defense (DOD) uses SQL Server for mission-critical applications that leverage data warehousing and near-real-time analytics capabilities.

Since 1997, the Hazus program at the US Federal Emergency Management Agency (FEMA) has maintained inventory and vulnerability databases, leveraging SQL Server to store state-level data according to geographic state and territory boundaries.[3]

MySQL and MariaDB

MySQL is a widely used, open source RDBMS that was initially developed by MySQL AB in the mid-1990s. Like most RDBMSs, it is based on Structured Query Language (SQL), which it uses for managing and manipulating databases. MySQL is known for its reliability, flexibility, and ease of use and is a popular choice for web applications, especially in combination with PHP in the LAMP (Linux, Apache, MySQL, PHP/Perl/ Python) stack. MySQL supports various storage engines, allowing users to choose the one that best suits their needs in terms of performance and features.

Over the years, MySQL has evolved to offer a wide range of features, including support for large databases, high availability, and replication. It also offers strong security features, including user authentication, role-based access control, and support for SSL encryption. MySQL is highly scalable and capable of handling databases of all sizes, from small projects to large-scale enterprise applications. It's now owned by Oracle Corporation, which in 2010 acquired Sun Microsystems (which had previously acquired MySQL AB in 2008). Despite concerns from the open source community about its continued development under Oracle, MySQL remains a cornerstone in the world of open source databases, and a variety of forks, such as MariaDB, have emerged to ensure its ongoing development and adaptability.

MariaDB was created by the original developers of MySQL and is designed to remain free under the GNU General Public License. It provides a drop-in replacement for MySQL, which means MariaDB can be easily substituted in place of MySQL without requiring significant changes to the codebase or database schemas. MariaDB also enhances MySQL's functionality with additional storage engines and more efficient querying.[4] MariaDB is widely used in various applications ranging from small-scale web services to large-scale enterprise applications, mainly due to its flexibility, ease of use, and robust community support.

---

3 FEMA. 2023. "Hazus Inventory National Database Fact Sheet." March. *https://www.fema.gov/sites/default/files/documents/fema_hazus-inventory-national-database-factsheet.pdf.*

4 Amazon Web Services. n.d. "What's the Difference Between MariaDB and MySQL?" Amazon Web Services, Inc. Accessed September 2024. *https://aws.amazon.com/compare/the-difference-between-mariadb-vs-mysql.*

Oracle Database

Oracle Database is a multimodel RDBMS developed and marketed by Oracle Corporation. First released in the late 1970s, it has grown into one of the most widely used and advanced databases in the world and is known for its robustness, scalability, and extensive feature set. Oracle Database is designed to manage large volumes of data and support complex applications, which makes it a popular choice for enterprises across various industries. It's also particularly renowned for its ability to handle high transaction loads and large-scale databases with high availability and reliability.

Although included in "Relational Databases" on page 88, Oracle Database supports multiple data models beyond relational table data that includes JSON, XML, vectors, and a handful of others. It allows organizations to manage diverse data types within a single system and offers advanced features such as Real Application Clusters (RAC) for high availability, Automatic Storage Management (ASM) for efficient data storage management, and Data Guard for disaster recovery. Oracle Database also includes powerful security features, such as encryption, data masking, and auditing that help protect sensitive data and comply with regulatory requirements.

Additionally, Oracle Database is highly optimized for performance with features like partitioning, parallel processing, and in-memory computing, which allows it to handle large-scale data processing and analytics workloads efficiently.

It's available in various editions, including Standard Edition and Enterprise Edition, that offer different levels of functionality to meet the needs of different organizations. Oracle also offers cloud-based versions of its database through Oracle Cloud. This includes the Oracle Autonomous Database, which, as its name implies, is a fully automated database that uses machine learning to perform routine management tasks without human intervention.

Also, like IBM Db2, Oracle's Autonomous Database supports hybrid storage models in which cold (i.e., infrequently accessed) data can be off-loaded to object storage to save on costs, while hot (i.e., frequently accessed) data remains on faster block or file storage.

Oracle Database is extensively utilized across various US federal government agencies to enhance operational efficiency and ensure data security. Notable use cases include the US Department of the Treasury's HR system, the COVID-19 Patient Monitoring System at the US Department of Health and Human Services (HHS), and various analytics projects in the US Air Force.[5]

---

5 Oracle. 2022. "FAQs for Autonomous Database." Oracle. Last modified June 10, 2022. *https://www.oracle.com/database/technologies/datawarehouse-bigdata/adb-faqs.html.*

PostgreSQL

PostgreSQL, also known as Postgres, is a powerful, open source RDBMS that has gained significant popularity in recent years. It is robust and scalable and is widely used for storing and managing large volumes of data in a secure and efficient manner. PostgreSQL is an object-relational database, which means it supports both object-oriented and relational data modeling approaches. It uses SQL as its primary language for creating, modifying, and querying databases. Like many of its peers, Postgres commonly uses file storage systems but can also operate on block storage systems.

It also excels in handling transactional data, processing orders, updating inventory, and managing customer accounts (i.e., OLTP). It's known for its reliability, performance, and flexibility and supports a wide range of data types including integers, strings, dates, timestamps, and JSON. It's used in simple web applications as well as in complex enterprise-level systems mainly because of its robust feature set that includes advanced indexing techniques based on generalized search trees (e.g., GiST and SP-GiST), transactional security, concurrency control, and backup and recovery mechanisms to ensure integrity and availability.

Another key feature of PostgreSQL is its extensibility. It has a rich ecosystem of extensions that includes support for various programming languages such as Python, Java, and C, as well as additional functionality for data analytics and reporting.

SQLite

SQLite is a very lightweight, open source RDBMS that is typically used for its simplicity and ease of integration. Unlike most other RDBMSs, SQLite is a serverless, self-contained database engine that does not require a separate server process to operate. Instead, it operates as a library that is directly embedded into the application using it. This design makes SQLite suitable for applications where simplicity and minimal configuration are important, such as in mobile apps, embedded systems, and small to medium-sized desktop applications.

An entire SQLite database is stored in a single file on disk, which makes it highly portable and requires almost no setup. Despite its small size, SQLite supports a wide range of SQL features including transactions, subqueries, triggers, and views. It adheres closely to the SQL standard and provides full ACID (atomicity, consistency, isolation, durability) compliance that ensures reliable and consistent data management, even in resource-constrained environments.

SQLite is not typically used for large-scale enterprise applications or scenarios requiring high concurrency because it has limited support for multiuser environments. Nonetheless, SQLite is widely used across a variety of platforms and industries and is often the default database engine for mobile applications and desktop application prototyping.

Sybase and SAP

Sybase is an RDBMS that was originally developed by Sybase, Inc., in the mid-1980s. Supposedly, it was one of the first commercially successful relational databases and is particularly known for its performance and efficiency in handling transaction-based applications. Sybase gained popularity in the financial services industry and other sectors that require high-performance data management systems. It introduced several innovations in database technology, such as the use of stored procedures and triggers to automate database operations.

In the 1990s, Sybase licensed its core technology to Microsoft, which then developed MSSQL based on the Sybase codebase. Over time, Sybase continued to evolve and was later acquired by SAP. Under SAP, Sybase became part of a broader suite of enterprise software solutions including integration with SAP's business applications and analytics tools.

Sybase's flagship product, Adaptive Server Enterprise (ASE), is known for its robustness and ability to handle high transaction volumes. It's suitable for mission-critical applications and supports various data types and complex queries. It's also optimized for environments that demand high availability and performance and strong security features like encryption and RBAC. Despite being less prominent in the market today compared to other RDBMSs, Sybase remains in use in many legacy systems and in the federal government; it continues to be supported by SAP.

Non-Relational Databases

As mentioned earlier in Part I, NoSQL is a category of database management system (DBMS) that diverges from the traditional relational database model. NoSQL provides a flexible and scalable way to handle large volumes of unstructured and semistructured data. NoSQL databases are designed to handle large-scale data storage and processing across multiple servers. Unlike traditional relational databases, NoSQL databases do not rely on fixed schemas, allowing for dynamic and unstructured data storage. They support various data models, such as key-value, document, column-family, and graph, catering to diverse use cases like near-real-time analytics, content management, and IoT. These databases can use distributed architectures to partition and replicate data across nodes to help ensure fault tolerance and consistent performance under high loads. This makes them a good alternative to traditional databases that might struggle handling larger data applications.

Many people think of NoSQL as "Not Only SQL"—as if NoSQL is a superset of relational databases. Perhaps erroneously, I prefer to think of NoSQL as "Not SQL". That is, everything that's not strictly a relational database is a non-relational database.

Document Stores and Key-Value Storage

The landscape of NoSQL databases has diversified significantly over the past decade to meet different application needs. Key-value stores, document-oriented databases, and multimodel solutions provide the flexibility, scalability, and performance necessary for modern use cases, ranging from web and mobile applications to IoT and near-real-time data processing. This section explores several of them and highlights their core features. Specifically, the technologies discussed in this section include Amazon DynamoDB, Apache Ignite, MongoDB, and Redis. Each offer similar but distinct approaches to data management and integration. The features most of interest include latency, throughput, and scalability.

Amazon DynamoDB and DocumentDB

Amazon DynamoDB is a fully managed key-value and document database offered by AWS. It's designed for applications requiring high throughput and minimal latency and has built-in support for scaling and high availability. DynamoDB supports key-value pairs and simple document structures but lacks the level of querying complexity that some other tools offer. One such tool is another Amazon service called DocumentDB.

Amazon DocumentDB is a fully managed document database service that is compatible with MongoDB, which makes it suitable for applications that require flexible, JSON-like document data structures. DocumentDB is designed for workloads that need to store, query, and index semistructured data with features that support rich indexing, aggregation, and complex querying capabilities. It's ideal for use cases where developers are already familiar with MongoDB or need a document-oriented database that can scale horizontally.

According to Amazon documentation, DocumentDB also uses "fault-tolerant storage that transparently handles the loss of up to two copies of data without affecting database write availability, and up to three copies without affecting read availability."[6]

In general, DocumentDB is better suited for complex document management and querying, while DynamoDB excels in high-speed key-value and simple document workloads.

---

6 Amazon Web Services. n.d. "What Is a Document Database?" Amazon Web Services, Inc. Accessed October 2024. *https://aws.amazon.com/nosql/document.*

Apache Ignite

Apache Ignite is an in-memory computing platform that provides a comprehensive set of features for high-performance computing and data management. It supports both key-value and SQL-based access patterns, which makes it adept for various types of applications. One of its core capabilities is distributed data caching, which allows it to store data in memory across multiple nodes, significantly reducing data retrieval times and enabling near-real-time processing. This feature is particularly beneficial for applications that require low-latency access to large datasets.

Additionally, Apache Ignite supports distributed computing through its compute grid and allows the execution of parallel computations across a cluster. This feature is important for applications requiring high computational power for purposes such as near-real-time analytics and complex event processing. Ignite also provides distributed persistence, which enables the platform to store data on disk in a way that is fully integrated with its in-memory capabilities. This means that even in the event of a complete cluster restart, the data can be quickly reloaded into memory without data loss.

Ignite's SQL grid functionality is another standout feature that offers full SQL-99 compliance, including support for distributed joins and transactions. This allows users to run complex queries across distributed datasets with ACID-compliant transactions that ensure data consistency and integrity. Moreover, Ignite includes a machine learning grid that supports the training and deployment of machine learning models directly within the cluster.

MongoDB

MongoDB is a popular NoSQL database that uses a document-oriented data model and stores data in flexible, JSON-like documents. This design allows MongoDB to handle various data types and structures, which makes it particularly well suited for large volumes of unstructured and semistructured data. Instead of rows and tables, MongoDB organizes data into collections of documents. Each document is an individual record that can contain nested fields, arrays, and other complex data structures. This flexibility facilitates rapid development and iteration, and developers can modify schemas without requiring complex migrations.

One of the key features of MongoDB is its ability to scale horizontally, distributing data across multiple servers (i.e., sharding). This distributed architecture helps ensure the database can handle heavy data loads and high request rates by adding more servers to the cluster. MongoDB also supports replication, which involves creating multiple copies of data across different nodes to ensure availability and durability in case of hardware failures.

In terms of querying, MongoDB provides a rich query language that includes capabilities for filtering, sorting, and aggregating data. It also supports indexing to optimize query performance. Unlike SQL databases, MongoDB's query language is tailored specifically for its document model that allows execution of complex operations directly on the document fields. Additionally, MongoDB's aggregation framework enables users to perform operations such as data transformation, grouping, and filtering in a manner similar to SQL's GROUP BY functionality.[7]

Redis

Redis, which is short for "remote dictionary server," is an open source, in-memory key-value store that is known for its high performance, flexibility, and simplicity. Unlike traditional databases, Redis operates primarily in memory, which allows it to deliver extremely fast read and write operations. This design makes Redis ideal for use cases that require high performance and low-latency data access but generally at lower scales than other DBMSs.

As a NoSQL database, Redis stores data as key-value pairs, but it supports a variety of data structures beyond simple strings, including lists, sets, sorted sets, hashes, and bitmaps. These built-in data structures enable developers to easily perform complex operations like pushing elements to a list, incrementing a counter, or querying a set. Redis also provides atomic operations that ensure they are completed fully without interference, even in a highly parallelized environment.

Another of Redis's strengths is its capability for persistence. While it operates in memory, Redis can periodically write data to disk or create a copy of its dataset to ensure durability in case of a system interruption. It offers two main persistence mechanisms: Redis Database Backup (RDB) snapshots and Append-Only File (AOF) logs—giving users the flexibility to choose between faster recovery times or more frequent data saving.

Graph Databases

Graph database technologies are used in various applications where understanding relationships between entities is crucial, such as social network analysis, recommendation engines, and knowledge graphs. Each technology has unique features and optimizations that make it suitable for various use cases and deployment environments. Here we discuss three such technologies: Amazon Neptune, Neo4j, and TigerGraph.

---

7 MongoDB. n.d. "$group (Aggregation Stage)." MongoDB Database Manual. Accessed February 2025. *https://www.mongodb.com/docs/manual/reference/operator/aggregation/group*.

Amazon Neptune

Amazon Neptune is a fully managed graph database service that supports both property graph models, using Gremlin and openCypher query languages, as well as Resource Description Framework (RDF) graph models, using SPARQL. Neptune is optimized for use cases like fraud detection, recommendation engines, knowledge graphs, and network security by enabling complex relationship-based queries and pattern discovery in vast networks with high performance and millisecond latency.

Key features of Neptune include serverless scalability and an architecture that separates storage and compute, which allows up to 15 read replicas to share storage without needing writes on the replicas. The Amazon Neptune Global Database provides fast local read access for globally distributed applications (i.e., across multiple AWS Regions).

Neptune is also built to be highly reliable and durable and features fault-tolerant, self-healing storage, point-in-time recovery, and continuous backups. Data is replicated across three availability zones (AZs) within a region, which ensures durability, while AWS charges only for a single copy.

Security is robust, with default encryption at rest, network isolation, advanced auditing, and fine-grained access control at the resource level. Additionally, Neptune meets various compliance standards, including FedRAMP (Moderate and High) and SOC (1, 2, and 3), and is HIPAA eligible. Being a fully managed service, Neptune eliminates the need for database management tasks such as hardware provisioning, software updates, configuration, and backups, which simplifies the maintenance of the graph databases.

Neo4j

Neo4j is a highly popular graph database management system designed to store, manage, and query data structured as graphs. Unlike traditional relational databases that use tables and rows, Neo4j represents data as nodes, relationships, and properties, making it particularly well suited for handling highly connected data. Its underlying architecture is based on the property graph model, which allows for efficient querying of complex relationships using Cypher, Neo4j's declarative query language.

In the context of data integration, Neo4j plays a crucial role by enabling organizations to merge and analyze data from diverse sources in a connected and coherent manner. Traditional data integration approaches often struggle with representing relationships between disparate datasets, especially when dealing with complex interdependencies. Neo4j addresses this challenge by naturally modeling these relationships, making it easier to uncover insights, detect patterns, and perform deep link analysis.

For example, in customer 360-degree views, Neo4j can integrate data from CRM systems, transaction records, social media interactions, and support logs to provide a unified understanding of customer behavior. Similarly, in supply chain management, Neo4j helps integrate data from multiple suppliers, logistics providers, and distribution channels to visualize and optimize the entire network. Additionally, it is widely used in fraud detection, where the ability to trace connections between entities like accounts, transactions, and devices is critical. Overall, Neo4j's graph-based approach makes it an effective tool for data integration scenarios that require flexible schemas, real-time insights, and deep relationship analysis.

TigerGraph

TigerGraph is a scalable, high-performance graph database designed for handling large-scale graph analytics and real-time deep link analysis. It uses a native parallel graph (NPG) architecture, which allows it to efficiently process and analyze massive amounts of highly connected data. TigerGraph is known for its ability to handle complex queries across large datasets quickly, making it suitable for enterprise-level applications that require real-time analytics. The database uses GSQL, a SQL-like query language tailored for graph processing, enabling users to write complex graph queries with ease.

In data integration, TigerGraph is leveraged to unify data from multiple heterogeneous sources by modeling them as interconnected graphs. This approach is particularly advantageous when the relationships between data points are as significant as the data itself. TigerGraph's architecture allows for seamless integration of structured, semistructured, and unstructured data, enabling comprehensive analysis and real-time decision making.

For instance, in financial services, TigerGraph can integrate transaction records, customer profiles, and third-party data to detect fraudulent activities by analyzing intricate transaction networks. In healthcare, it supports the integration of patient records, clinical trial data, and medical research to facilitate personalized treatment plans and drug discovery. Additionally, in supply chain optimization, TigerGraph enables the integration of supplier data, logistics, and inventory management systems to provide a holistic view of the supply chain network. Overall, TigerGraph's ability to process deep link analytics at scale makes it an effective solution for complex data integration challenges that require real-time insights and advanced analytics.

Vector Databases

The growth of unstructured and semistructured data, coupled with advancements in artificial intelligence and machine learning, has necessitated new ways of storing, managing, and querying data. Traditional databases, which primarily store data in tabular formats, often struggle with the complex, high-dimensional nature of modern datasets, particularly when it comes to tasks like similarity search, image recognition, and natural language processing. This is where vector databases come into play.

As touched on in Part I, a vector database is specifically designed to handle vector embeddings—numerical representations of data objects such as text, images, or other multimedia. These embeddings are produced by machine learning models and capture the essential features and properties of the data in a compact, high-dimensional vector space. By leveraging the mathematical properties of these vectors, a vector database enables efficient similarity searches and pattern recognition across massive datasets. This makes vector databases an essential tool for modern AI and machine learning applications, where the ability to quickly and accurately retrieve relevant information is critical.

Unlike traditional databases, which use indexes based on exact matches, vector databases use algorithms such as approximate nearest neighbor (ANN) search to find the closest vector representations to a given query. This allows for more flexible and nuanced querying, where results are ranked based on their similarity to the query, rather than exact matches. This capability is particularly useful in applications such as recommendation systems, semantic search, and anomaly detection, where understanding the underlying relationships between data points is more important than finding identical records.[8]

The structure of a vector database is optimized for scalability and performance. It typically includes features like sharding and replication to handle large-scale data storage and access. Additionally, it offers robust support for dynamic data changes, backups, and security measures, making it a reliable choice for enterprise applications. By integrating these capabilities, vector databases provide a comprehensive solution for the storage and management of complex, high-dimensional data, bridging the gap between raw data and actionable insights.

Vector databases represent a paradigm shift in data management, driven by the needs of modern AI and machine learning applications. They offer a powerful alternative to traditional data storage and querying methods, which enables organizations to unlock the previously unrealized potential of their unstructured and semistructured data.

LanceDB

LanceDB is an open source database optimized for handling vector data and is commonly used in applications like machine learning, recommendation systems, and natural language processing. It's designed to efficiently store, index, and query high-dimensional vectors like embeddings generated by AI models. LanceDB offers seamless integration with popular data processing frameworks and libraries, including Python-based tools often used in data science workflows.

---

8 Elastic Platform Team. 2024. "Understanding the Approximate Nearest Neighbor (ANN) Algorithm." *elastic* (blog), Elasticsearch B.V. April 17. *https://www.elastic.co/blog/understanding-ann*.

It utilizes an Apache Arrow–based columnar format, which allows efficient data storage and in-memory processing that speeds up analytical queries. LanceDB also features support for vector search operations, which can enable fast similarity searches that are useful for finding related images, documents, or other content. LanceDB can be used as a standalone database or can be integrated into existing data pipelines.

LanceDB supports operations such as filtering, sorting, and aggregating, which makes it versatile for both vector and nonvector data management. Its design focuses on providing scalable and performant solutions for handling large datasets and ensuring low-latency querying and efficient resource utilization.

Pinecone

Pinecone is a cloud-based vector database used for vector search in production applications. Even with billions of items, it provides ultra-low query latency, and indices are updated in near real time.

Pinecone's vector search solution allows users to combine search results with metadata filters—for example, product category, price, or customer rating.

Additionally, Pinecone handles the routine task of data backup automatically, but it also gives users the flexibility to selectively back up specific indices for future use. With Pinecone's user-friendly API, developers can build high-performance vector search applications regardless of their choice of programming language.

Also, Pinecone's cloud native architecture makes it cost-effective, and it uses a pay-per-use pricing model so users pay for only what they need.

Pinecone has numerous real-world applications across various industries. It provides fast and fully deployment-ready search and similarity functionality for handling high-dimensional text and audio data, which makes it ideal for audio and textual search tasks.

Related to natural language processing, Pinecone can power advanced applications like document classification, semantic search, text summarization, and sentiment analysis. It also enhances user experience by enabling personalized suggestions through efficient recommendations.

Pinecone supports fast retrieval of image and video content, which is especially useful for surveillance and image recognition tasks. It also excels at detecting patterns in time-series data using similarity search, which aids in recommendations, clustering, and labeling. As a vector-based database, Pinecone efficiently handles high-dimensional data at scale.

Weaviate

Weaviate is an open source vector database designed for building AI-native applications. It combines vector search with keyword search techniques, supports retrieval-augmented generation (RAG), and enables use cases like hybrid search, generative feedback loops, and personalized AI systems. Weaviate is a developer-friendly, cloud-indifferent database that is optimized for performance. It emphasizes privacy, scalability, and community engagement.

Wide-Column Databases

Wide-column NoSQL databases organize data in tables with rows and columns resembling traditional relational databases, but the names and formats of the columns can differ between rows in the same table. These databases group related columns of data together.

Examples of wide-column data stores include Apache Cassandra, Google Bigtable, and HBase, all of which are known for their ability to manage distributed data across multiple nodes while providing high availability and fault tolerance.

Apache Cassandra and HBase

Originally developed at Facebook and now maintained by Apache, Cassandra is a distributed, wide-column store database designed for handling large amounts of data across many commodity servers with no single point of failure. It's known for its high availability and scalability and is suitable for applications with heavy write and read requirements.

Cassandra employs a peer-to-peer architecture in which all nodes in a cluster are considered equal. This eliminates the traditional leader-follower roles found in other database systems. The Cassandra architecture ensures that data is distributed and replicated across multiple nodes and remains operational in the event of node failures. Cassandra uses a partitioned row store model where data is organized by partition keys and stored in a distributed fashion across the cluster. This model provides excellent performance for write-heavy workloads and allows for efficient retrieval of data by partition key. Cassandra also offers tunable consistency, where users can configure the level of consistency required for reads and writes. This helps balance the trade-offs between consistency, availability, and partition tolerance.

Cassandra is great for use cases such as near-real-time big-data applications, IoT data management, and online transaction processing where uptime and speed are critical. With its ability to scale linearly by simply adding more nodes to the cluster, Apache Cassandra has become a popular choice for organizations wanting to manage large-scale, distributed data with minimal downtime.

Another Apache project called HBase is a distributed, scalable, and open source NoSQL database modeled after Google's Bigtable. It's designed to handle large datasets across many servers and is built on top of the Hadoop Distributed File System (HDFS). HDFS is designed to manage large amounts of structured data. It provides a fault-tolerant way of storing sparse datasets that are common in many big-data use cases.

HBase supports random, near-real-time read and write access to large datasets, which makes it suitable for applications that require fast query and update capabilities like online analytics and transaction processing. It features strong consistency and high availability and supports automatic sharding and replication. HBase integrates tightly with Hadoop and can be used alongside tools like Apache Hive and Apache Pig for complex data processing and analysis.

Also, the schemaless design of HBase allows for flexible column-oriented storage, which enables the dynamic addition of columns without altering the table structure. While powerful and scalable, managing HBase does require expertise in distributed systems, mainly because it involves configuration and tuning of nodes and clusters to achieve optimal performance and reliability.

AWS Keyspaces

Amazon Keyspaces is a fully managed, serverless database service that is compatible with Apache Cassandra. It can run existing Cassandra workloads in the cloud without the need to provision, patch, or manage servers. The service supports the use of the same Cassandra application code and developer tools, which helps ensure a seamless transition to a cloud environment. Also, it can automatically adjust the scale of tables to match fluctuating application traffic and support thousands of requests per second with virtually unlimited throughput and storage capacity. The data is encrypted by default, and point-in-time recovery can be used for continuous backup of table data.

Azure Cosmos DB

Azure Cosmos DB is a globally distributed, multimodel database service designed to provide high availability, low latency, and scalability for applications of any size. It supports data models such as document, key-value, graph, and column-family, and it offers APIs for SQL, MongoDB, Cassandra, and Gremlin. With automatic and seamless data replication across multiple Azure regions, Cosmos DB ensures consistent, fast access to data worldwide.

The service offers comprehensive SLAs for throughput, latency, availability, and consistency, and it allows developers to select the best consistency level for their applications, ranging from strong to eventual consistency. Azure Cosmos DB is serverless and elastically scalable, which can provide instant scalability for both storage and throughput based on demand. It also features built-in security and automatic indexing.

Azure Cosmos DB also supports graph databases through Apache Gremlin, which allows for property graph storage and querying and makes it suitable for applications that require globally distributed data with low latency and high availability. Some of the specific benefits of the Gremlin API include elastically scalable throughput, fast queries and traversals with a widely adopted graph query standard, automatic indexing, tunable consistency levels, and an inherent compatibility with Apache TinkerPop.

Google Bigtable

Google Bigtable is a fully managed, scalable, and high-performance NoSQL database service designed for large-scale applications. It's built to handle massive datasets, often involving billions of rows and thousands of columns, making it ideal for use cases such as near-real-time analytics, time-series data, IoT data, and machine learning. Bigtable is a key-value database that uses a distributed architecture, which ensures low-latency access to data while supporting high throughput.

Its underlying infrastructure is similar to technologies like Apache HBase, but as a Google Cloud product, it benefits from seamless integration with other Google Cloud services such as Dataflow and BigQuery. Bigtable also provides strong consistency, automatic scaling, and redundancy across regions. It's designed for workloads where speed and efficiency are critical. Offering a schemaless design in which data is organized into tables with rows and columns but doesn't enforce any predefined schema facilitates flexibility.

Data Warehouses

Data warehousing tools are specialized systems designed to store, retrieve, and analyze large volumes of data, often comprising large volumes of historical records. These tools are typically used for decision support and are optimized for complex analytical query (i.e., OLAP) tasks. By centralizing data from multiple sources, including operational databases and external systems, data warehouses enable organizations to perform in-depth analytics, trend analysis, and reporting. Their primary focus is on delivering insights from data to support strategic decision making.

Amazon Redshift

Amazon Redshift is a fully managed, column-oriented, petabyte-scale data warehouse service in the cloud that is designed to facilitate fast and efficient analysis of large datasets. It is part of the AWS ecosystem and is engineered to handle complex queries and large-scale data analytics with minimal setup and maintenance efforts. Redshift achieves high performance through its columnar storage format, which allows for significant compression and efficient retrieval of data needed for queries. The columnar storage, combined with parallel processing capabilities across multiple nodes in a cluster, enables Redshift to execute complex queries quickly on large datasets.

Redshift integrates well with other AWS services like Amazon S3 for data storage, AWS Glue for data cataloging and ETL, and Amazon QuickSight for business intelligence and visualization. It also supports a wide range of SQL-based query tools and BI applications, which makes it accessible for analysts and data scientists familiar with SQL. Redshift's architecture allows users to start small with a single-node cluster and scale up as needs grow and without significant reconfiguration. One of Redshift's standout features is its cost-effectiveness. It has the ability to scale compute and storage independently and charges for only what is used (i.e., pay as you go).

Security features include automated backups, encryption, and access configurations to protect data. In addition, Redshift offers features such as Redshift Spectrum that allows users to query and analyze data directly in S3 without first loading it into Redshift, as well as concurrency scaling that automatically adds capacity to handle multiple concurrent queries. These features, combined with its performance, scalability, and integration within the AWS ecosystem, make Amazon Redshift a popular choice for organizations wanting to run large-scale data warehousing and analytics workloads in the cloud.

Lastly, Redshift supports the concept of *external tables*, where the data resides in an object store and the database can query it as if it were part of the database. This feature is commonly seen in databases designed to process large datasets.

Apache Doris, Druid, Hadoop, and Hive

Apache Doris is an open source, modern data warehouse for near-real-time analytics. It consists of push-based microbatch, pull-based streaming data ingestion, and a storage engine with near-real-time append and pre-aggregation capabilities. Doris is also capable of federated querying of data lakes such as Hive, Iceberg, and Hudi as well as databases such as MySQL and PostgreSQL.

Apache Druid is a high-performance, near-real-time analytics database designed for fast query performance and the ingestion of large volumes of event-driven data. It's specifically built to handle use cases that require low-latency queries on massive datasets and is therefore a popular choice for interactive analytics, operational intelligence, and business intelligence applications. Druid combines features from both data warehouses and time-series stores and offers a unique architecture that excels in scenarios where data is ingested continuously and needs to be queried almost immediately.[9]

Druid's architecture is based on a distributed and scalable design where data is stored in segments that are distributed across a cluster of servers. It supports both near-real-time and batch data ingestion and can facilitate streaming data from sources like Apache Kafka or batch data from Hadoop. Druid also supports a columnar storage format that, combined with advanced indexing techniques like compressed indices, allows it to deliver subsecond query responses, even for complex, high-dimensional queries.

Additionally, Druid provides features such as roll-up aggregation during ingestion, which reduces data storage requirements and improves query performance by summarizing data before storing it. Druid's flexibility, high availability, and ability to handle both streaming and historical data with low query latency make it an ideal solution for applications like monitoring and alerting, near-real-time dashboards, and exploratory data analysis in industries ranging from finance to telecommunications.

The HDFS is a distributed filesystem designed to run on commodity hardware and provide high-throughput access to large datasets. It's a key component of the Apache Hadoop framework and is optimized for storing and processing vast amounts of data across a large number of nodes. HDFS splits large files into smaller blocks, typically 128 MB or 256 MB in size, and distributes them across multiple nodes in a cluster. This distribution not only facilitates parallel processing by enabling data locality, where computation is performed close to where the data is stored, but also provides fault tolerance. Data blocks are replicated across multiple nodes (the default is three copies). This replication ensures that the data remains accessible even if one or more nodes fail. HDFS is designed to handle very large files, provide a high level of fault tolerance, and support high aggregate data bandwidth.

Apache Hive is a data warehouse software built on top of Apache Hadoop and is designed to facilitate the management and analysis of large datasets stored in a distributed environment. It provides a SQL-like interface, called HiveQL, enabling users to query and manage data stored in the HDFS using a syntax similar to traditional SQL. Hive is ideal for data warehousing applications, as it allows for easy integration and analysis of data across various sources without needing extensive programming skills.

Hive is also particularly useful in big-data contexts because it can handle both structured and semistructured data; it supports various file formats, including text, ORC, and Parquet; and it can integrate with other tools in the Hadoop ecosystem, such as

---

9 Apache Software Foundation. n.d. Apache Druid (website). Apache Software Foundation. Accessed October 2024. *https://druid.apache.org.*

Apache Pig and Apache Spark. Additionally, Hive's architecture includes a metastore, which stores metadata information, and a query engine that transforms HiveQL queries into MapReduce, Tez, or Spark jobs, optimizing them for efficient execution on the Hadoop cluster.

One of the strengths of Hive is its ability to partition and bucket data, which enhances query performance by reducing the amount of data processed. However, due to its reliance on batch processing, Hive is not suitable for near-real-time query processing and is better suited for batch-oriented data analysis tasks. Overall, Apache Hive simplifies the process of querying and analyzing large datasets on Hadoop and is accessible to a broader audience through its SQL-like interface and integration capabilities.

Cloudera Data Warehouse

Cloudera Data Warehouse (CDW) is a cloud native, self-service analytics solution designed to provide scalable, high-performance data warehousing capabilities. It's part of Cloudera Data Platform (CDP), which integrates data management and analytics across hybrid and multicloud environments.

CDW enables organizations to run SQL analytics on large volumes of data and leverages distributed computing for efficient querying and processing. It supports a variety of data sources and formats and enables users to analyze structured and semistructured data with low latency. Built on open source technologies such as Apache Hive and Impala, CDW also offers robust integration with machine learning and data engineering workflows that provide a unified experience for data-driven decision making. The platform is designed with enterprise-grade security, governance, and compliance in mind, featuring fine-grained access controls, encryption, and metadata management. With its elastic scaling capabilities, CDW allows businesses to optimize performance and cost by dynamically adjusting resources based on workload demands.

IBM Db2 Warehouse

IBM Db2 Warehouse is known for its always-on workloads, providing simple, governed access to data and eliminating data silos across the hybrid cloud.

Data engineers, developers, and data scientists can efficiently store, share, and analyze governed data from multiple sources, including hybrid cloud environments and open formats. The platform seamlessly integrates with other relational databases like Db2, data lakes, and IBM watsonx.data lakehouse, streamlining the data ecosystem for analytics and AI applications. Designed specifically for the cloud, it operates natively on cloud object storage.

Snowflake

Snowflake is used in data aggregation, complex data analysis, report generation, providing business insights, and other use cases. For rapidly growing organizations, it might make sense to move data to Snowflake (if the organization is currently using something like PostgreSQL). Snowflake has virtually unlimited scalability and compute that can be spun up or down easily to accommodate any workload. Its built-in cost optimization features and storage-compute separation helps keep costs low. Also, because Snowflake is a fully managed platform, upgrading operating systems and other supporting components will not be an issue, and security is off-loaded to the service provider.

On the face of it this may seem counterintuitive, but with Snowflake's pay-as-you-go model, you pay only for the compute that is actually used, and this can be turned off when not required.

Further, like Redshift, Snowflake supports the concept of "external tables," where the data resides in an object store and the database can query it as if it were part of the database. This feature is commonly seen in databases designed to process large datasets.

Data Lakes and Lakehouses

Object storage services like Amazon S3, Google Cloud Storage, and Azure Blob Storage are designed for storing large amounts of unstructured data such as files, images, and logs. They generally provide the scalability, durability, and cost-effectiveness that data lakes, data lakehouses, and archival storage require. In addition to Amazon S3, Azure Blob Storage, and Google Cloud Storage, there are several other great options for building data lakes and data lakehouses.

Amazon Simple Storage Service

Amazon offers a comprehensive suite of services to help organizations build and manage data lakes. It enables efficient storage and analysis of vast amounts of data, and at the core is Amazon Simple Storage Service (Amazon S3), providing a durable, scalable, and secure foundation for your data lake.

With AWS Lake Formation, you can expedite the creation of secure data lakes, reducing the time from months to days. AWS Glue facilitates seamless data movement between your data lake and various analytics services. This integrated ecosystem allows you to store all your data cost-effectively, foster innovation through comprehensive analytics, utilize purpose-built tools for optimal performance, and simplify management with serverless options.

Apache Hudi and Iceberg

Apache Hudi, short for "Hadoop upserts, deletes, and incrementals," is an open source data management framework that provides efficient data lake operations by enabling incremental data processing on large-scale datasets. Hudi is designed to simplify the management of large analytical datasets stored on Hadoop-compatible distributed storage systems, such as Amazon S3 or HDFS, by enabling capabilities like upserts (updates and inserts), deletes, and efficient handling of changing data.

Hudi organizes data into files based on a combination of unique keys and timestamps that allow it to manage data updates and deletes efficiently without needing to rewrite entire datasets. This incremental processing capability makes Hudi particularly useful in streaming data scenarios, such as in data pipelines for near-real-time analytics or ETL workflows. Hudi provides two main storage types: copy on write (CoW) and merge on read (MoR). CoW writes data directly to new files on disk during updates, offering simpler management at the cost of higher write amplification, while MoR enables faster writes by keeping updates in delta files and merging them with base files during query time.

Moreover, Hudi integrates well with big-data processing engines like Apache Spark, Apache Hive, and Presto, enabling efficient querying and analysis of both historical and near-real-time data. It also supports features like time-travel queries, which allow users to access previous versions of their datasets, and data compaction, which optimizes storage by merging small files into larger ones. Apache Hudi's ability to handle incremental data processing, coupled with its rich feature set, makes it a powerful tool for managing and querying large-scale, evolving datasets in modern data lake architectures.[10]

Apache Iceberg, first developed at Netflix, is an open source table format designed for managing large-scale data lakes with an emphasis on performance, scalability, and data integrity. It provides a robust, flexible structure for organizing data into tables that can handle both batch and streaming data efficiently. Unlike traditional table formats, Iceberg supports schema evolution, partitioning, and versioning without requiring the entire dataset to be rewritten. This makes it a prime candidate for dynamic and evolving data environments where seamless updates, deletions, and temporal queries allow users to access data as it existed at specified points in time.

Iceberg is designed to work with various data processing engines such as Apache Spark, Apache Flink, and Trino and provides interoperability and flexibility across different systems. By abstracting the complexity of underlying storage formats, like

---

10 Apache Software Foundation. n.d. Apache Hudi (website). Apache Software Foundation. Accessed October 2024. *https://hudi.apache.org.*

Parquet and Avro, Apache Iceberg simplifies data management and enhances query performance, leading to reliable and efficient data lakes.

Azure Blob Storage

Microsoft Azure Blob Storage is a scalable object storage solution for unstructured data such as text and binary data. It's an alternative to Amazon S3 and is designed for applications requiring high availability, scalability, and security. Like S3, Azure Blob Storage offers different access tiers (*hot*, *cool*, *cold*, and *archive*) to manage costs effectively based on data access patterns:

Hot tier
> A high-performance storage tier designed for frequently accessed or updated data. It offers the fastest access but comes with the highest storage costs.

Cool tier
> A cost-effective storage option for data that is seldom accessed or modified. Data must remain here for at least 30 days. It has lower storage costs but higher access costs than the hot tier.

Cold tier
> This tier is for data that is rarely accessed or modified but still requires quick retrieval. Data must be stored for at least 90 days. It offers lower storage costs and higher access costs than the cool tier.

Archive tier
> An offline storage option intended for infrequently accessed data, with less strict access speed requirements (usually within hours). Data must be stored for at least 180 days.

Azure Blob Storage also integrates well with other Azure services, which makes it a popular choice for big-data analytics and machine learning workloads, and as a backend for web and mobile applications.

Delta Lake

Delta Lake is an open source storage framework that allows the creation of a flexible lakehouse architecture compatible with various compute engines such as Spark, PrestoDB, Flink, Trino, Hive, Snowflake, Google BigQuery, Athena, Redshift, and others.[11] It enhances the reliability of data lakes by introducing a transactional storage layer on top of the data stored in cloud environments.

---

11 Delta Lake. n.d. Delta Lake (website). Linux Foundation Projects. Accessed October 2024. *https://delta.io*.

Traditional data lakes often face inefficiencies and challenges when processing large datasets. Delta Lake addresses these problems by providing a solution that operates on top of data lakes to improve performance and reliability.

Delta Lake is often used as the underlying storage mechanism in a medallion architecture (also called a *multi-hop architecture*). The term *medallion architecture* is used for architectures in which data is copied or conditioned multiple times before it reaches its destination. The reliability and transactional features of Delta Lake ensure that data remains consistent and accessible as it moves through the different layers of the architecture.[12]

Figure 6-1 shows an example medallion (or multi-hop) architecture.

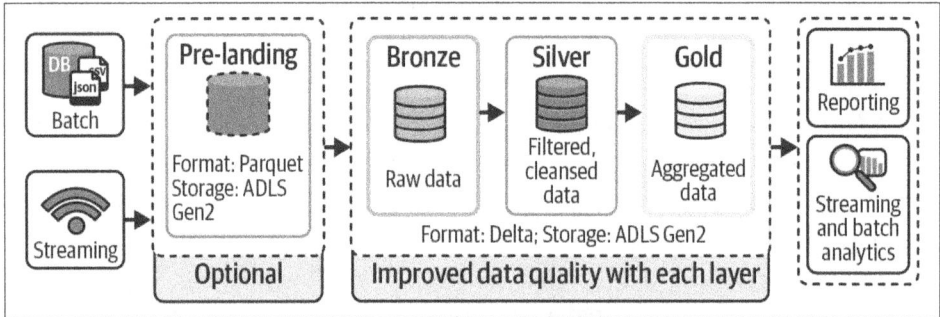

Figure 6-1. Multi-hop architecture

Features of a multi-hop architecture include:

- Combining of streaming and batch loads
- Implementation of ETL process in cloud, using fast processing and memory optimization techniques
- Change data capture
- Better data management and security features at each layer
- User-level access at different layers

Databricks was included in this chapter because it's so tightly associated with data lakes. However, it would have also been appropriate to include it with data ingestion tools in Chapter 7.

---

12 Lans, Rick van der. 2023. "The Multi-Hop Data Architecture Addiction." LinkedIn. November 9. *https://www.linkedin.com/pulse/multi-hop-data-architecture-addiction-rick-van-der-lans-5xuke.*

Google Cloud Storage

Google Cloud Storage (GCS) is an enterprise-level object storage service designed for developers and businesses. GCS offers a unified, scalable storage solution for structured and unstructured data and, like Amazon S3 and Azure Blob Storage, provides multiple storage classes—namely, standard, nearline, coldline, and archive. GCS is known for its high performance, low latency, and strong integration with other Google Cloud services.

Google Drive, one of Google's services, is a consumer-oriented service that allows users to store files in the cloud, synchronize files across devices, and share files with others. It is part of Google's suite of productivity tools and offers integration with Google Docs, Sheets, and Slides. Google Drive provides a user-friendly interface and collaborative features, making it suitable for personal use, education, and small businesses.

IBM Cloud Storage Services

IBM Cloud Storage Services offer a range of cloud solutions, including object storage, block storage, and file storage. IBM Cloud Object Storage is particularly noteworthy for its scalable and resilient architecture designed to handle large volumes of unstructured data. It integrates with IBM's AI and analytics tools and provides advanced data management and analysis capabilities. IBM's storage solutions are designed with a strong emphasis on security and compliance and are therefore suitable for industries with stringent regulatory requirements.

IBM Cloud Object Storage entails built-in encryption, multi-region support, and seamless integration with the IBM Cloud ecosystem, and it supports data-driven workloads for AI, data lakehouses, media content, cloud native applications, backup, and archiving.

Conclusion

Data stores and management systems form the backbone of modern data architectures and integrations. Understanding the different types of databases, including relational and non-relational systems, is important for designing efficient, scalable, and reliable data storage solutions. Relational databases such as IBM Db2, MariaDB, MySQL, PostgreSQL, SQLite, and others offer structured, schema-based storage with robust transactional support. These systems continue to evolve with enhanced features for things like hybrid cloud environments, advanced security, and high availability.

Non-relational databases, like MongoDB and Neo4j, are designed to handle unstructured and semistructured data, which provides flexibility and scalability for applications with different data needs. They are particularly suited for distributed environments and enable efficient handling of large-scale datasets and near-real-time analytics.

As data engineering requirements continue to grow, selecting the appropriate data store depends on multiple factors, including the nature of the data, performance needs, and scalability requirements. Understanding the system capabilities allows organizations to optimize their data infrastructure and employ the best storage option that meets business needs while maintaining performance, security, and cost-efficiency.

In the next chapters, we explore how these systems integrate with larger data pipelines and discuss additional technologies that provide the appropriate capabilities.

## CHAPTER 7

Data Ingestion and Streaming Tools

Data ingestion tools facilitate linking operational applications with analytical tools that produce reports and can provide organized data for machine learning models. Ingestion tools also greatly affect the data processing abilities of an organization, because data that cannot be accurately and reliably ingested in a timely manner will lose its usefulness. In this chapter, we cover some of the more well-known contemporary data ingestion and streaming tools.

By understanding the strengths and trade-offs of these tools, organizations can design robust and scalable ingestion pipelines that align with their strategic objectives. And, as data continues to grow in volume, velocity, and variety, selecting the right tools and frameworks will remain crucial for maintaining competitive advantage.

Apache Beam, Flink, Spark, and Storm

Apache Beam is an open source, unified programming environment for defining both batch and streaming data processing pipelines. It allows developers to build pipelines that can run on a variety of *execution engines* (or *runners*), such as Apache Flink and Apache Spark (which we'll go over shortly). Beam abstracts the complexities of parallel computing and simplifies the development of data-intensive applications. It supports key features like windowing, event-time processing, and a rich set of built-in transforms, making it flexible for near-real-time and batch workloads.

Beam can read your data from a diverse set of supported sources regardless of where the data resides, on premises or in the cloud. Beam writes the results of your data processing logic to most of the popular data sinks. Figure 7-1 shows a visual representation of Beam's batch and stream unified programming model.

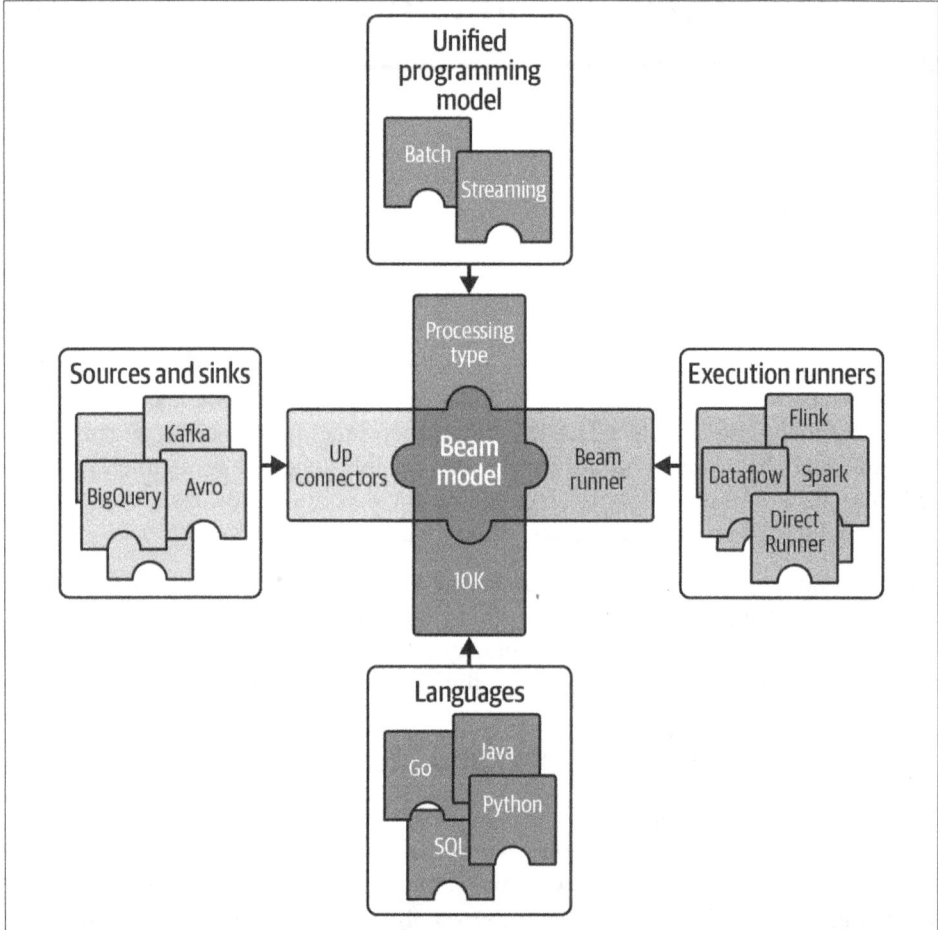

Figure 7-1. Beam's batch and stream unified programming model

Figure 7-2 shows a screenshot of the Beam Playground that is available online (*https://play.beam.apache.org*). Beam Playground is an interactive environment for toying around with Beam examples without needing to install Beam within your own environment.

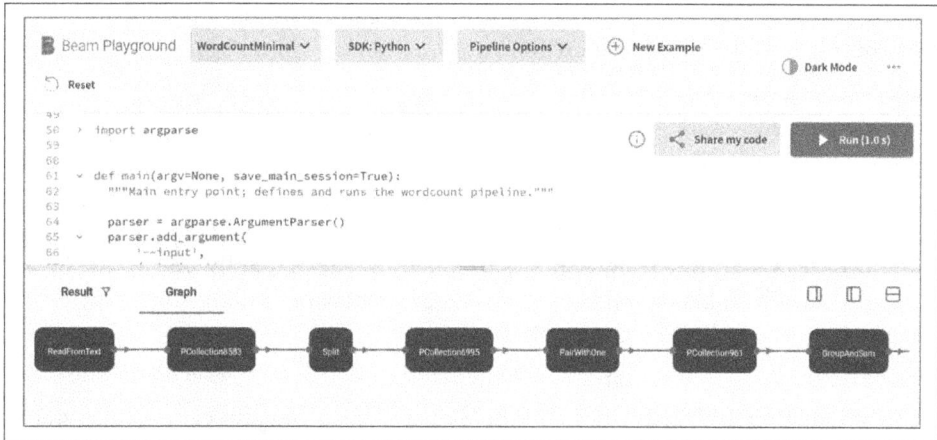

Figure 7-2. Screenshot of Beam Playground

As stated previously, one of the available execution engines for Beam is Apache Flink. Apache Flink is an open source stream processing framework designed for large-scale, distributed, near-real-time data processing. It provides an efficient, fault-tolerant architecture that allows it to process both bounded (batch) and unbounded (streaming) data with low latency. Flink excels at event-driven applications due to its ability to handle out-of-order data with stateful computation, which helps ensure accurate results in sometimes complex use cases.

One of Flink's key strengths is its native support for exactly-once processing semantics where each message is delivered precisely once. This helps maintain data consistency during failures, which makes Flink well suited for mission-critical applications.

Also, Flink's distributed runtime scales horizontally across clusters and integrates well with streaming ecosystems like Confluent. Its APIs are designed for ease of use and offer high-level abstractions for stream and batch processing in Java, Scala, and Python. This versatility is useful for developers building data-intensive applications.

Flink performs batch processing on top of its stream processing engine using event windows, whereas Spark, another execution engine available for Apache Beam, performs stream processing on top of its batch processing engine. Spark does this by breaking streams into microbatches that can then be processed through a distributed computing system. Spark is designed for processing large-scale data quickly and efficiently, and its APIs are available in multiple languages, including Java, Scala, Python, and R. It also integrates well with Hadoop ecosystems as well as with various data sources like HDFS, Amazon S3, and modern data lakes. The US Department of

Veterans Affairs (VA) uses Apache Spark to access and read multiple VA-supported data sources through JDBC and ODBC.[1]

Using Apache Spark with another Apache framework called Storm, organizations can create a hybrid data processing architecture where Storm captures and processes near-real-time data streams and sends the processed data to a shared storage layer or a message queue like Kafka. Spark can then consume this data for further batch processing, analysis, or model training. Apache Storm is designed for processing large streams of data with low latency. It was originally developed at Twitter (now X) and is highly scalable, fault-tolerant, and capable of processing millions of messages per second. It is used to build complex event processing (CEP) systems that require near-real-time analytics, continuous computation, and near-real-time data processing.

The computation architecture of Apache Storm is based on directed acyclic graphs (DAGs) where each node performs a specific task. The nodes can be spouts or bolts. Spouts are sources of streams in a Storm topology that are responsible for pulling data from external sources such as message queues or databases. Bolts are the processing units that transform or analyze the data streams.[2]

The flexibility of Storm's topology model allows developers to create fairly robust and intricate data processing pipelines that can be tailored to various use cases such as near-real-time analytics, machine learning, and ETL tasks. Apache Storm includes features like automatic failover, guaranteed message processing, and scalability, which make it a useful tool for processing high-velocity data streams. However, it is often compared to Apache Flink. As one Flink developer commented, "Compared to Apache Storm, the stream analysis functionality of Flink offers a high-level API and uses a more lightweight fault-tolerance strategy to provide exactly-once processing guarantees." Also, Apache Storm does not have batch capabilities. Therefore, Flink might, in some respects, be considered an improvement on Storm.[3]

Apache NiFi

The value of intelligence to national security often depends on its perishability, which led the NSA and the United States Intelligence Community (IC) to develop and implement NiagaraFiles, or NiFi, to prioritize and manage critical dataflows. NiFi can automate aspects of data management, transformation, and storage and enable data transfer across systems and agencies. It embeds contextual metadata, which

---

1 US Department of Veterans Affairs. 2024. "VA Technical Reference Model v 25.9: Apache Spark." October 29, 2024. *https://www.oit.va.gov/Services/TRM/ToolPage.aspx?tid=10273*.

2 Apache Software Foundation. n.d. "What Is Apache Flink?—Architecture." Apache Software Foundation. Accessed May 2024. *https://flink.apache.org/what-is-flink/flink-architecture*.

3 Penchikala, Srini. 2015. "Fabian Hueske on Apache Flink Framework." *InfoQ*. April 28, 2015. *https://www.infoq.com/news/2015/04/hueske-apache-flink*.

---

helps ensure a robust chain of custody for information. Apache released NiFi as open source software, allowing global contributors to view, modify, and enhance the technology. NiFi is now widely used by companies like ExxonMobil, AT&T, and British Gas and, presumably, by at least some of the US intelligence agencies. It has also been incorporated into Cloudera.

Figure 7-3 shows NiFi's browser-based user interface for creating and managing dataflows. It provides a visual canvas where users can drag and drop processors to design complex workflows. These processors represent individual data processing tasks, such as ingesting data, transforming it, or routing it to various destinations. The canvas allows users to connect processors with directed edges that define the flow of data and enables the building of highly customizable and interactive pipelines.

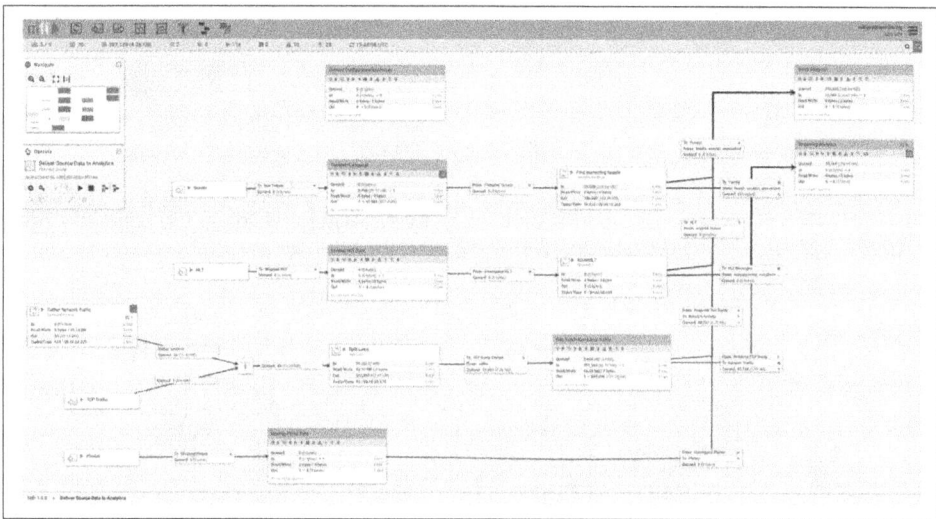

Figure 7-3. NiFi graphical interface

The interface also supports near-real-time monitoring, which offers users insight into the health and performance of dataflows through visual indicators and metrics. Users can pause, stop, or resume dataflows directly from the interface and can set parameters, manage processor configurations, and define properties via accessible dialog boxes. NiFi's GUI is further enhanced by features like zooming, searching, and a breadcrumb navigation system that can help immensely for large workflows.

AWS Glue and Amazon Kinesis

For an out-of-the-box solution, AWS Glue is an ETL service that simplifies data prep for analytics. It allows organizations to extract, cleanse, and consolidate data at scale and even suggests schemas for storing data. It also allows data architects to integrate data with different methods, such as ETL, ELT, batch, and streaming. Different subservices within Glue handle different aspects of data ingestion:

AWS Glue Data Catalog
Allows data scientists to query data efficiently and observe how data changes over time

AWS Glue DataBrew
Offers a visual interface that allows data analysts to transform data without writing code

AWS Glue Sensitive Data Detection
Automatically identifies, processes, and masks sensitive data

AWS Glue DevOps
Allows developers to track, test, and deploy data integration jobs more consistently

For public sector use cases, AWS Glue is available in AWS GovCloud (US-West Region). For instance, a PySpark-based AWS Glue job is being used by the Smithsonian to process multiple large-scale datasets and generate AWS Neptune files. Figure 7-4 shows an example ETL architecture that employs AWS Glue.

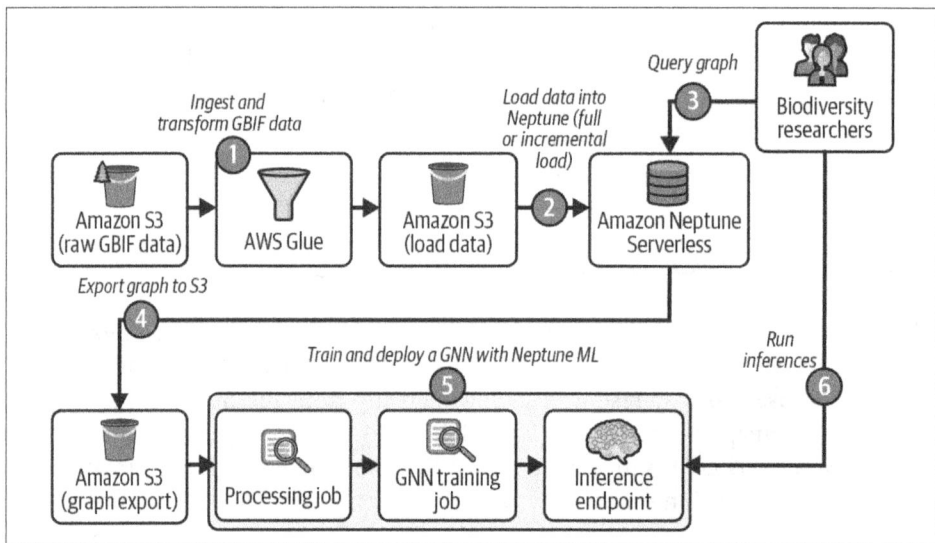

Figure 7-4. Example ETL architecture with AWS Glue

In addition to AWS Glue, Amazon has a service called Kinesis that is fully managed and is designed for near-real-time data collection, processing, and analysis. It enables users to ingest large streams of data such as video, IoT telemetry, and application logs and provides low-latency processing. Kinesis supports both near-real-time and microbatch analytics; it integrates with the Apache Kafka ecosystem and offers scalability for handling data from various sources. It can be used for applications like monitoring, fraud detection, and IoT analytics, and it works well with other AWS services as well as with other cloud service providers (CSPs) for hybrid cloud solutions. Like AWS Glue, Kinesis is available in AWS GovCloud.

Azure Event Hubs

Azure Event Hubs is a fully managed, scalable, and near-real-time data ingestion service. It enables streaming of millions of events per second from a plethora of different sources. Like Amazon Kinesis, Azure Event Hubs meshes well with the Apache Kafka ecosystem.

Event Hubs also works well with other Azure services and supports both near-real-time data ingestion and microbatching with customizable retention times. As a managed service, Event Hubs offers elastic scalability, which allows you to adjust from streaming megabytes to terabytes of data as needed. Further, by connecting with Azure Stream Analytics, a serverless streaming solution can pretty easily be deployed.

Confluent and Kafka

Apache Kafka is an open source distributed event streaming system. It was originally designed for creating high-throughput, low-latency, near-real-time data pipelines and implementing stream processing. Confluent is Kafka's fully managed counterpart.

I include Kafka and Confluent together in this section because the creators of Confluent originally developed Kafka. Confluent is a commercialized version of Kafka that has enhanced capabilities.

Both allow organizations to publish, subscribe, store, and process large volumes of data in a fault-tolerant and scalable manner. Their architectures are based on a distributed commit log that helps ensure durability and replication of data across multiple servers. They also provide connectors through their Kafka Connect framework, which enables integration with a wide range of data sources such as databases, filesystems, cloud storage, and applications.

Whenever I hear the terms *data mesh*, *stream processing*, or *denied, degraded, intermittent, and limited* (DDIL), Confluent and Kafka typically come to mind.

With the US DOD's relatively recent shift toward adopting modern, Agile, and cloud native computing environments, Confluent has become an important tool for the department's software factories. Specific government use cases for Confluent and Kafka involve log and event management and streaming data from edge devices. For example, the National Aeronautics and Space Administration (NASA) uses Confluent Kafka to stream sensor data and alerts in its General Coordinates Network (GCN).[4] In fact, if you're registered in the GCN, the following Python code will allow you to become a consumer of alerts that other users produce:[5]

```
##  Install the gcn-kafka module from the Conda repo
conda install -c conda-forge gcn-kafka

##  Create a Kafka consumer
from gcn_kafka import Consumer
consumer = Consumer(client_id='YOUR CLIENT ID',
                    client_secret='YOUR CLIENT SECRET KEY')

##  List available Kafka topics
print(consumer.list_topics().topics)

##  Subscribe to topics and receive alerts
consumer.subscribe(['gcn.classic.text.FERMI_GBM_FIN_POS',
                    'gcn.classic.text.LVC_INITIAL'])
while True:
    for message in consumer.consume(timeout=1):
        if message.error():
            print(message.error())
            continue
        print(message.value())
```

To facilitate data transformation and enrichment during ingestion, Confluent offers KSQL and Kafka Streams. They both support near-real-time processing to manipulate and analyze data as it flows through the system. Moreover, Confluent integrates security protocols like encryption and authentication to ensure that ingested data is protected from unauthorized access, which helps with adherence to compliance and governance requirements. For organizations moving toward cloud native architectures, Confluent provides fully managed services that help facilitate ingestion of data into cloud environments with minimal operational overhead.

---

4 "The General Coordinates Network (GCN) is a public collaboration platform run by NASA for the astronomy research community to share alerts and rapid communications about high-energy, multimessenger, and transient phenomena." (NASA. n.d. NASA General Coordinates Network [website]. Accessed March 2025. *https://gcn.nasa.gov.*)

5 NASA. n.d. GCN Kafka Client for Python. NASA General Coordinates Network GitHub repository. Last modified August 2025. *https://github.com/nasa-gcn/gcn-kafka-python.*

Conclusion

Data ingestion tools play an important role in enabling organizations to transform raw data into actionable insights. The diverse ecosystem of tools, ranging from open source platforms like Apache Beam, Flink, and Spark to enterprise-grade solutions such as AWS Glue, Azure Event Hubs, and Confluent Kafka, underscores the breadth of capabilities available for implementing modern data pipelines.

These tools support both batch and streaming data processing and offer flexibility that caters to a wide array of use cases—from near-real-time analytics and machine learning to ETL workflows and event-driven architectures. Furthermore, advancements in no-code/low-code platforms like Matillion, Meltano, and Workato democratize data integration by allowing nontechnical users to contribute to data science and engineering processes.

## CHAPTER 8

Comprehensive Integration Suites

All-encompassing data integration platforms are the cornerstone of modern data-driven enterprises and provide all the necessary infrastructure to unify, transform, and leverage data effectively across diverse systems. At their core, these platforms are designed to address the challenges of managing and utilizing data spread across multiple locations—often in "silos"—by offering a comprehensive suite of tools and features.

True data integration platforms typically encompass key functionalities such as data catalogs for discovering and inventorying data assets, data conditioning tools to cleanse and rectify inconsistencies in data, and data connectors to facilitate movement and transformation between systems. They also generally include robust mechanisms for data ingestion that enable organizations to gather and import data for immediate use or future analysis, and data governance tools that safeguard the availability, security, usability, and integrity of critical information.

Furthermore, these platforms usually support data migration processes that ensure smooth transitions across computing environments. Their ETL and ELT capabilities as well as their MDM frameworks help establish consistent definitions and a consistent, unified source of truth.

The best modern enterprise-grade data integration platforms elevate their utility through advanced features tailored to meet contemporary demands such as automation, user-friendly interfaces, and platform guidance or recommendations. Automation streamlines data pipelines, reducing manual intervention and enhancing efficiency. User-friendly interfaces often include drag-and-drop functionalities. Platform-provided guidance democratizes data operations for users of varying technical expertise.

The top integration platforms also support complex transformations and offer assistance with intricate calculations and data manipulation. Security and compliance are also central to these platforms. They help ensure that data handling adheres to stringent regulations and typically employ state-of-the-art encryption to protect sensitive information.

This chapter delves into the intricacies of some of the more recognizable comprehensive integration platforms and explores how their tools and features allow organizations to harness the full potential of their data assets. It also attempts to outline the pivotal role of data integration platforms in driving operational efficiency and informed decision making.

AWS Glue, Amazon Elastic MapReduce, and Amazon Q

AWS Glue is a fully managed ETL service designed to simplify and automate data integration tasks. It allows organizations to prepare, clean, and transform data from multiple sources and make it ready for analytics, machine learning, or other business applications. AWS Glue does not require users to manage infrastructure, and it automatically scales resources based on workload demands. One of its key features is the AWS Glue Data Catalog, which acts as a centralized metadata repository and enables easy data discovery and schema management. Additionally, AWS Glue supports both visual and code-based ETL development.

There are currently three modes of working with AWS Glue: AWS Glue for Apache Spark, AWS Glue for Ray, and AWS Glue for Python Shell. This makes Glue accessible to data engineers as well as less tech-savvy analysts. With built-in connectors for AWS services such as Amazon S3, RDS, and Redshift and for third-party databases, Glue streamlines many of the integration processes, particularly with job scheduling and workflow orchestration.

Another cloud-based Amazon offering that complements AWS Glue is Amazon Elastic MapReduce (EMR). EMR is a big-data platform designed to process vast amounts of data quickly and cost-effectively. It's built on popular open source frameworks like Apache Hadoop, Apache Spark, and Presto and is meant to simplify the creation and management of big-data environments by abstracting the complexities of infrastructure setup, configuration, and scaling.

EMR's managed cluster model lets users process large datasets across distributed computing environments, which makes it well suited for tasks such as data transformation, streaming data processing, log analysis, machine learning, and near-real-time analytics. It's also able to run distributed computing jobs, which enables efficient execution of ETL workflows at scale. For example, EMR can be used to clean and condition raw data and convert data into standardized formats for integration with downstream systems. Users can write ETL pipelines that process structured and unstructured data.

In addition to AWS Glue, EMR's integration with other AWS services—such as Amazon S3 for storage and Amazon Redshift for analytics—further enhances its utility in data integration projects. It allows for automated and efficient data ingestion, processing, and transfer across these services. Organizations also benefit from EMR's scalability, as it dynamically adjusts resources to handle varying workloads and with a pay-as-you-go pricing model.

One of the newer offerings from Amazon that is used in tandem with AWS Glue is Amazon Q. With Q, you can build data integration pipelines using natural language. It can generate AWS Glue code for ETL processing and also help troubleshoot jobs.

Azure Data Factory

Azure Data Factory (ADF) is a fully managed, cloud-based, and "serverless" data integration service from Microsoft that allows users to orchestrate and automate data movement and transformation at scale. It enables organizations to construct data pipelines that can move and process data from various sources, such as on-premises databases, cloud storage solutions, and SaaS applications, and deliver it to destination systems like data lakes or SQL databases. With its ability to integrate and schedule complex workflows, ADF supports data transformation using various other Azure technologies such as HDInsight and SQL-based transformations within the service itself.

ADF provides a code-free UI for designing data workflows as well as a robust set of APIs for more customized development needs. Additionally, ADF includes features such as monitoring, logging, and security integrations to ensure reliable data operations. The service is highly scalable and can handle both simple, scheduled data transfers in addition to more complex, enterprise-level data integration tasks. ADF is widely used for modern data warehousing, big-data analytics, and business intelligence projects. It's also sometimes considered to be an upgrade from SQL Server.

ADF has been used at the US Department of Veterans Affairs (VA) as well as the US Federal Trade Commission (FTC). At the FTC, ADF has been used to securely connect, transfer, transform, and load data between multiple cloud data sources.

Databricks

Databricks is a platform widely used for ETL and ELT processes. It leverages Apache Spark's capabilities to handle large-scale data processing and incorporates Delta Lake and MLflow, which provide a storage layer and support for MLOps, respectively.

For data ingestion, Databricks inherently supports various data sources, including cloud storage systems like Amazon S3, Azure Data Lake Storage, and Google Cloud Storage in addition to popular databases and APIs. Databricks provides tools to extract data from these sources, transform it directly within the storage system, and load it into a target data store. Transformations can include a wide range of operations such as filtering, aggregating, and joining. Support for various programming languages include Python, SQL, Scala, and R.

Databricks Delta Lake is often used in ELT processes because it provides ACID transactions and scalable metadata handling and unifies streaming and batch data (see Figure 8-1).

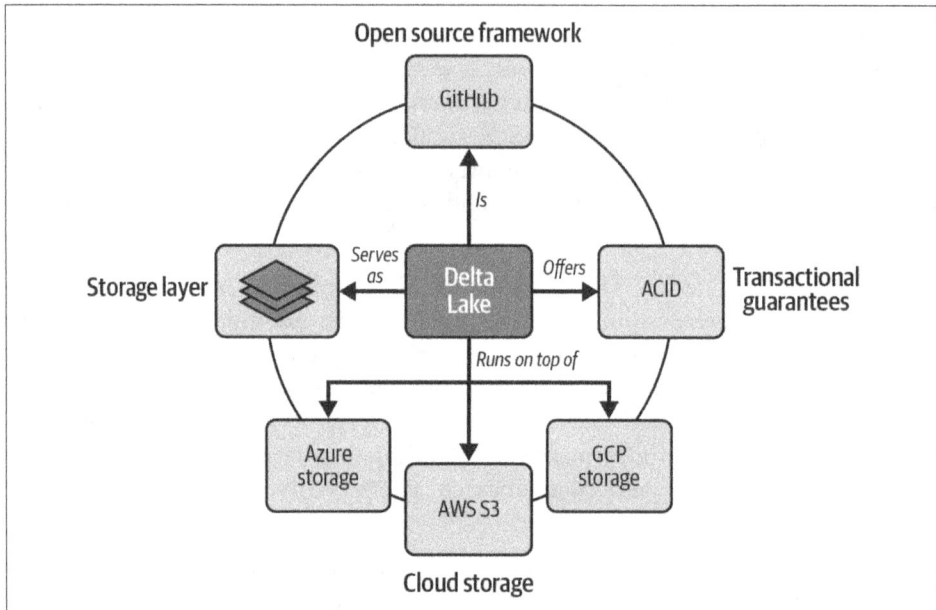

Figure 8-1. Delta Lake concept diagram

Databricks also integrates with various BI tools and data visualization platforms to enable easy access to processed data for analysis and reporting, and it includes notebooks and workflows that allow teams to easily collaborate.

In 2021, Databricks launched an open source protocol called Delta Sharing for securely sharing data across organizations in near real time and independent of the platform where the data resides.[1]

Databricks is used by many US federal government agencies, including the Department of Defense, the Department of Homeland Security, the Postal Service, the Food and Drug Administration, the Army Corp of Engineers, and the Department of Transportation. In November 2024, Databricks received Provisional Authorization (PA) for the DOD's Cloud Computing Security Requirements Guide Impact Level 5 (IL5), but it has been available within the DOD's big-data platform, ADVANA, for many years and has previously obtained FedRAMP High authorization.[2]

The United States Postal Service (USPS) Office of the Inspector General (OIG) ensures integrity, accountability, and efficiency in USPS operations, and to address challenges such as increasing data volumes and complex infrastructure, the USPS OIG has transitioned its computing environment to a cloud-based lakehouse architecture. This modernization has allowed for centralized data management, improved data reliability, and enhanced analytics and machine learning capabilities. With the new system, the OIG detects potential postal crimes, optimizes operations, and develops innovative solutions like Informed Delivery, which provides digital previews of incoming mail and mitigates fraud.

At the USPS, lakehouses have improved efficiency immensely and cut total costs by approximately 40%. Analytical processes that previously took months now take days, which allows auditors and investigators to improve customer-facing services.[3]

---

1 Databricks. 2021. "Databricks Unveils Delta Sharing, the World's First Open Protocol for Real-Time, Secure Data Sharing and Collaboration Between Organizations." Databricks. May 26, 2021. *https://www.databricks.com/company/newsroom/press-releases/databricks-unveils-delta-sharing-the-worlds-first-open-protocol-for-real-time-secure-data-sharing-and-collaboration-between-organizations*.

2 Databricks. 2024. "Databricks Achieves Authorization for DoD IL5 on AWS GovCloud." PR Newswire. November 18, 2024. *https://www.prnewswire.com/in/news-releases/databricks-achieves-authorization-for-dod-il5-on-aws-govcloud-302305459.html*.

3 Databricks. n.d. The Data Intelligence Platform for Federal Agencies (website). Databricks. Accessed November 2024. *https://www.databricks.com/solutions/industries/federal-government*.

Figure 8-2 shows the Databricks user interface.

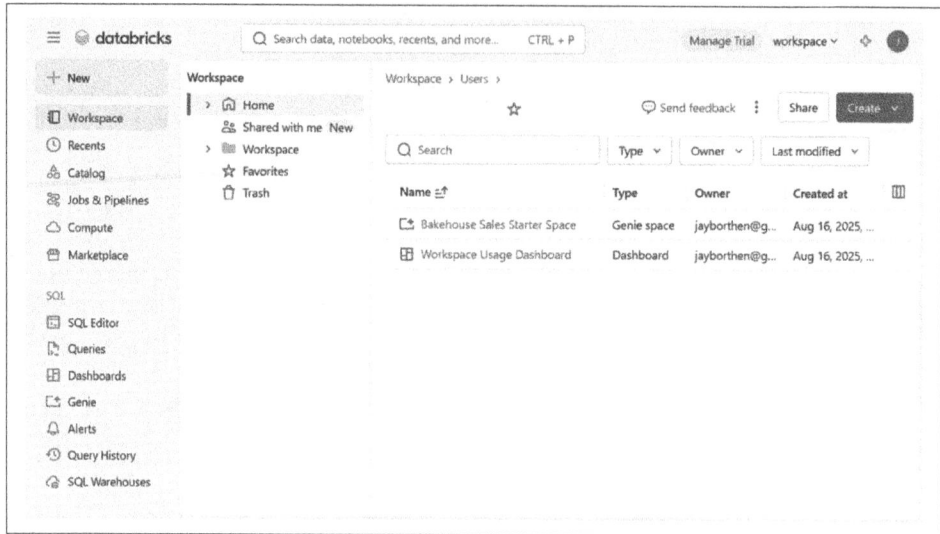

Figure 8-2. The Databricks user interface

Fivetran

Similar to most of the other product offerings mentioned in this chapter, Fivetran is a managed enterprise data integration platform. Like its peers, it's designed to automate the process of data ingestion and transformation to enable organizations to centralize their data from various sources into data warehouses or data lakes for analysis.

Also like most of its peers, Fivetran provides prebuilt connectors that can automatically extract data from a wide range of sources, including databases, SaaS applications, and event logs, and load it into a destination such as Amazon Redshift, Google BigQuery, or Snowflake.

What sets Fivetran apart is its focus on reliable data movement and minimal configuration. Once a connector is set up, Fivetran automatically manages schema changes and ensures data is continuously synced with minimal latency that provides a near-real-time reflection of the source systems in the data warehouse. The "ready-to-analyze schema" and automation significantly reduce the maintenance burden on data engineering teams, which allows them to focus on more strategic tasks rather than on managing data pipelines.

Fivetran is available in AWS GovCloud, but it's not readily apparent whether Fivetran is deployed within the US federal government.

IBM DataStage and App Connect

IBM's DataStage is the data integration component of the IBM InfoSphere Information Server platform that facilitates ETL. It's well suited for handling large volumes of data in complex environments—on premises or in the cloud—and supports a wide range of data sources including databases, enterprise applications, and big-data platforms. One of the core strengths of DataStage is its ability to perform complex data transformations at scale, leveraging its parallel processing and enterprise connectivity capabilities. It also employs user-friendly features such as a drag-and-drop GUI. Dataflows (or jobs) can be configured without needing extensive coding experience.

IBM's broader InfoSphere suite provides enhanced data governance, metadata management, and data quality tools.

IBM App Connect provides hundreds of prebuilt connectors and customizable templates to accelerate integration projects using low-code tools. IBM App Connect is also considered an application integration software and acts as middleware between different application platforms. It's deployable on premises as well as in the cloud as a scalable, fully managed Integration Platform as a Service (iPaaS) on AWS.

IICS and PowerCenter

Informatica Intelligent Cloud Services (IICS) is a comprehensive suite of data integration and data management tools and is generally considered to be a low-code solution. It has a range of capabilities to facilitate data operations across various environments, and in addition to data integration functionalities, it includes features for application integration.

IICS supports a variety of integration patterns and use cases including ETL, ELT, and near-real-time data streaming and synchronization. Its data integration capabilities allow users to connect to a wide range of data sources, both on premises as well as in the cloud, and process data through an intuitive interface. IICS was authorized as FedRAMP Moderate in February 2022.

A second Informatica product called PowerCenter streamlines ETL into consolidated data warehouses. It provides tools like data profiling, data quality management, and metadata management to ensure data integrity and accuracy. With its user-friendly visual interface, PowerCenter simplifies the development of data integration workflows. PowerCenter is particularly suited for traditional enterprise environments requiring robust ETL functionalities, strict governance, and the reliability of legacy systems to handle large, complex datasets effectively.

IICS and PowerCenter are both data integration tools but differ significantly in various aspects. IICS is a cloud-based solution optimized for modern cloud ecosystems, while PowerCenter is an on-premises tool renowned for its data transformation capabilities. IICS eliminates the need for installing client applications on personal computers. PowerCenter can sometimes be complicated to install and may require expert assistance. However, workflow design in PowerCenter allows engineers to create process flows in various formats, whereas IICS requires selecting a design pattern up front. IICS is highly cloud-compatible, supports single, multi-, and hybrid cloud environments, and can scale automatically based on demand and data volume. Additionally, IICS has a more modern user interface, template-driven development, and APIs for continuous delivery. IICS can automatically convert many PowerCenter assets to its platform, which makes migration between the two essentially seamless.

Microsoft SQL Server Integration Services

Microsoft SQL Server Integration Services (SSIS) is a data integration and workflow automation tool that is part of the Microsoft SQL Server suite. SSIS provides a platform for building high-performance data transformation and migration solutions that enable organizations to extract, transform, and load data from various sources into a centralized database or data warehouse. It supports sources such as relational databases, flat files, XML, and cloud services. With its user-friendly graphical interface, SSIS allows developers to design and manage data workflows through drag-and-drop components. Additionally, SSIS offers robust features for error handling, logging, and performance tuning that help ensure reliable and efficient data processing.

It is commonly used for tasks such as data warehousing, data conditioning, and data synchronization. Organizations often use SSIS to streamline their data management processes and enhance the quality and accessibility of their data assets.

MuleSoft

MuleSoft, a Salesforce company, offers a comprehensive integration solution called Anypoint Platform. It enables users to connect applications, data, and devices with low-code tools and prebuilt connectors (450+). The platform allows organizations to create a flow of data across different environments, including on-premises, cloud, and hybrid systems.

The Anypoint Platform offers tools for building, deploying, and managing APIs that serve as the building blocks for integrating various software and systems. This API-led approach enables organizations to standardize and reuse integrations, which reduces the complexity and cost of connecting disparate systems. MuleSoft also supports near-real-time data integration that allows for timely and accurate data exchange, and the platform provides data transformation capabilities that help ensure that data is appropriately formatted and compatible across different systems. MuleSoft has been recognized as a leader in both iPaaS and API management.[4]

Oracle Data Integrator and GoldenGate

Oracle Data Integrator (ODI) is a comprehensive data integration platform. According to UD Analytics, it covers most, if not all, data integration requirements from "high-volume, high-performance batch loads, to event-driven, trickle-feed integration processes" and service-oriented-architecture (SOA)-enabled data services. Oracle Data Integrator facilitates developer productivity and improved user experience with a flow-based declarative user interface and integration with Oracle GoldenGate.

GoldenGate is a managed service that functions as a near-real-time data mesh platform. It utilizes replication to ensure high data availability and supports near-real-time data analysis.

Pentaho

Pentaho, currently owned and maintained by Hitachi Vantara, is a pretty comprehensive data integration and business analytics platform that helps organizations manage and integrate data from a wide variety of sources. Pentaho Data Integration (PDI), also known as Kettle, is the core component of the platform. It provides ETL capabilities and supports both batch and near-real-time processing, making it suitable for various use cases, from traditional data warehousing to big-data analytics. Pentaho also has a drag-and-drop interface that simplifies the creation of complex data pipelines and enables users to design integration jobs without extensive programming knowledge. Additionally, Pentaho has a fairly extensive library of connectors for big-data technologies like Hadoop, Spark, and NoSQL databases.

Qlik, Talend, and Stitch

Qlik offers a comprehensive suite of tools for data analytics, data integration, and data management and is designed to support near-real-time data capture and delivery. Its flagship offering in the 1990s was QlikView, which has since been superseded by Qlik Sense (on-premises) and Qlik Cloud Analytics (SaaS) that together form Qlik's *Data Analytics* portfolio. Qlik Sense is favored by government clients for its transparency, controllability, and security, while Qlik Cloud Analytics is optimized for cloud-based deployments.

---

4 MuleSoft. n.d. MuleSoft from Salesforce (website). Salesforce, Inc. Accessed September 2024. *https://www.mulesoft.com*.

Qlik's *Data Integration* portfolio, comprising Qlik Replicate and Qlik Compose, excels in managing heterogeneous environments and enables near-real-time data movement between on-premises and cloud systems as well as cross-cloud transfers.[5] Paired with Qlik Catalog, the platform facilitates automated schema synchronization, data instantiation, and robust cataloging and supports the creation of data warehouses, marts, and lakes.

Qlik is one of only a handful of platforms that do change data capture (CDC) well. The CDC capabilities ensure up-to-the-minute data availability while minimizing latency. Log-based CDC, specifically, is Qlik Replicate's default CDC method for RDBMS, but other CDC methods are available.

Qlik's architecture is designed for scalability and stability and trusted by over 2,500 clients, including half of the current Fortune 100 companies. The platform has also facilitated over 200,000 database and mainframe migrations to AWS, Azure, and Google Cloud. Qlik's automated tools (see Figure 8-3) simplify mapping, target table creation, and deployment of analytics-ready structures. Its cataloging and search capabilities make data accessible and manageable at scale.

It can also integrate with existing geospatial data present in applications like ArcGIS.

The diagram in Figure 8-3 shows an example of Qlik's data warehouse automation.

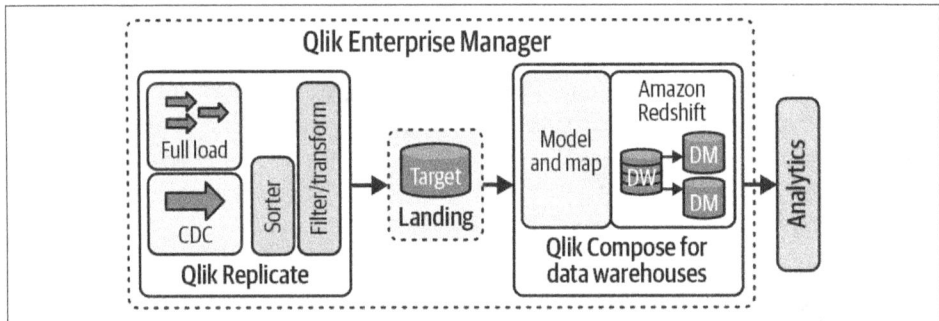

Figure 8-3. An example of Qlik's data warehouse automation

Within the past few years, Qlik has obtained additional capabilities with the acquisition of Talend and Stitch. Qlik announced the acquisition of Talend in early 2023. Talend offers data integration and management tools with low-code development features, provides robust ETL and ELT capabilities (such as 1,000+ data source connectors), and facilitates collaboration and scheduling.

---

5 US Analytics. n.d. "Financial Report Logs Reporting: User Guide for Oracle Data Integrator." US Analytics. Accessed January 2025. *https://www.us-analytics.com/guide-financial-report-logs-reporting-oracle-data-integrator.*

Talend's wide range of tools for data connectivity, transformation, and governance enable smooth integration of data from various databases, applications, and systems. Its interface and collection of prebuilt connectors allow users to unify and appropriately condition data. With strong capabilities for managing complex data workflows and supporting near-real-time data processing, Talend is a popular option for organizations seeking reliable data extraction and integration solutions. It's particularly well suited for businesses looking to enhance data quality in their data warehouses and carry out complex transformations across multiple data sources.[6]

Qlik Stitch is a cloud-based data integration platform that offers a no-code, drag-and-drop ETL pipeline creation solution. It was designed to simplify the ETL process. As part of the Qlik data integration ecosystem, Stitch offers robust capabilities for seamless and scalable data movement, enabling organizations to unify data from diverse systems for analysis and reporting. It supports over 100 data sources, including popular databases, SaaS applications, and cloud platforms, making it a versatile tool for organizations with varied data landscapes. Stitch's automated approach reduces the manual effort involved in data preparation that helps ensure efficient and reliable data replication. In the same vein, Stitch also incorporates CDC technology to identify and replicate only modified data, which optimizes resource usage and enhances data freshness in near-real-time scenarios.

Relational databases and queries that were originally developed in the 1980s for transactional systems are not always well suited for modern analytics. Traditional query-based tools often exclude data and restrict users to shallow exploration of data, which can often lead to missed insights and opportunities. Qlik Sense leverages the unique Associative Engine that allows users of all skill levels to explore data without restrictions. It enables dynamic exploration with interactive selection and search, instantly recalculating analytics and highlighting relationships using color coding. By maintaining context across all visualizations and including both related and unrelated values in analyses, the Qlik Associative Engine uncovers insights that query-based tools can often miss. This innovative technology represents more than 30 years of dedicated development and remains one of Qlik's key differentiators.

TIBCO

TIBCO is an integration platform that aids in data integration by providing a suite of tools designed to connect, unify, and manage data across various systems and applications. TIBCO's integration capabilities are centered around its TIBCO Cloud Integration and TIBCO BusinessWorks products, which allow organizations to connect on-premises, cloud, and hybrid environments. These tools offer a comprehensive set

---

6 Warchol, Katarzyna. 2024. "Qlik + Talend—the Future of Data Integration." Inetum Polska. March 14, 2024. *https://www.nearshore-it.eu/articles/qlik-talend-the-future-of-data.*

of connectors and adapters that facilitate dataflows between different applications, databases, and services. TIBCO also supports near-real-time data integration and provides advanced data transformation and mapping capabilities. With its strong focus on API management and event-driven architecture, TIBCO enables organizations to create scalable and flexible data integration solutions that can adapt to changing business needs. TIBCO is well suited for organizations wanting to reduce the complexity of their data integration processes, enhance data accuracy, and improve overall system interoperability.

TIBCO Cloud Integration provides a low-code platform for integrating applications, data, and devices across hybrid environments. It supports near-real-time data integration and offers a range of connectivity options suitable for enterprise-scale projects.

TIBCO BusinessWorks provides a graphical development environment that allows users to build and manage integration workflows without requiring extensive coding. BusinessWorks supports a wide range of integration patterns, including service-oriented architecture (SOA), microservices, and API-led connectivity. It is commonly used for automating business processes, orchestrating services, and enabling near-real-time data exchange between disparate systems. The platform includes features for data transformation, error handling, and support for various communication protocols. It's widely employed in industries that need reliable and scalable integration solutions.

Conclusion

Data integration platforms are essential tools for organizations striving to consolidate, transform, and utilize their data assets effectively. The breadth of options discussed in this chapter underscores the diversity of capabilities and features available to meet varying data integration needs. From platforms like Amazon EMR and Azure Data Factory, which excel in cloud-based big-data processing, to tools such as Fivetran that prioritize automation and ease of use, the landscape of integration solutions is expansive and highly customizable. These platforms empower organizations to streamline complex data workflows, bridge disparate systems, and maintain data quality while adhering to stringent governance and security requirements.

The integration platforms covered in this chapter also highlight the evolving role of technology in managing data across diverse environments, from on-premises legacy systems to modern cloud architectures. As organizations continue to adopt hybrid and multicloud strategies, the ability to integrate data securely and efficiently has become a cornerstone of operational success. The platforms discussed not only address traditional data integration challenges but include innovations like machine learning integration, low-code interfaces, and near-real-time analytics as well. Together, they illustrate the transformative power of data integration in driving organizational agility, enhancing collaboration, and unlocking the full potential of enterprise data assets.

Introducing the Example Data Integration Solution

In Part III, we finally get our hands dirty and build a data integration solution from the ground up. Chapter 9 describes our starting point, including givens, assumptions, and objectives of the example integration solution. You'll examine the actual solution architecture toward the end of Chapter 9, followed by the hands-on implementation of a batch integration in Chapter 10, and a streaming integration in Chapter 11.

The major CSPs have serverless equivalents of many of the procedures we will cover in this part. However, starting with bare-bones Amazon EC2 Instances will mimic an environment that can be replicated independent of any particular CSP, and the Qlik part of the solution should be able to be duplicated on-prem, given similar hardware and operating systems.

## CHAPTER 9

Introducing the Example Solution

In this chapter, we introduce the example solution, which will be detailed in Chapters 10 and 11. We will discuss the objectives of the example, describe its initial state, and give you a big-picture overview of its architecture. By providing this high-level overview of the example scenario, this chapter aims to provide a tangible starting point for the hands-on portions in Chapters 10 and 11 and preview what's to come.

Objectives

The goals of the example data integration in Chapters 10 and 11 include the following:

Demonstrate the ease with which a purpose-built data integration platform can handle the ETL process.

> The example will show how a modern data integration platform can simplify the traditional extract, transform, load (ETL) workflow. Rather than requiring extensive custom scripting or manual configuration, the platform streamlines data ingestion, transformation, and delivery across multiple sources and destinations. By highlighting automation, low-code interfaces, and built-in connectivity, the demonstration reveals how integration tasks that once demanded significant effort can now be executed with speed and repeatability.

Illustrate some of the concepts discussed in Part I, including batch and stream processing.

> Concepts such as batch and streaming integration, data silos, and pipeline orchestration are brought to life through the practical implementation. The example includes both static data sources (e.g., CSV files and relational databases) as well as near-real-time data streaming from IoT devices, allowing readers to see firsthand how the platform accommodates different data velocities and

varieties. This reinforces foundational ideas around temporal granularity, latency tolerance, and architectural choices when designing for different use cases.

Provide a general guide for setting up data integration platforms.

Although the example uses specific tools, it provides a blueprint for data integration that can be applied in a variety of environments and with many different tools. It walks through setup considerations including source and target selection, deployment options, cloud infrastructure utilization, and configuration of key components. The goal is not just to teach how to replicate this particular solution but to provide a reusable approach to building and deploying data integration solutions.

Initial State

The starting point for the example integration solution includes a local CSV file, a small PostgreSQL database on an Ubuntu server, and a digital humidity and temperature (DHT) sensor that streams data from a Raspberry Pi. The CSV file contains data from the US Energy Information Administration (EIA); the PostgreSQL database contains data from the US Department of Energy.[1] Figure 9-1 displays the initial state of the example solution. Note that there are no connections from or to any of the data sources.

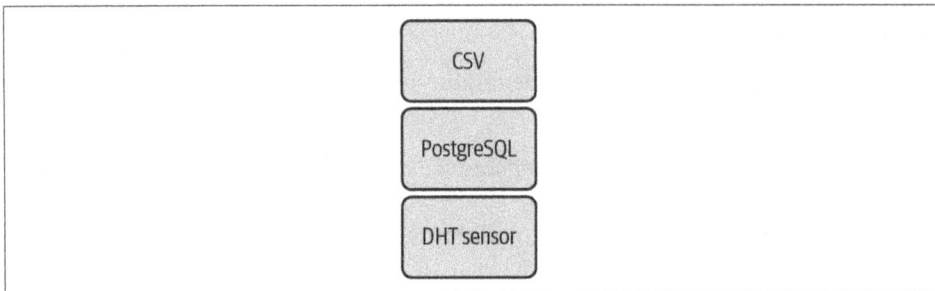

Figure 9-1. Initial state

At the end of the integration, the two batch datasets (i.e., the CSV file and the PostgreSQL database) that could be considered to be in their own silos will be merged into a single location so the data can be used for hypothetical business intelligence (BI) purposes.

---

1 The process used to create the database is shown in Appendix A.

Planned Architecture

Before beginning the actual hands-on implementation of a data integration solution, you would typically perform requirements gathering, analysis of alternatives, and detailed process planning in addition to data discovery and profiling. However, the objective here is not project management, so we will forego deep dives into management practices and will instead focus on presenting different components of an example data integration.[2]

As with any project, you want the solution to be as simple as possible without compromising capability. However, there are always constraints and challenges that create complexity. With the example solution, to keep things interesting and more realistic, some complexity is intentionally being introduced.

Figure 9-2 shows the planned architecture.

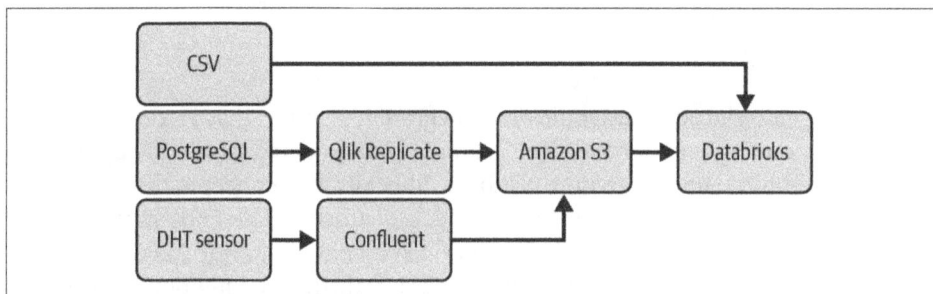

Figure 9-2. Planned architecture

The example shows how integration is carried out on the Qlik platform. I chose Qlik because it's the platform with which I'm currently most familiar and also because I have a readily accessible license. Similarly, we're using AWS because, although I started my journey into the Cloud with Azure, I am currently most familiar with AWS. Finally, we're using Databricks and Confluent because I am currently interacting with them on a client project, they're readily available, and they're versatile. Specifically, we're using Confluent Cloud so that we don't need to run our own Kafka cluster.

You should note that there are costs associated with Qlik, AWS, Databricks, and Confluent. AWS, Databricks, and Confluent have consumption licenses that you can utilize on somewhat of an as-needed basis without costs becoming too overburdensome. Qlik, on the other hand, is exclusively designed for enterprise-level data integrations, and it would likely be prohibitively expensive for an individual to obtain

---

2 A resource I highly recommend that thoroughly covers data management is Piethein Strengholt's *Data Management at Scale* (O'Reilly).

a license. However, as we saw in Part II, there are many good options available, each with their own pros and cons that need to be considered for each specific use case.

To accommodate the deployment of Qlik, the planned data integration solution consists of one EC2 Instance that leverages Windows Server to host Qlik Replicate (which is considered a component of the broader Qlik Data Integration offering). Databricks will also be leveraging AWS via CloudFormation and required compute resources.

> Security is a crucial aspect of data management, and meticulous planning and thorough vetting of security practices should occur in tandem with the development and implementation of a data integration solution. Security is sporadically addressed here but is not the primary focus, so security and hardening best practices (principle of least privilege, etc.) have not been consciously adhered to.

Conclusion

This chapter introduced an example data integration solution that incorporates both batch and streaming components. The example aims to demonstrate the capabilities of a purpose-built data integration platform, illustrate key concepts from earlier in the book, and guide readers in setting up such platforms. The chosen architecture uses Qlik Replicate on an AWS EC2 Instance, Confluent Cloud for Kafka streaming, and Databricks for processing, demonstrating a realistic yet intentionally complex solution.

In Chapter 10, we'll implement a batch solution, and in Chapter 11, we'll implement a streaming solution.

Implementing a Batch Solution

In this chapter we walk through the steps of implementing the data integration solution introduced in Chapter 9. By the end of this chapter, you will have gained practical experience in building a batch solution that is scalable and reliable.

Setting Up Qlik Replicate

In the following sections, we'll set up Qlik Replicate in a Windows Server EC2 Instance, and we will copy data located in a PostgreSQL database into an AWS S3 bucket to form the beginning of a small data lake.

Setting Up a Windows Server EC2 Instance for Qlik Replicate

First, we create a Windows Server EC2 Instance with the following specs. These specs align with Qlik's *Basic System* recommended hardware configuration but with an additional 8 GB of memory:[1]

```
t3.xlarge
4 vCPUs
x86_64 Architecture
16 GiB Memory
EBS Root Device Type
GP3 Volume Type
320 GiB HD
3000 IOPS

AMI: Microsoft Windows Server 2025 Base
AMI ID: ami-07fa5275316057f54
```

---

1 *GB ≈ GiB.*

Log in to AWS and navigate to the EC2 dashboard. In the EC2 Instance console, click the "Launch instances" button and select "Launch instances" from the drop-down menu, as shown in Figure 10-1.

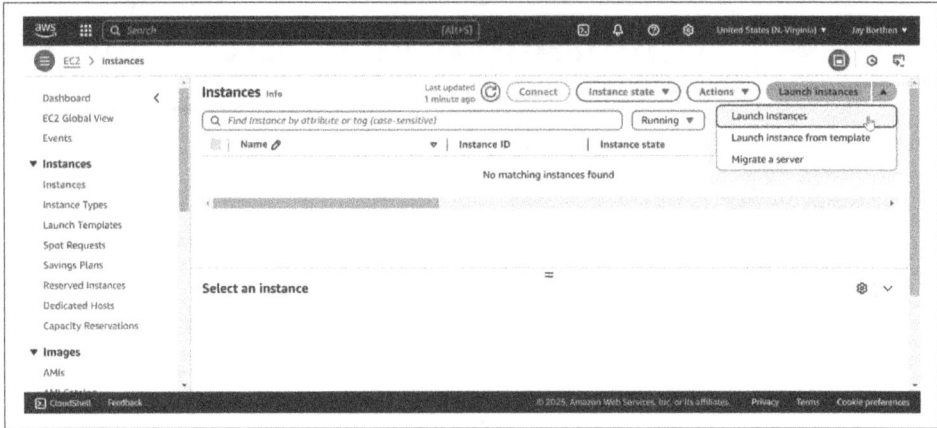

Figure 10-1. Launch instances

Name the instance. Here we'll use the name "Qlik Replicate (Windows Server)." Then, under Application and OS Images (Amazon Machine Image) and the Quick Start tab, select the Windows panel. Under Amazon Machine Image (AMI), if not already selected, select Microsoft Windows Server 2025 Base, as shown in Figure 10-2.

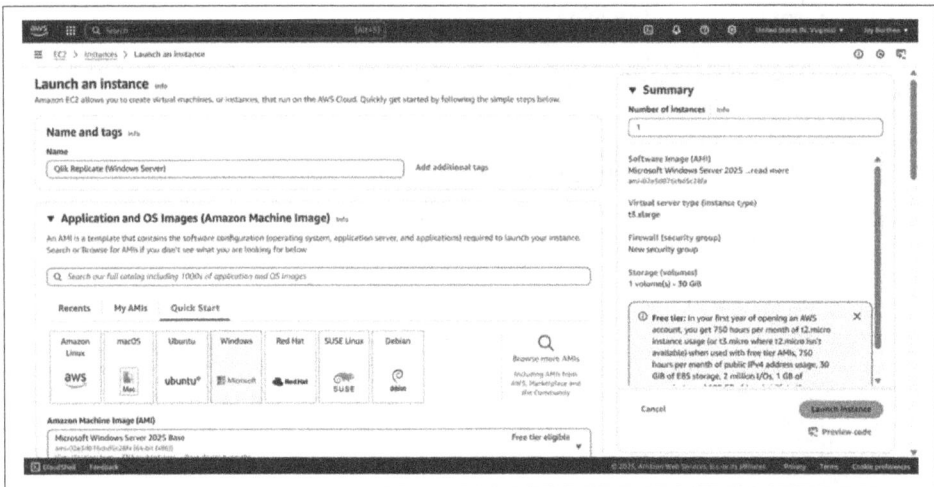

Figure 10-2. Launch an instance

Scroll down. Under "Instance type," select "t3.xlarge," and then either select an existing key pair or click "Create new key pair." Here, we're going to create a new key pair.

After you've clicked "Create new key pair," a "Create key pair" dialog box, as shown in Figure 10-3, should appear. Name the key pair. We'll use the name "BDIS Windows RDP Key Pair." Make sure the "Key pair type" is RSA and the "Private key file format" is set to *.pem*. Then click the "Create key pair" button.

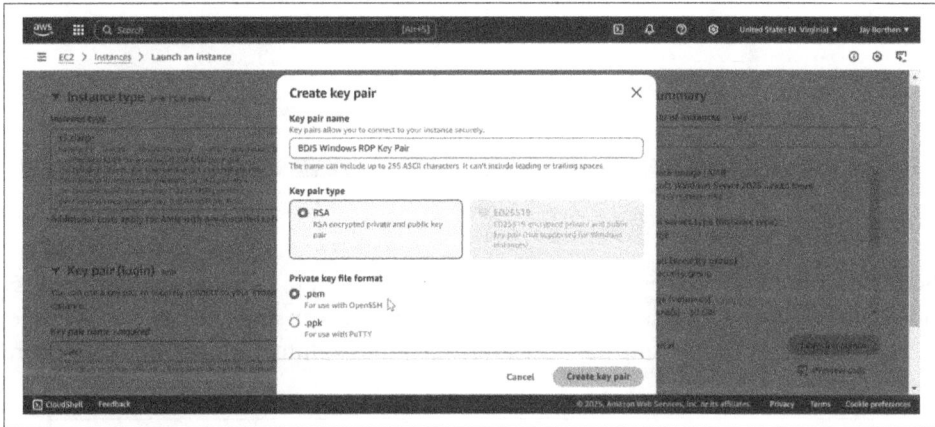

Figure 10-3. Create key pair

After you've hit the "Create key pair" button, a Save As pop-up window should show up. Save the *.pem* file in an accessible location for later.

Then, back in the "Launch an instance" interface, scroll down to the "Network settings" section, as shown in Figure 10-4, and create or select a security group. Here, we are going to allow RDP traffic, which will open port 3389 with TCP.

> We are allowing traffic from anywhere to access the remote desktop. This is not a recommended practice. Allowing only specific IP addresses is best.

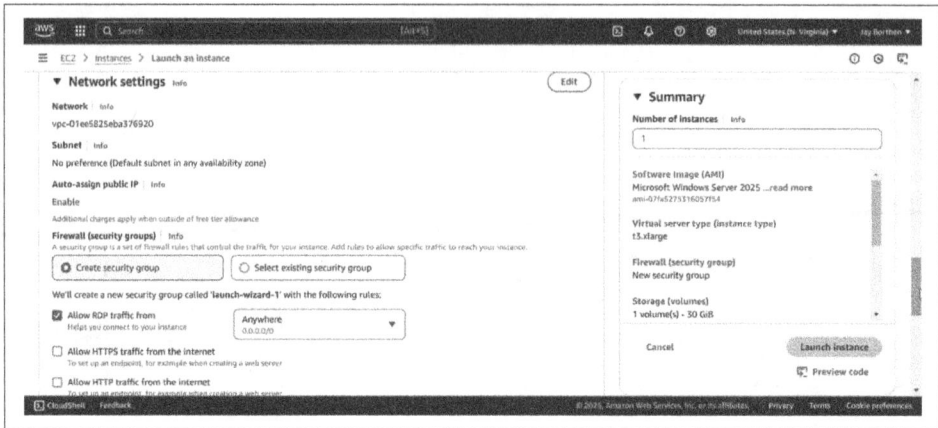

Figure 10-4. Network settings

Scroll farther down. Under the "Configure storage" section, as shown in Figure 10-5, make sure you have an adequate amount of storage and an appropriate root volume. In this tutorial, we'll be using 320 GiB and a gp3 root volume, which should be more than adequate.

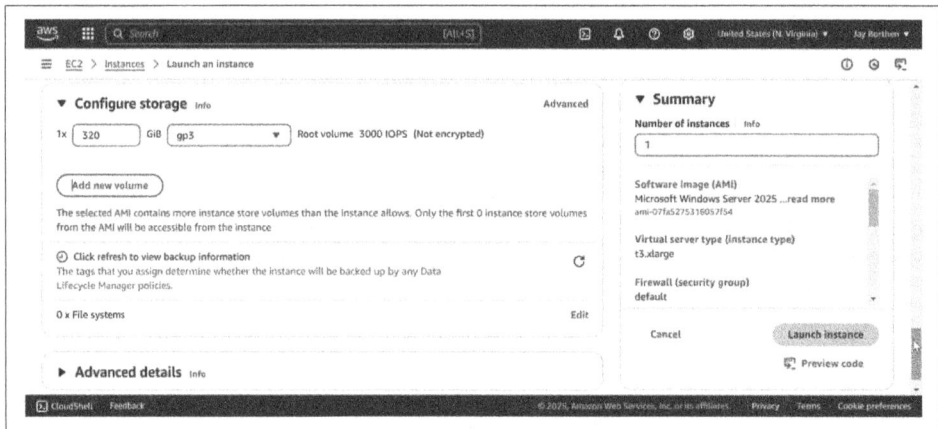

Figure 10-5. Configure storage

Finally, click the "Launch instance" button. You should see something similar to what's shown in Figure 10-6.

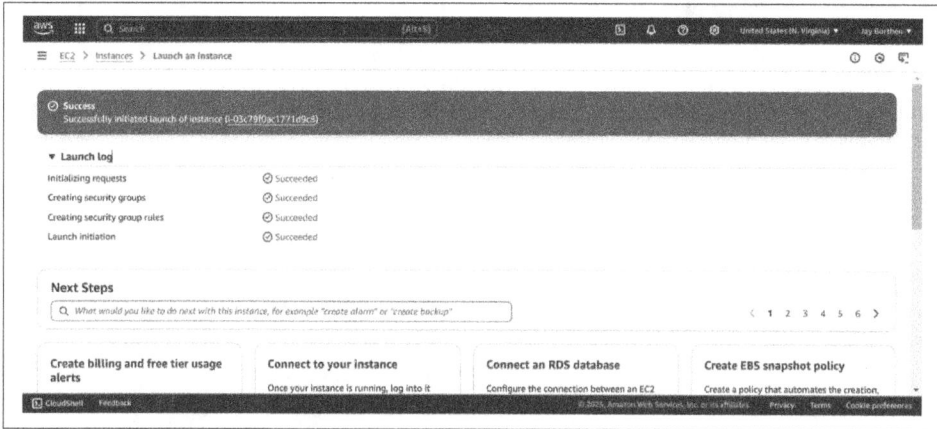

Figure 10-6. Successfully initiated launch of instance

Navigate back to the Amazon EC2 Instances console. When the Windows Server EC2 Instance is running, select the checkbox next to the Windows Server EC2 Instance and then click the Connect button, as shown in Figure 10-7.

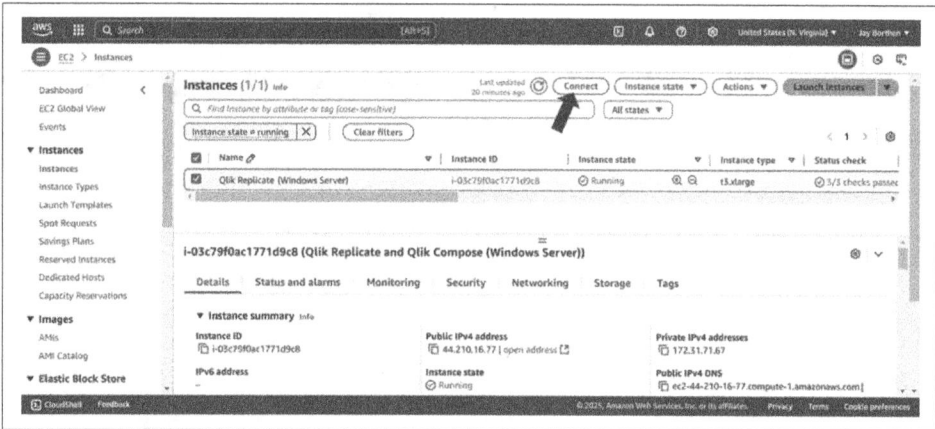

Figure 10-7. Selecting the Windows Server EC2 Instance

In the "Connect to instance" screen, as shown in Figure 10-8, navigate to the "RDP client" tab, and click the button labeled "Download remote desktop file."

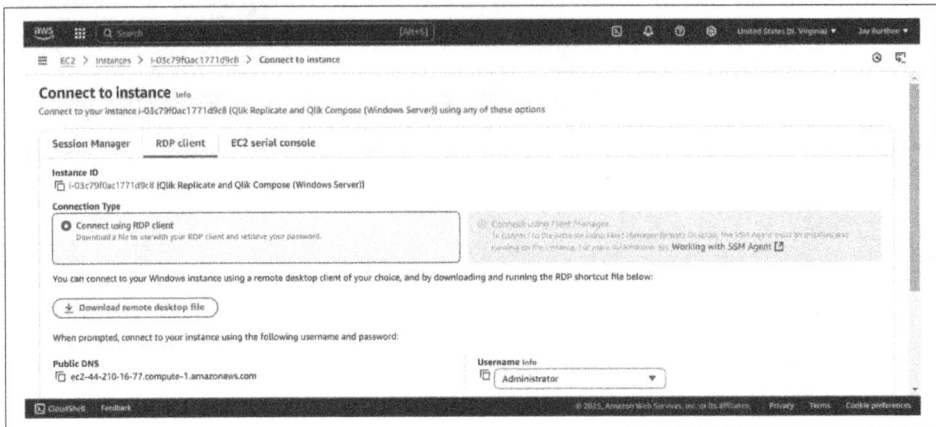

Figure 10-8. Downloading the remote desktop file

Scroll farther down the page, below the "Download remote desktop file" button, until you see "Get password."

Click "Get password," and then on the subsequent screen, click the button labeled "Upload private key file," as shown in Figure 10-9.

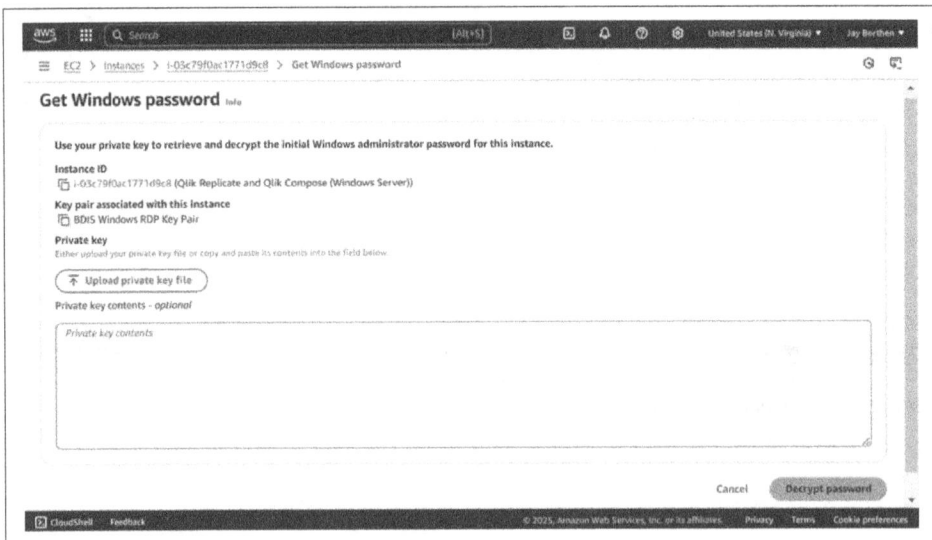

Figure 10-9. Uploading the private key file

In the pop-up window, find your private key file from earlier that ends with *.pem*, and double-click it. After the private key file is uploaded, click the "Decrypt password" button and copy the given password. This password is required to log in to the Windows Server RDP, so keep it in a safe place.

Find the RDP file that was downloaded previously and double-click it to run it. It might look something like what is shown in Figure 10-10.

Figure 10-10. Qlik Replicate RDP

Select the Connect button if prompted and enter the password you just found into the Windows Security interface, and then click the button to continue. A Windows Server screen, similar to the one shown in Figure 10-11, should appear.

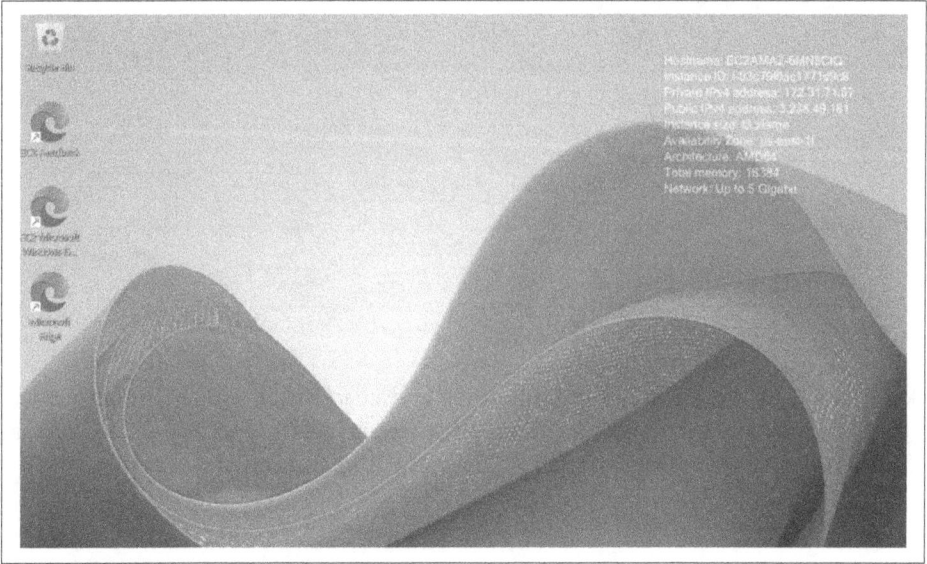

Figure 10-11. Windows Server interface

Installing and Downloading Qlik Replicate

Now that we have the EC2 Windows environment set up, we need to download and install Qlik Replicate. The prerequisites for installing Qlik Replicate on a Windows computer include the following:

- .NET Framework 4.8 or later.
- Visual C++ Redistributable for Visual Studio 2015. (If it is not installed or if an older version is installed, it will be installed automatically during installation.)
- TLS 1.2 or later must be supported in the underlying OS.
- Port 443 must be opened for outbound and inbound communication.

To download and install Qlik Replicate, first navigate to *https://community.qlik.com/t5/ Product-Downloads/tkb-p/Downloads* from the Windows Server environment. The Qlik site will likely ask you to sign in, and after you do so, you should see a site similar to the one shown in Figure 10-12.

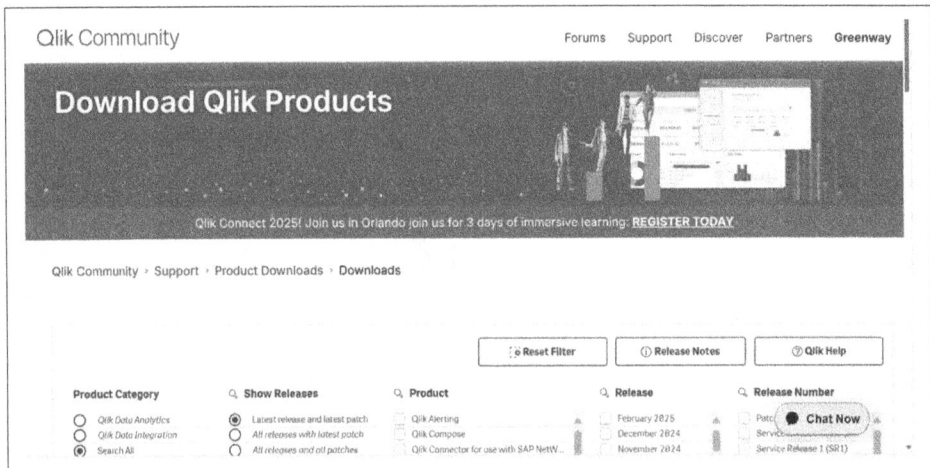

Figure 10-12. Qlik product download site

Scroll down to the area with radio buttons and checkboxes. Under Product, select Qlik Replicate, and then select the desired release and release number. In this case, as shown in Figure 10-13, we're selecting November 2024 and Initial Release.

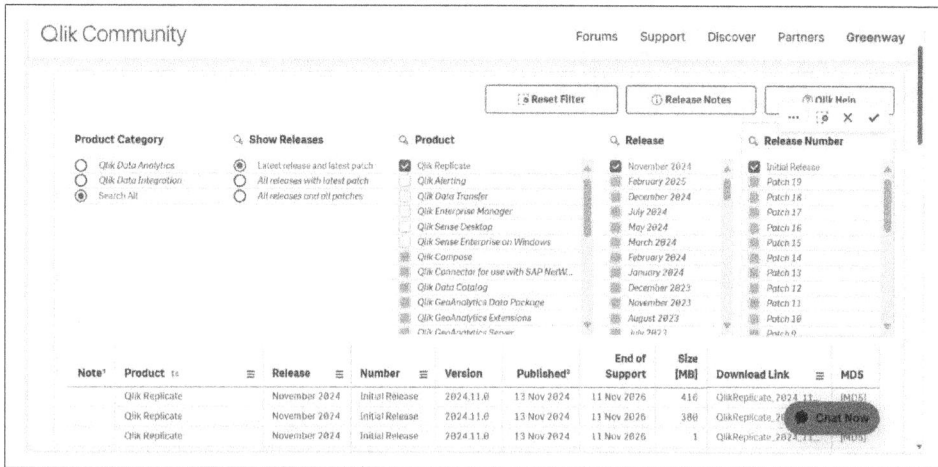

Figure 10-13. Qlik product selection site

Scroll farther down the page and you will see relevant downloadable assets. Click the Download Link corresponding to Windows. In our case, we are downloading *QlikReplicate_2024_11_0_Windows_X64.zip*.

After it's downloaded, find the **.zip* file, extract it, navigate into the extracted folder, as shown in Figure 10-14, and then double-click on the extracted executable file to run it.

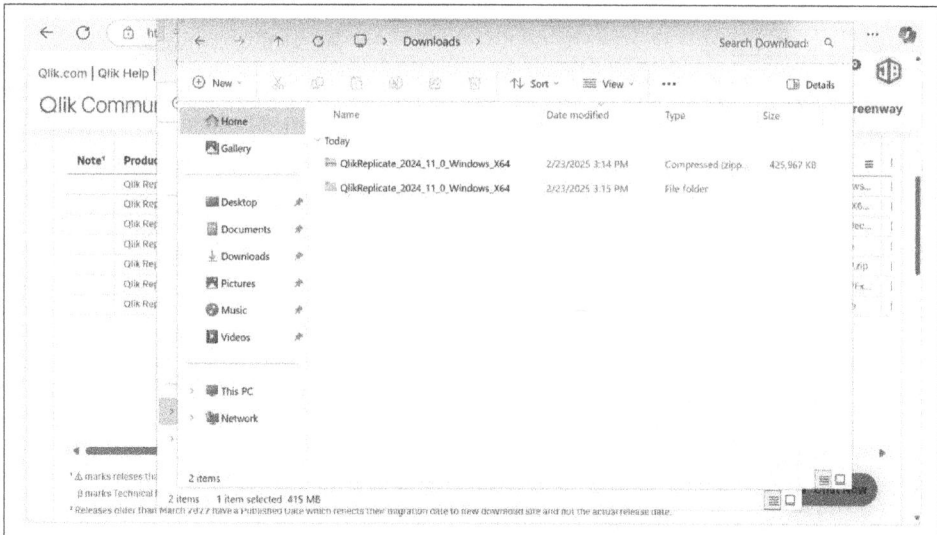

Figure 10-14. Installing Qlik Replicate in Windows Server

After you have double-clicked the Qlik Replicate executable, InstallShield should open and walk you through the installation. We will "Install a local Replicate Server" and use the default destination folder, *C:\Program Files\Attunity\Replicate*.

After you've gone through the InstallShield Wizard, Qlik Replicate will be configured and installed. Click Finish after installation. Qlik Replicate should now be present in the Start Menu, as shown in Figure 10-15.

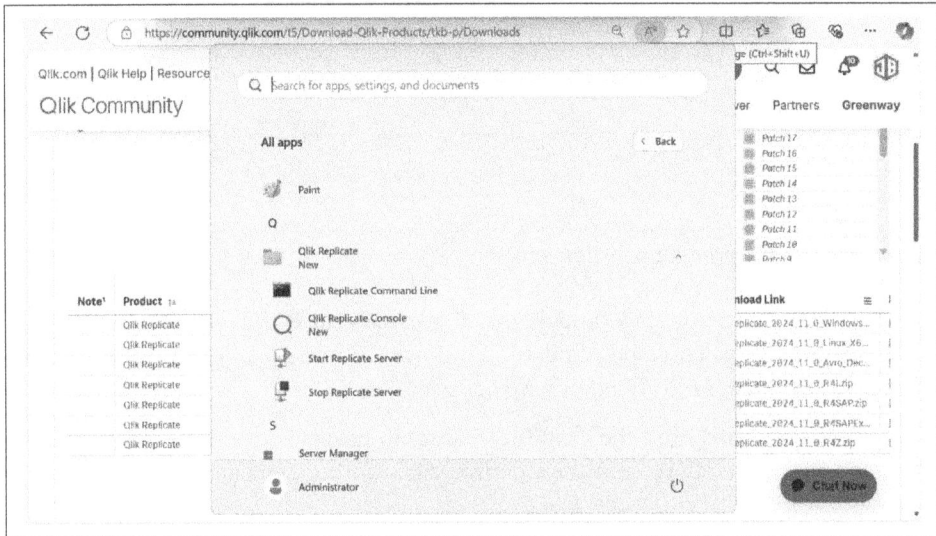

Figure 10-15. Qlik Replicate installed in Windows Server

Open the Qlik Replicate console application. As shown in Figure 10-16, your browser will prompt you for a username and password, which are your domain username and password. For this demo, our EC2 Instance username is "administrator," and the password is what was found in "Setting Up a Windows Server EC2 Instance for Qlik Replicate" on page 141 after downloading the Windows Server RDP.

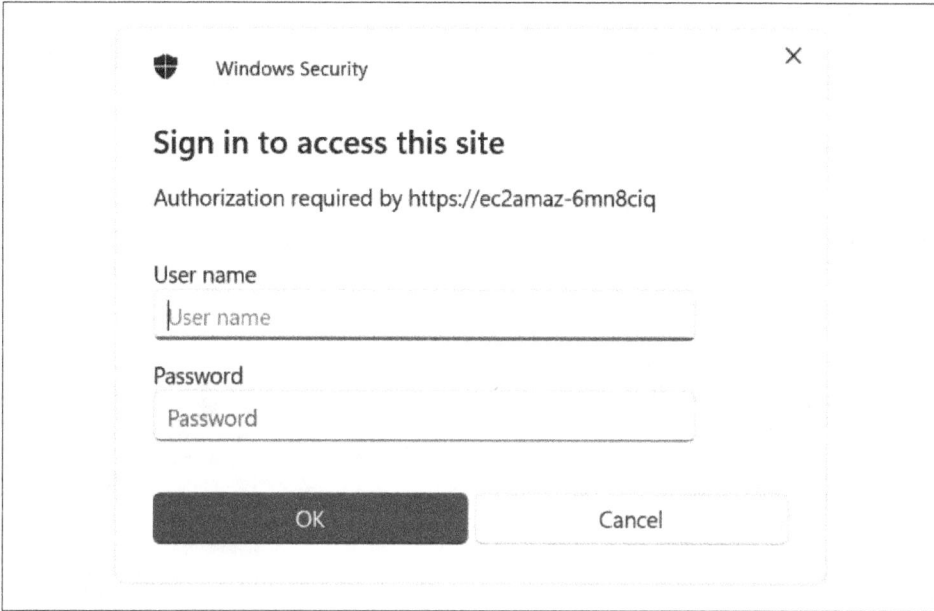

Figure 10-16. Qlik Replicate console authentication screen

After successfully signing into the Qlik Replicate console, you should see something like what is shown in the screenshot image in Figure 10-17.

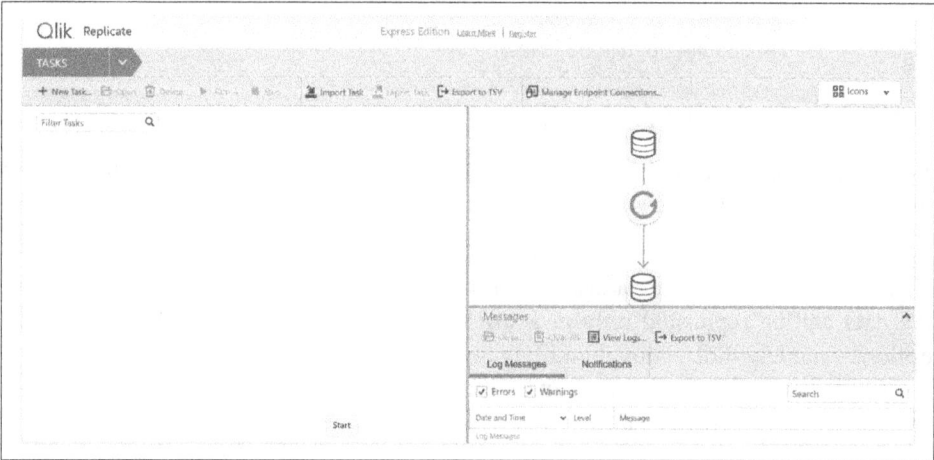

Figure 10-17. The Qlik Replicate console

To register the application, you will need to copy the Qlik license files to the Windows Server EC2 Instance. These files will likely be text files that were provided by Qlik via email. Assuming the Clipboard option is enabled in your Windows Server Remote Desktop, you should be able to simply copy the license text files from your local desktop to the Windows Server (EC2) environment.

After the license files are present in the Windows Server environment, click on the Register link at the top of the Replicate console. The Register License window should pop up, as shown in Figure 10-18. Click the Load button, navigate to the corresponding license file, select it, and click the Register License button.

Figure 10-18. Qlik Replicate license screen

Setting Up Endpoint Connections

Assuming Qlik Replicate is registered, click on the + New Task button at the top left of the interface. A New Task dialog box should show up and look similar to what is shown in Figure 10-19.

Name the task and provide a description if desired. Then select Unidirectional, since the data will be replicated only in a single direction. The other Replication Profile options—namely Bidirectional and Log Stream—allow syncing of data between locations and using the database's transaction log as a source for replicating changes, respectively. Log Stream enables CDC, which is described in Chapter 2.

Make sure that Full Load is selected under Task Options so that Qlik Replicate loads all of the source data to the target endpoint. The Apply Changes option tells Qlik Replicate to process changes; the Store Changes option stores changes in either Change Tables or an Audit Table. For now, though, the Full Load option is the only one required.

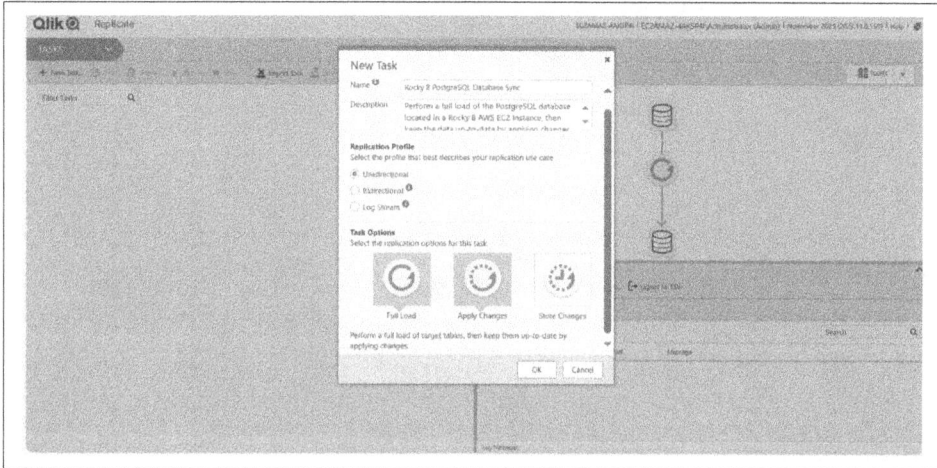

Figure 10-19. New task

After clicking the OK button, click on Manage Endpoint Connections. In the pop-up window as shown in Figure 10-20, select + New Endpoint Connection.

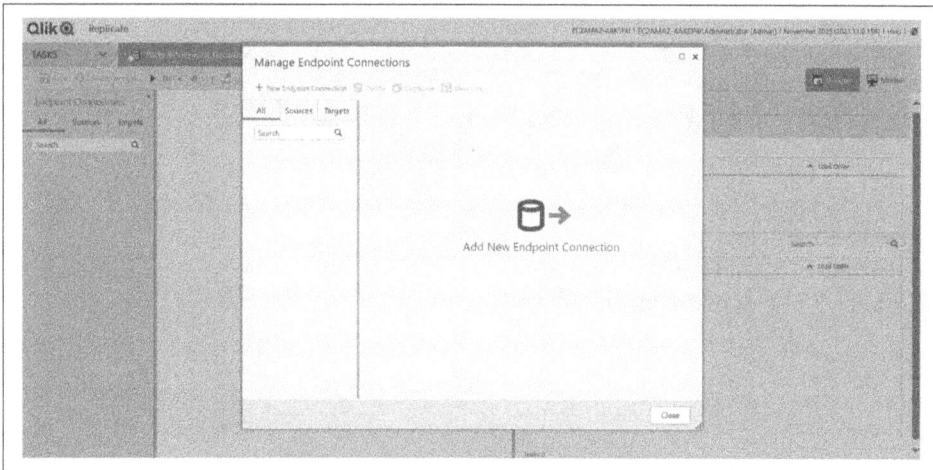

Figure 10-20. Manage endpoint connections

Name the endpoint connection to be created and provide a description if desired. Make sure the Role is designated as Source. Then select PostgreSQL for Type. The dialog will expand and additional fields will become available. Fill in the fields with their appropriate values. Then click the Test Connection button, as seen in Figure 10-21. If everything has been filled in correctly, you should see a notice that the connection was successful.

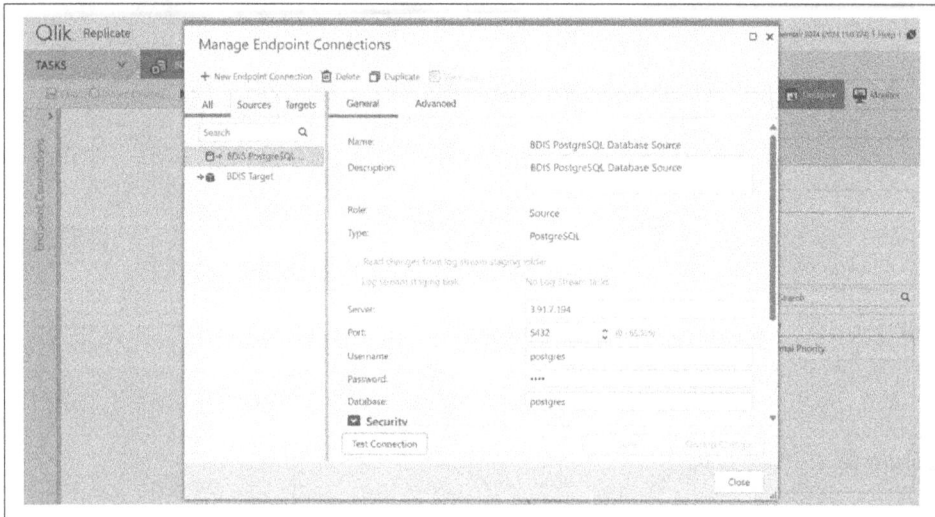

Figure 10-21. Test connection

> If you receive an error indicating that *libpq.dll* cannot be loaded, verify the ODBC package is installed on the Replicate machine—in our case, the Windows Server instance. The ODBC *.msi* file can be found at the PSQL ODBC download site.

Repeat the same steps for the target. In this case, our target is an Amazon S3 bucket. After the target is connected, you should see something similar to what is shown in Figure 10-22. This is the Qlik Replicate Designer. It shows the dataflow and the selected tables from the source.

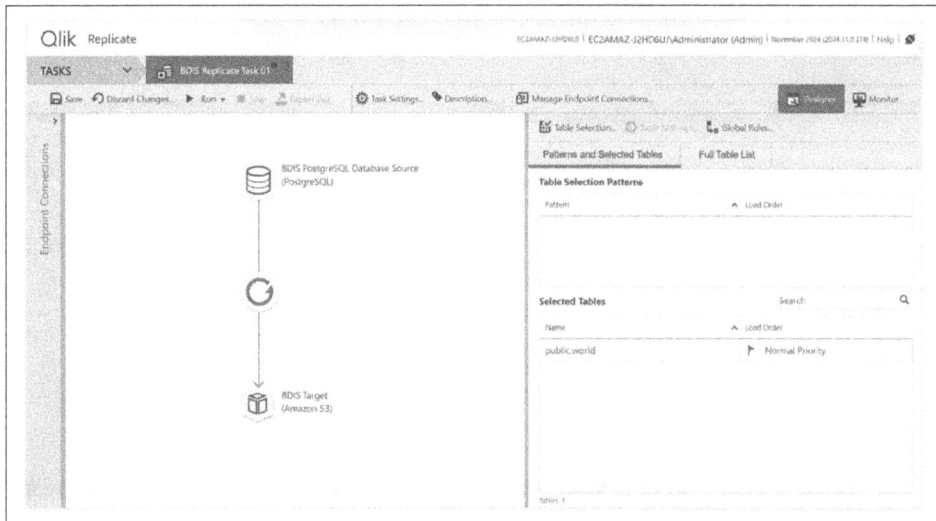

Figure 10-22. Replicate Designer

After selecting the desired tables, select Run at the top of the interface. The Monitor window will show the progression of the replication process and will look something like what is shown in Figure 10-23.

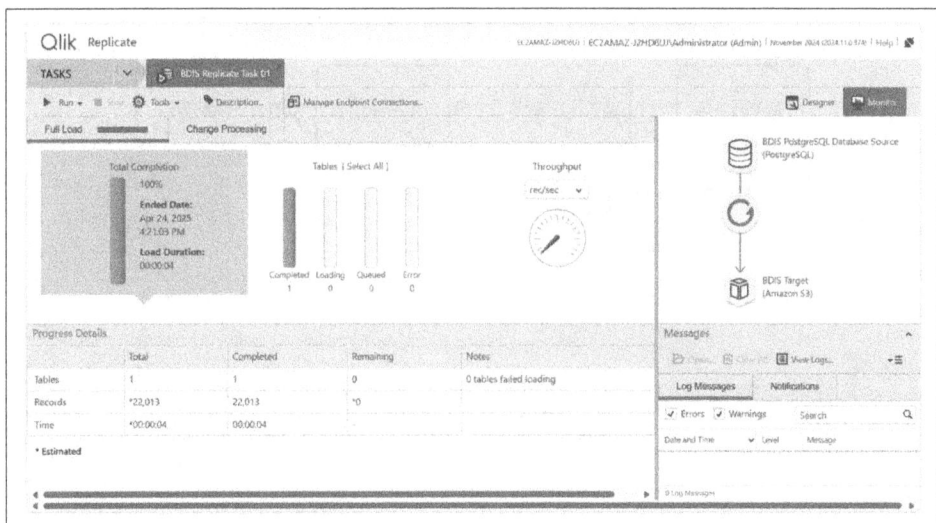

Figure 10-23. Replicate Monitor

After the replication task is complete, check the target location for the previously selected tables. You should see something similar to what's in Figure 10-24.

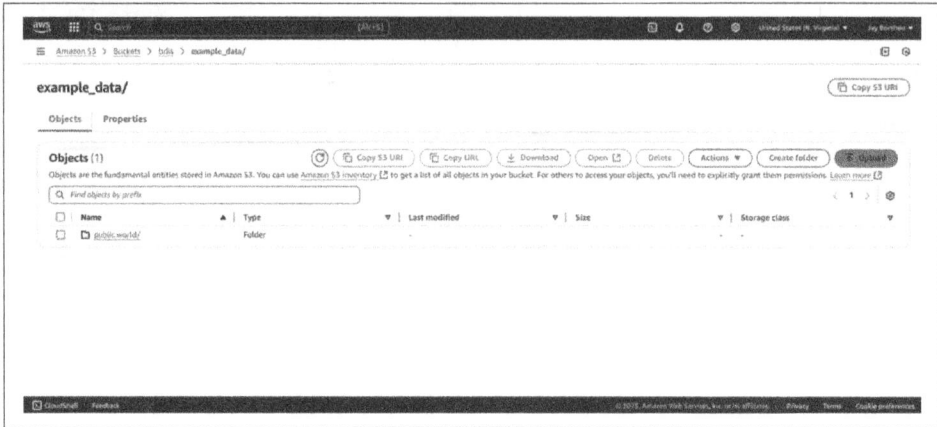

Figure 10-24. AWS S3 example data

We've now finished the first leg of our example integration, as shown in Figure 10-25. Now we need to set up the Databricks environment.

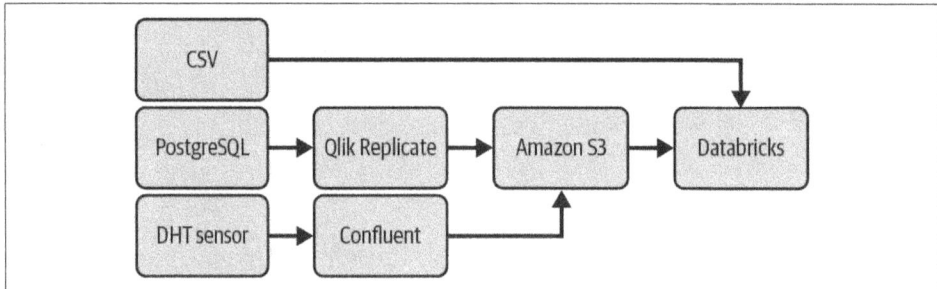

Figure 10-25. Integration status

Setting Up Databricks

As discussed in Part II, Databricks simplifies data integration by providing a unified platform that connects data sources and enables organizations to consolidate and process data at scale. With support for structured, semistructured, and unstructured data, Databricks offers features like Delta Lake for efficient data storage, transformation, and versioning. Its ability to integrate with popular data lakes, warehouses, and cloud services ensures interoperability while leveraging collaborative tools like notebooks and ML workflows. Databricks helps accelerate data integration pipelines.

Setting Up Databricks in AWS

First, sign in to your AWS account. You will need it later. Then, if you don't already have a Databricks account, navigate to the Databricks website (*https://data bricks.com*). Then click on the Try Databricks button.

Fill out the form and click the Continue button at the bottom. On the next screen, make sure AWS is selected and click the Continue button.

You may need to verify your account via email, but after doing so, you should see something similar to Figure 10-26.

Enter a workspace name in the provided textbox. (In this example, I'm using the workspace name Example Workspace.) Also select the appropriate AWS region from the drop-down menu and press the "Start quickstart" button.

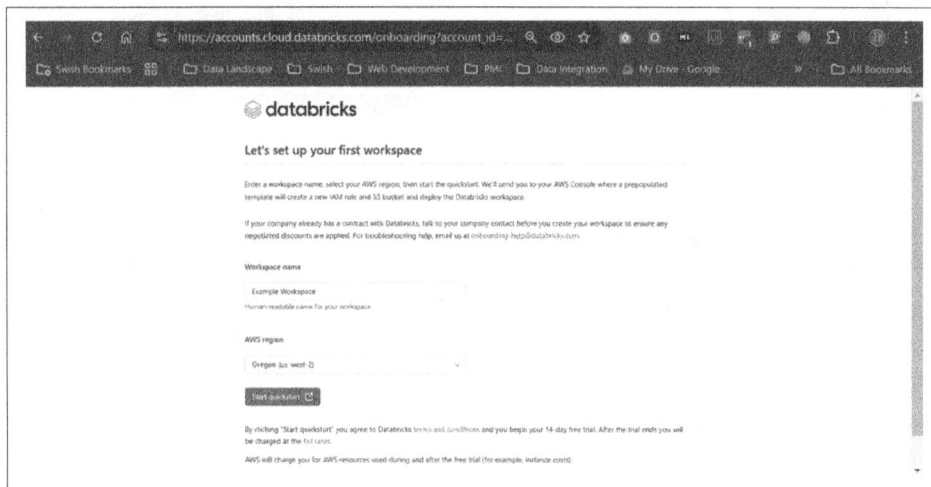

Figure 10-26. Databricks workspace setup

Assuming you are signed in to your AWS account, you should see something similar to Figure 10-27.

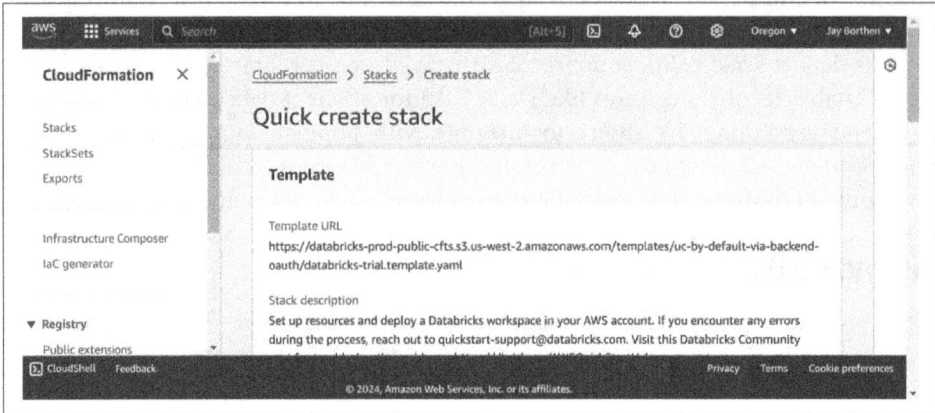

Figure 10-27. AWS CloudFormation Databricks stack creation

Scroll down and create a name for the stack, if desired/required. I'm leaving it as is, as shown in Figure 10-28.

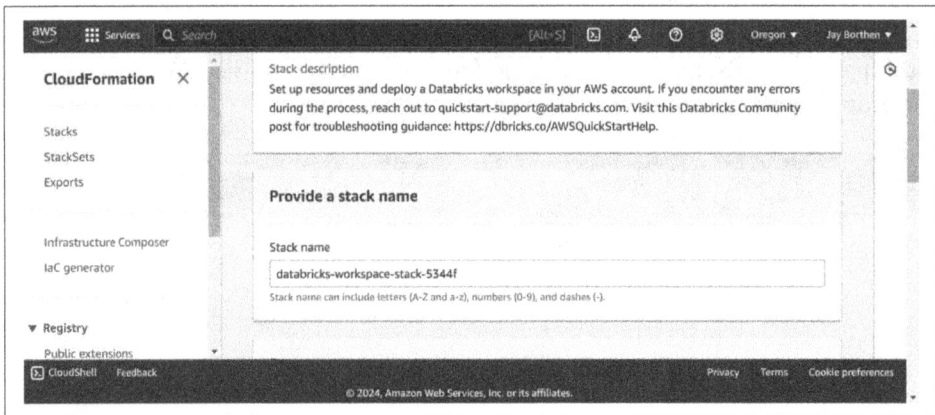

Figure 10-28. AWS CloudFormation stack name

Scroll down farther and change the Databricks account ID, if needed. Also, the workspace name should have copied over from the Databricks setup screen. (In this example, the name of the workspace is Example Workspace, as mentioned previously and as shown in Figure 10-29.)

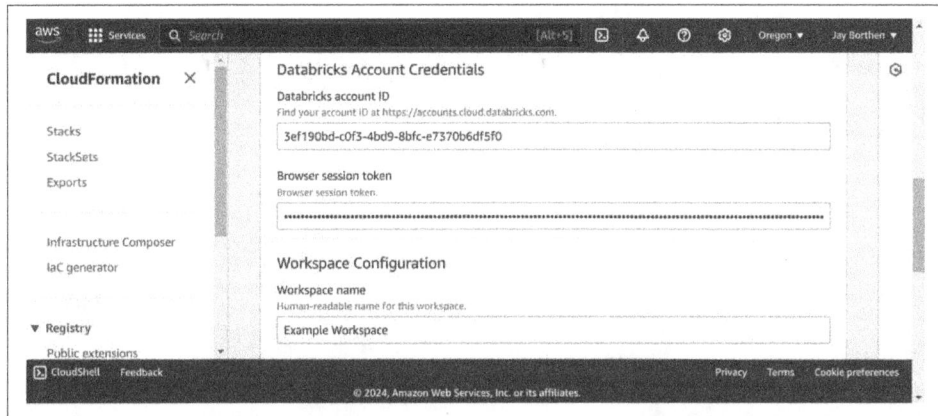

Figure 10-29. AWS CloudFormation Databricks account credentials

Scroll down farther and you will see a place to specify permissions (i.e., IAM roles), as shown in Figure 10-30. Also remember to acknowledge that AWS CloudFormation might create additional IAM resources. Click the "Create change set" button.

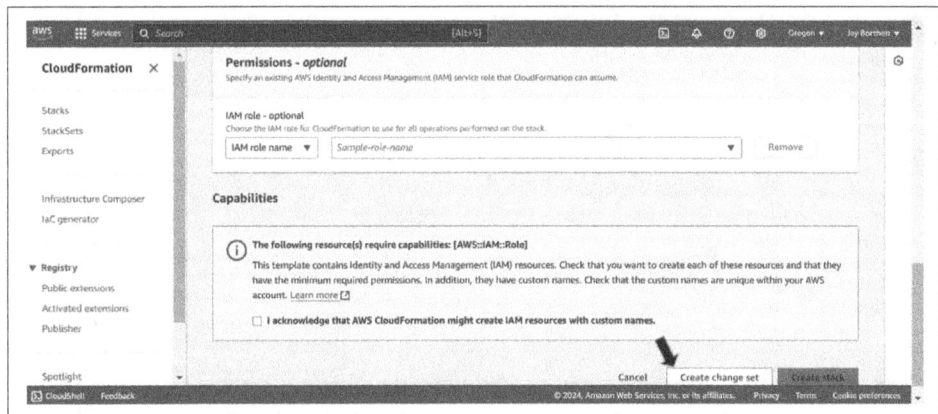

Figure 10-30. AWS CloudFormation permissions settings and creating a change set

A change set is a preview of how this stack will be configured before creating the stack. This allows you to examine various configurations before executing the change set. If you would like to create a change set, fill in the form controls, similar to what's shown in Figure 10-31, and select the "Create change set" button. Otherwise, click Cancel.

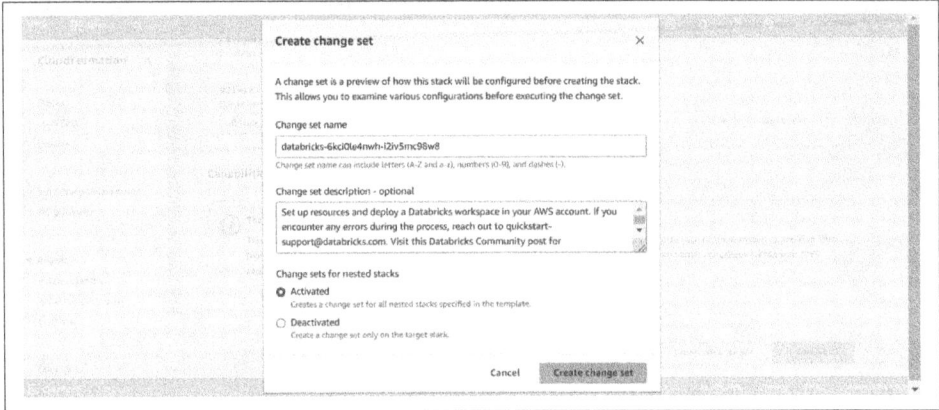

Figure 10-31. AWS CloudFormation "Create change set" window

Once you are back in the CloudFormation stack setup console, click the "Create stack" button, as shown in Figure 10-32.

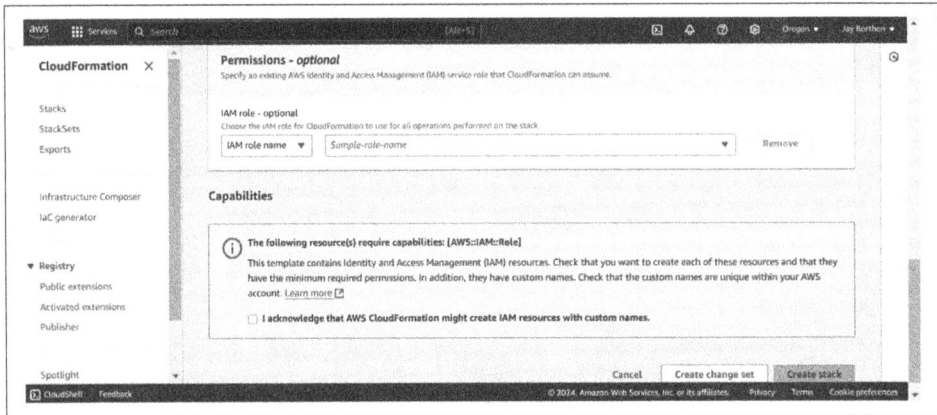

Figure 10-32. AWS CloudFormation stack creation completion

CloudFormation will then show you that the stack is being created. This may take five to ten minutes.

When the creation of the stack is complete, you will receive an email like what is shown in Figure 10-33.

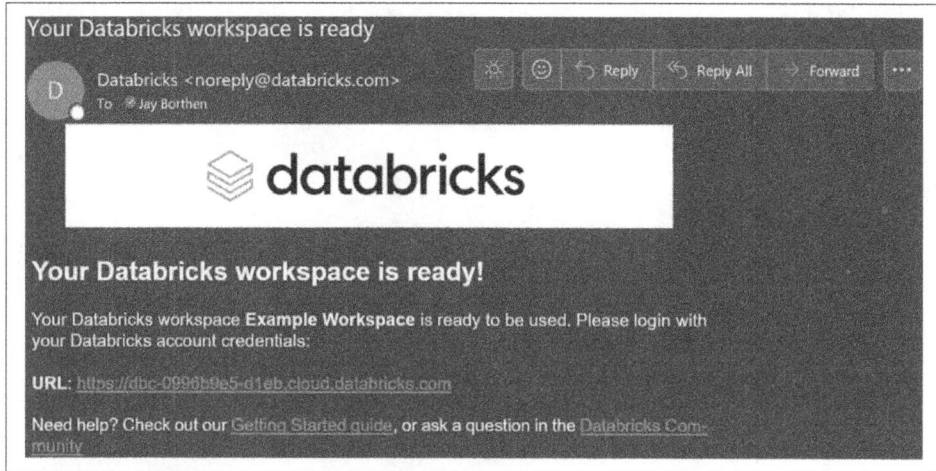

Figure 10-33. Databricks workspace setup complete

The status of the stack in the console will also indicate that the stack creation is complete, as can be seen in Figure 10-34.

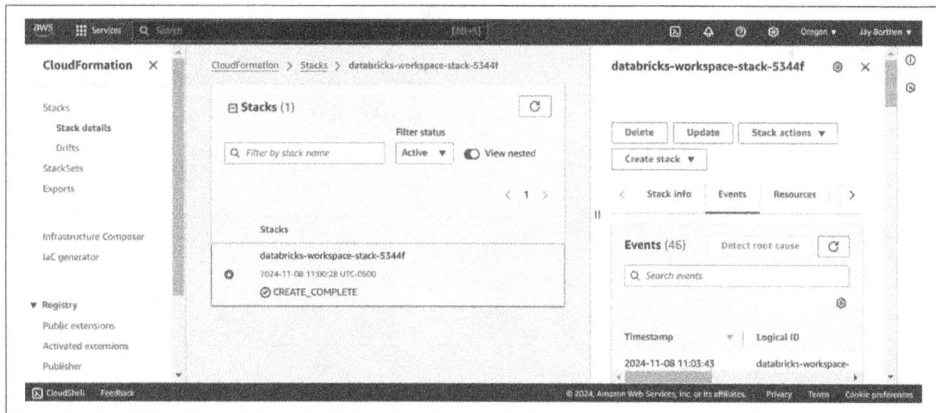

Figure 10-34. AWS CloudFormation stack setup complete

Notice that you are given a URL in your email. (Alternatively, you can find the URL under the Outputs tab in the right panel of the CloudFormation console, as shown in Figure 10-35. Once the Outputs tab has been selected, scroll to the bottom of that panel, and the WorkspaceURL will be shown.)

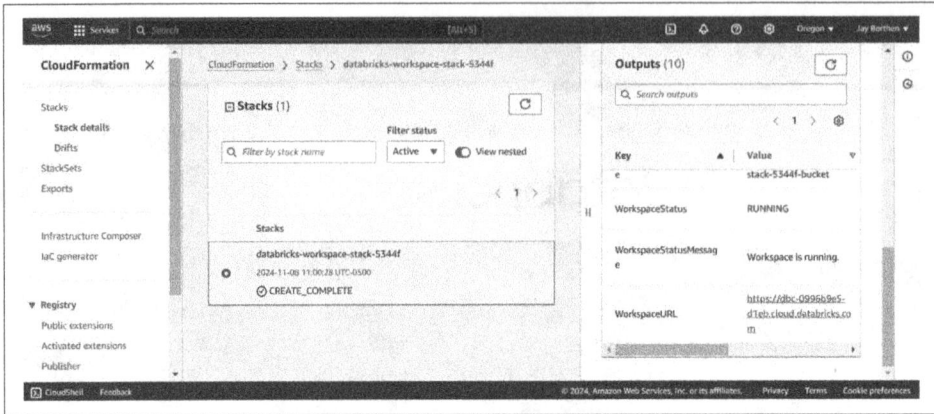

Figure 10-35. AWS CloudFormation Outputs tab

Navigate to that URL in your browser, and as shown in Figure 10-36, you will be greeted with the Databricks console, with your workspace shown in the upper right.

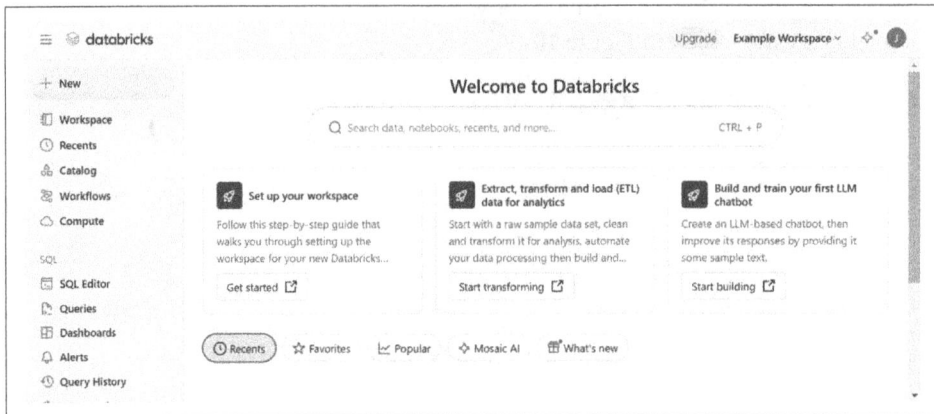

Figure 10-36. Databricks welcome screen

Connecting Databricks

Now we'll bring in a raw *.csv* file and then connect Databricks to S3.

Go to Catalog in the left-hand menu, as shown in Figure 10-37.

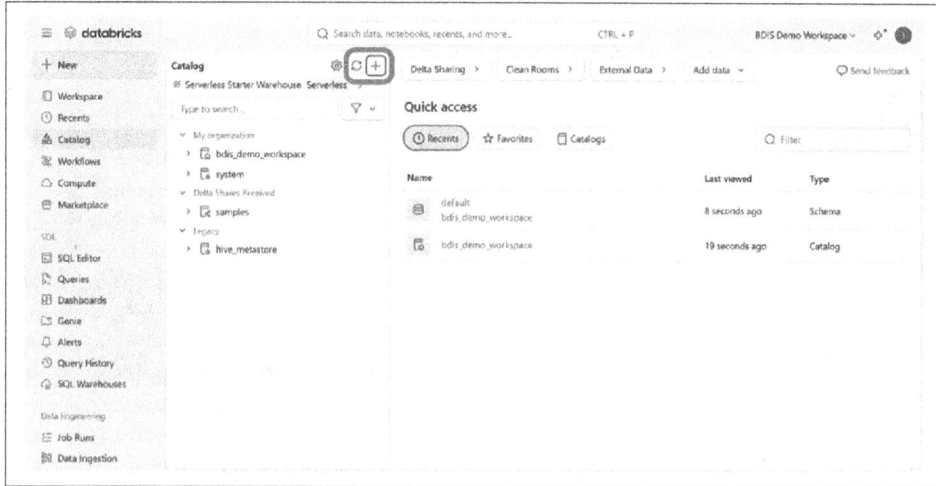

Figure 10-37. Databricks catalog

Click the plus sign (+) at the top right of the Catalog container and select "Add data" from the drop-down menu, as shown in Figure 10-38.

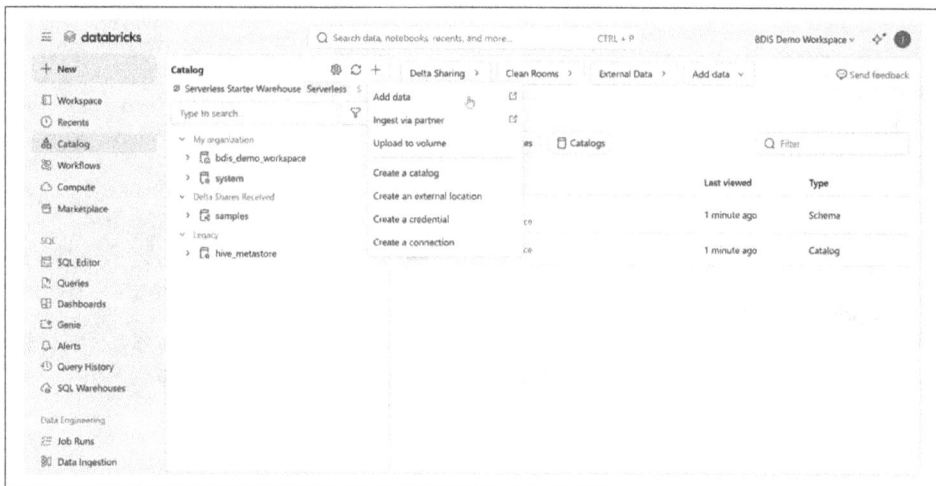

Figure 10-38. Add data to Databricks

Next, when the "Upload files to volume" dialog box appears, as shown in Figure 10-39, drag and drop your data file or browse for it.

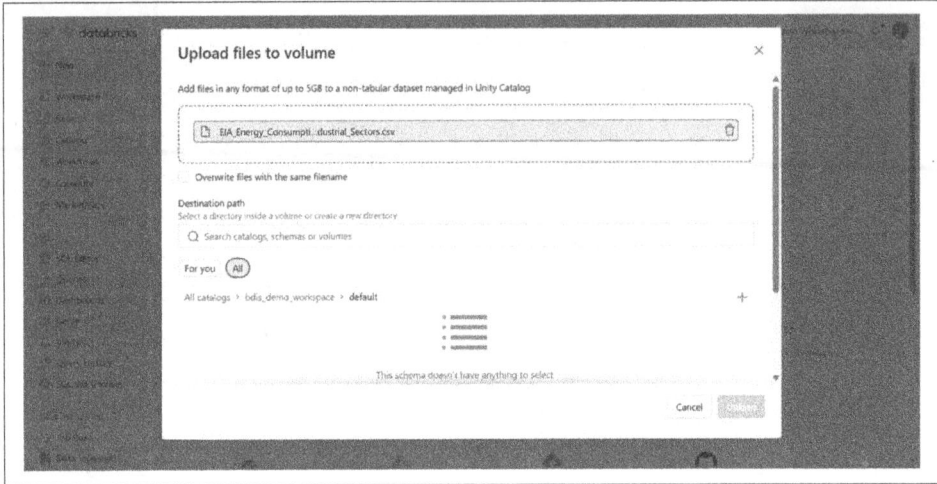

Figure 10-39. Upload files to volume

Then scroll down and select or create a volume. Here, we'll create a volume in the default catalog under *bdis_demo_workspace*, as shown in Figure 10-40.

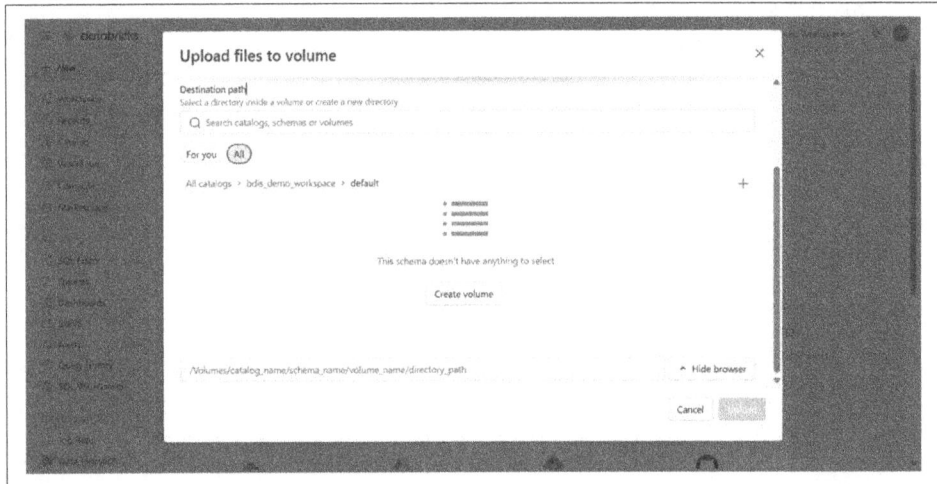

Figure 10-40. Select or create volume

Name the volume, ensure "Managed volume" is selected under "Volume type," and provide a comment if desired. Then click the Create button, as shown in Figure 10-41.

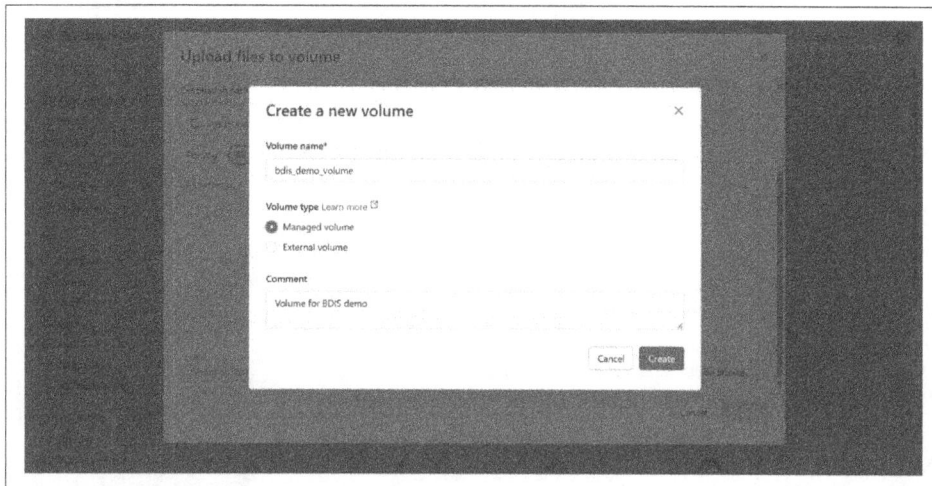

Figure 10-41. Create a new managed volume

Databricks primarily recommends managed volumes as the solution for storing and managing access to nontabular data and recommends using external volumes to store nontabular data files that are read or written by external systems in addition to Databricks.

Managed volumes provide a fully managed storage experience, and all interactions with files in managed volumes go through Unity Catalog. External volumes bring data governance to cloud object storage. For example, when you drop an external volume, you remove the volume from Unity Catalog, but the underlying data remains unchanged in the external location.

Once the volume is created or one is selected, click the Upload button. Navigate back to the Catalog tab and drill down through the catalog where the data file was just uploaded, and you should see the volume and the data file present, as shown in Figure 10-42.

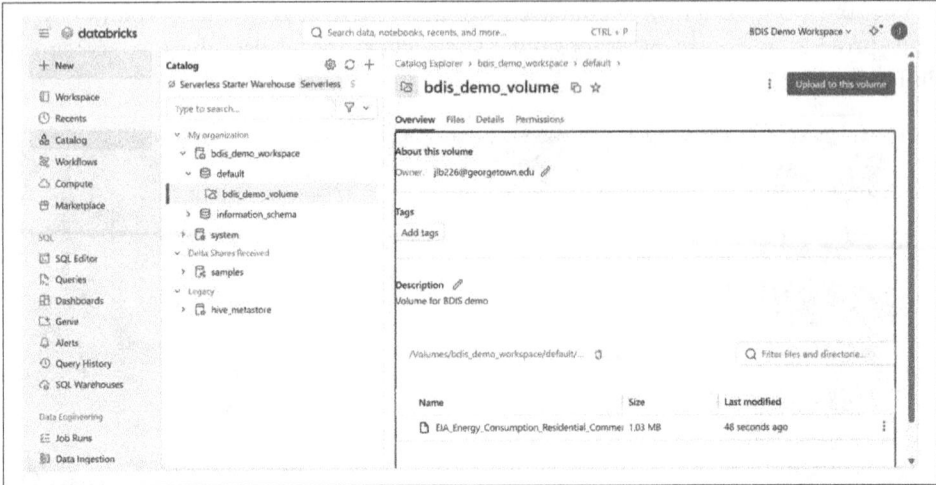

Figure 10-42. Databricks demo volume

Next, click the plus sign (+) at the top right of the Catalog container again and then select "Create an external location" from the drop-down menu, as shown in Figure 10-43.

Figure 10-43. Create an external location

Verify AWS Quickstart is selected, as shown in Figure 10-44, and click Next.

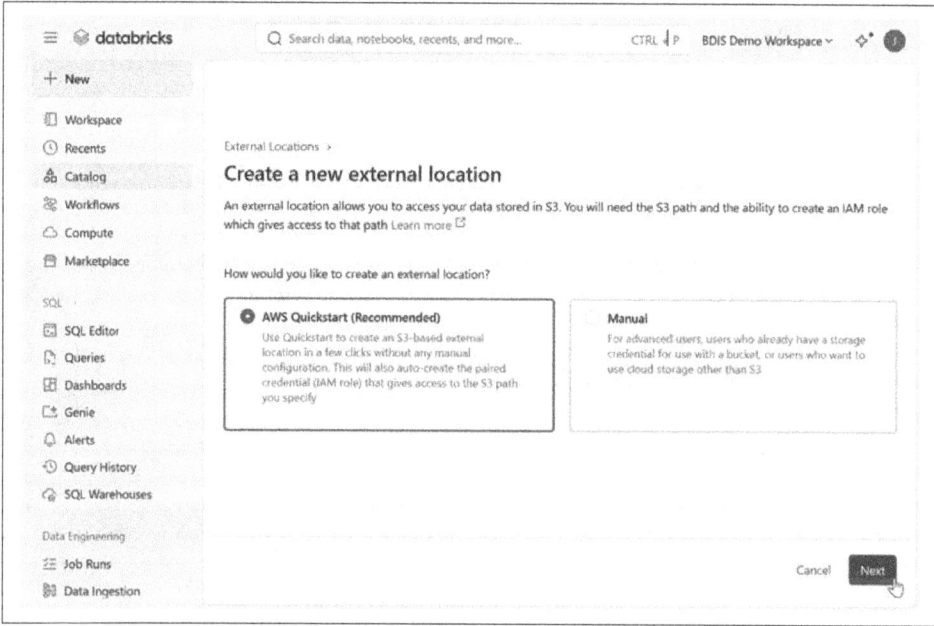

Figure 10-44. Create a new external location quickstart

Next, fill in the bucket name of the Amazon S3 bucket we used previously (i.e., "bdis"). Select "Get token," and your personal access token will be generated, as shown in Figure 10-45. Copy the token for later and then click the "Launch in Quickstart" button, shown at the bottom of Figure 10-45.

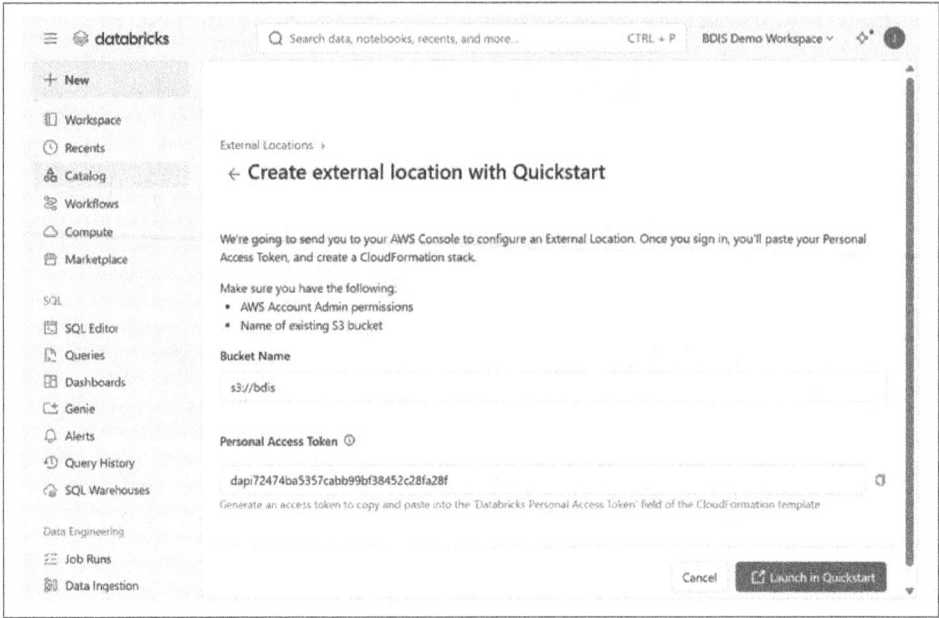

Figure 10-45. Bucket name and personal access token

You should be taken to AWS CloudFormation, as shown in Figure 10-46. Fill in the Databricks Personal Access Token field with the personal access token value you copied in the previous step.

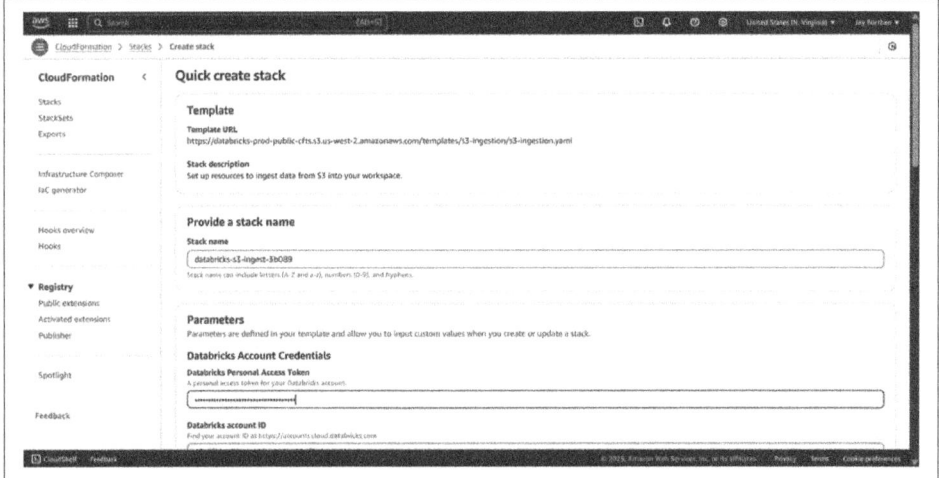

Figure 10-46. AWS CloudFormation Databricks account credentials

After scrolling down and verifying that the "Data bucket name" is correct, scroll to the bottom, check the CloudFormation resources acknowledgement, and then click the "Create stack" button, as shown in Figure 10-47.

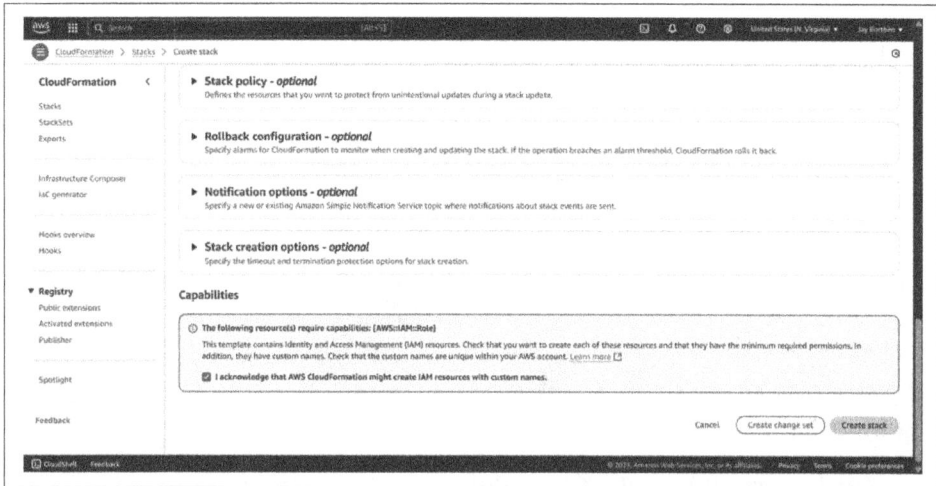

Figure 10-47. Create stack

When the stack has been created, go back to the Databricks interface, as shown in Figure 10-48, and click Ok.

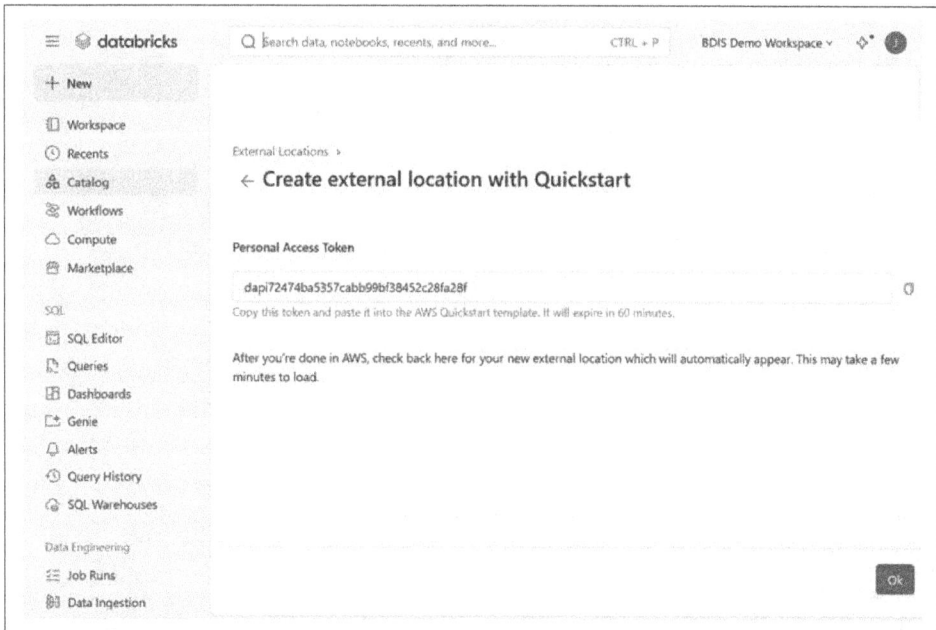

Figure 10-48. External location creation

Navigate back to the Catalog tab, select the plus sign (+) again, and select "Add data" from the drop-down menu, as shown in Figure 10-49.

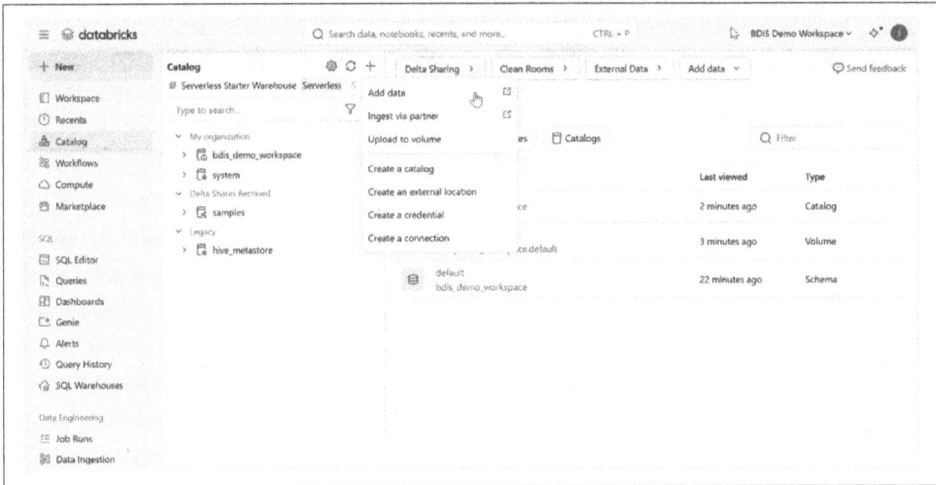

Figure 10-49. Select "Add data" from the drop-down menu

Click on "Create Delta table from S3," as shown in Figure 10-50.

Make sure the drop-down menu under the "Create Delta table from S3" title is accurate, and you should see the example data folder from S3 that we replicated data into, which was shown in Figure 10-24.

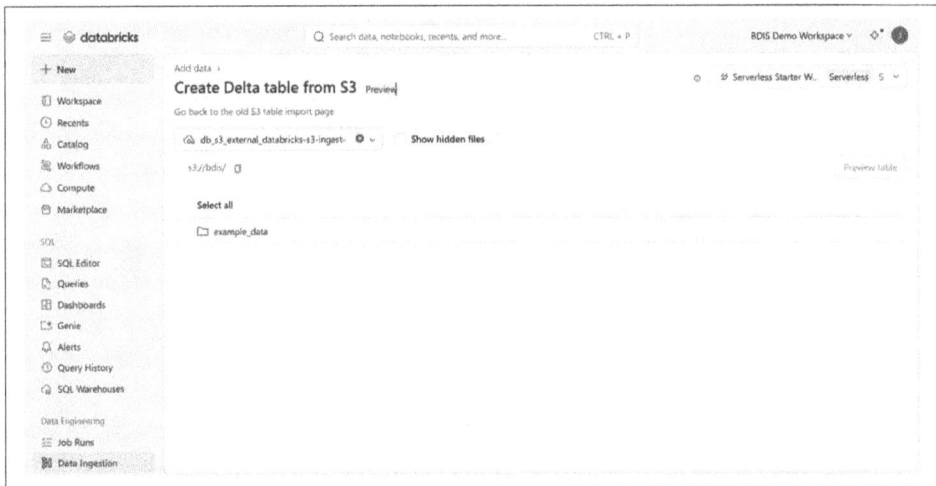

Figure 10-50. Example data folder from S3

Click through the folder until you get to the *.csv* file, checkmark the file, and then click "Preview table" on the right, as shown in Figure 10-51.

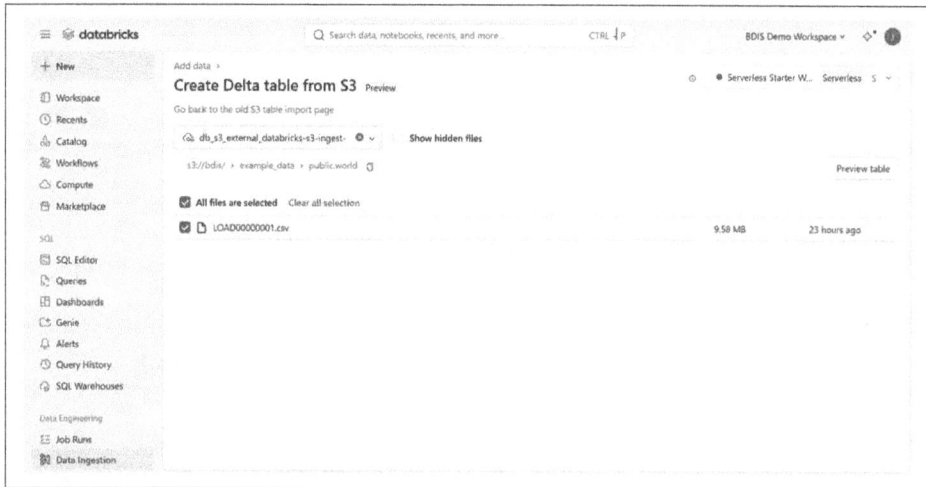

Figure 10-51. Example CSV file

After a few moments, you should see a subset of the data similar to what is shown in Figure 10-52. Click "Create table."

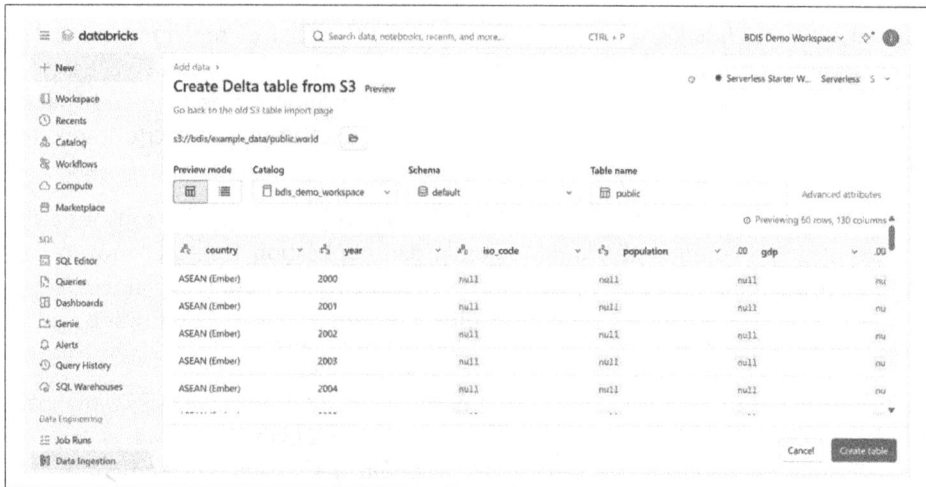

Figure 10-52. CSV data view

As you see in Figure 10-53, the data should now be present in the catalog near the data we loaded to the volume earlier. We have now implemented a batch solution via Databricks.

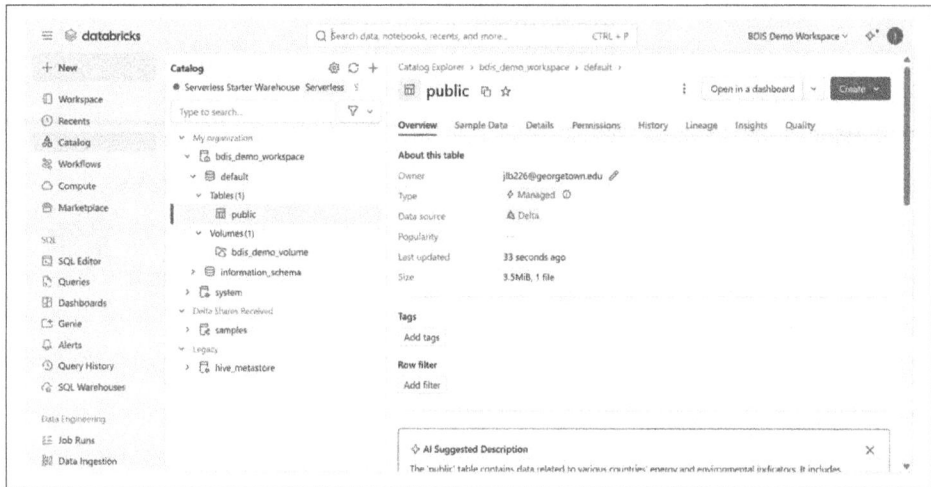

Figure 10-53. Data present in the catalog

Conclusion

This chapter provided a detailed, hands-on walkthrough for implementing a data integration solution using Qlik Replicate and Databricks within an AWS environment. We started by deploying Qlik Replicate on a Windows Server EC2 Instance, where the setup process included selecting appropriate instance specifications and configuring access.

After downloading and installing Qlik Replicate, we registered the software with license files and configured a unidirectional data replication task that moved data from a PostgreSQL source into an Amazon S3 bucket. The chapter explained how to connect both the source and target endpoints and run a full-load replication task to populate the initial data lake.

Then we shifted to Databricks and illustrated how to set up a Databricks workspace on AWS using CloudFormation. Once the Databricks environment was active, we uploaded a CSV file into a managed volume in Unity Catalog and then configured an external location that linked Databricks to the S3 bucket. By connecting to the S3 bucket, users can browse, preview, and create Delta tables from the replicated data. We have thus formed a functional data pipeline that enables scalable ingestion, storage, and transformation in a cloud-based data lake architecture.

In Chapter 11, we'll add streaming data to our pipeline.

Implementing a Streaming Solution

In this chapter, we embark on building a simple IoT pipeline using a Raspberry Pi and a DHT22 humidity and temperature sensor. This setup will enable continuous environmental data collection, which we will stream in near real time to Confluent Cloud using Apache Kafka. The goal is to create a foundational system that combines hardware, software, and cloud infrastructure to demonstrate end-to-end data streaming.

We begin by assembling the physical components and configuring the Raspberry Pi running Ubuntu, then proceed to connecting and programming the sensor. After that, we'll establish a Kafka cluster in Confluent Cloud, set up topics, and configure producer and consumer applications using Python. Finally, we'll create a connector to persist the streaming data to Amazon S3. By the end of this chapter, you'll have a fully integrated pipeline capable of capturing, streaming, and storing sensor data in a scalable and cloud native environment.

Raspberry Pi and Sensor Setup

We'll now set up a Raspberry Pi with a humidity and temperature sensor and feed streaming data to Confluent. The setup involves several steps, beginning with the assembly and configuration of the hardware components. By the end of this chapter, you will have a fully functional system that continuously monitors and streams humidity and temperature data and streams the data via Confluent Kafka.

Bill of Materials

This is a pretty simple project from a hardware perspective. We need only the Raspberry Pi, its power supply, the humidity and temperature sensor, and three jumper wires to connect the sensor to the Raspberry Pi. Figure 11-1 shows the entire bill of materials (BOM).

Part	Thumbnail	Quantity	Description
Raspberry Pi		1	Raspberry Pi 4 Model B—8 GB RAM
Raspberry Pi power supply		1	Raspberry Pi 4 power supply (US)
Humidity and temperature sensor		1	DHT22 temperature and humidity sensor module breakout
Jumper wires		3	6" M/F jumper wires

Figure 11-1. Bill of materials

We'll also need access to an internet connection from the Raspberry Pi 4 Model B, which has WiFi capability, and it's assumed that Ubuntu is being used as an operating system. Specifically, the example uses Ubuntu version 22.04.5 LTS (code-named Jammy).

It's important not to use the Raspbian operating system, because one of the important packages used in the Python code is not readily compatible.

Sensor Configuration

The sensor can be connected to the Raspberry Pi using pins 1, 6, and 7. Pin 6 is also designated as GPIO pin 4, which is important for the Python code. Figure 11-2 shows the configuration.

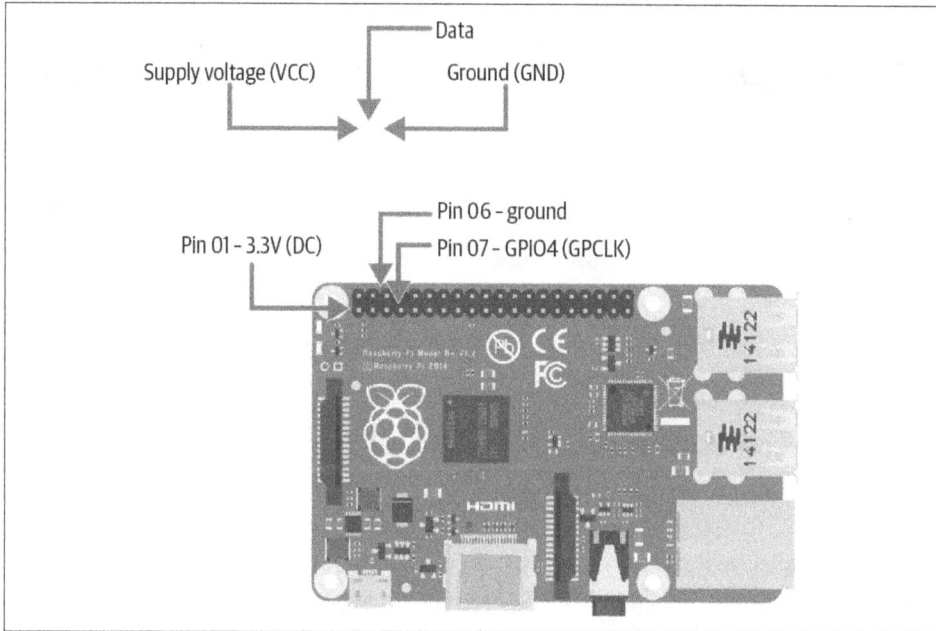

Figure 11-2. Humidity and temperature sensor connection configuration (Source: Electronics for You 2025 (https://electronicsforyou.com))

The quantity of sensor pins and their arrangement order differ among different sensor manufacturers, so make sure the correct sensor pins are being connected to the correct Raspberry Pi pins by observing the pin labels that should be present on the sensor.

Creating a Confluent Cloud Cluster

When the sensor is connected to the Raspberry Pi, and assuming you have an active Confluent Cloud account, navigate to Confluent Cloud with your Raspberry Pi Ubuntu browser, as shown in Figure 11-3, and create a new Kafka cluster by selecting Add Cluster. You may need to select an environment as well.

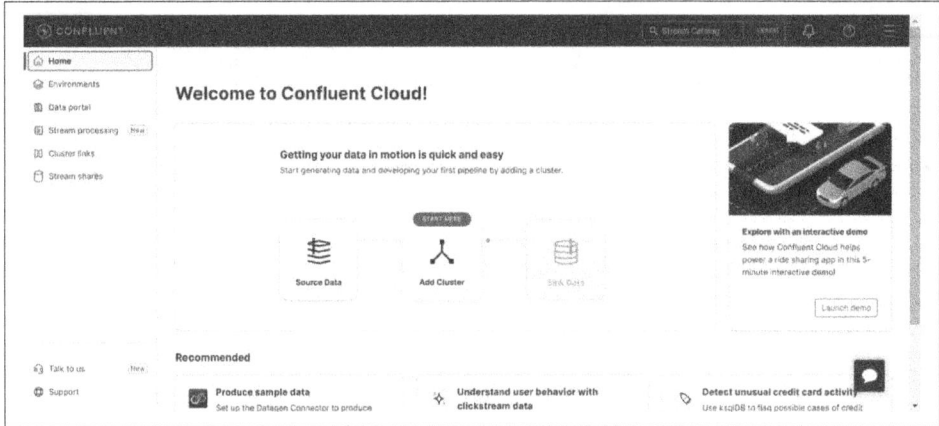

Figure 11-3. Confluent Cloud home screen

For this example, we'll use the basic cluster configuration, so click the "Begin configuration" button on the far left as shown in Figure 11-4.

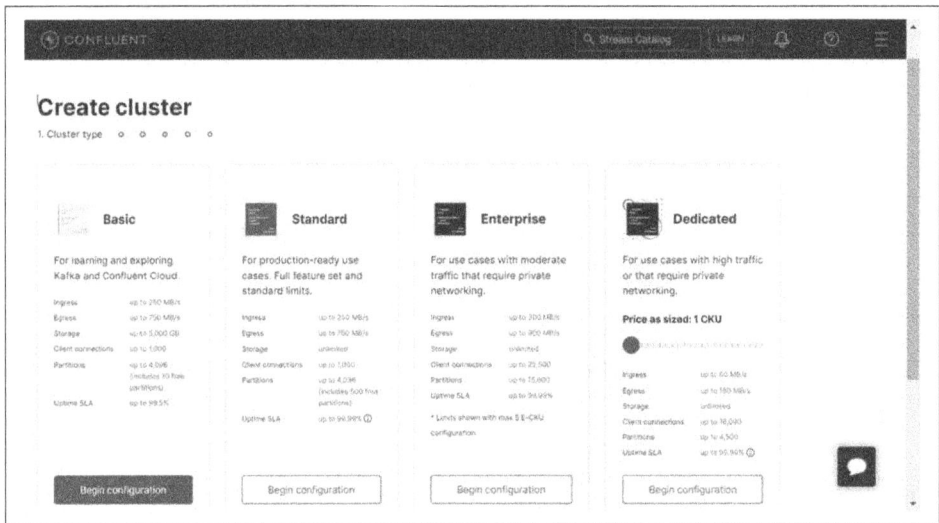

Figure 11-4. Create cluster

Select the appropriate Region and Availability and click Continue, as shown in Figure 11-5.

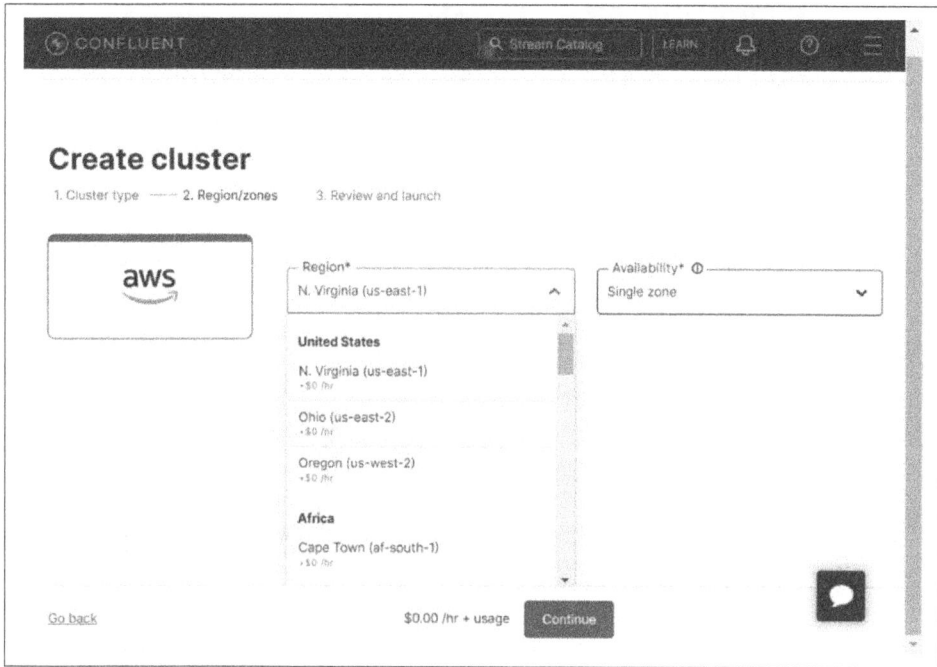

Figure 11-5. Choose the region and availability

Name the cluster, and then click the "Launch cluster" button. We'll use the name *bdis_kafka_cluster_01*. See Figure 11-6.

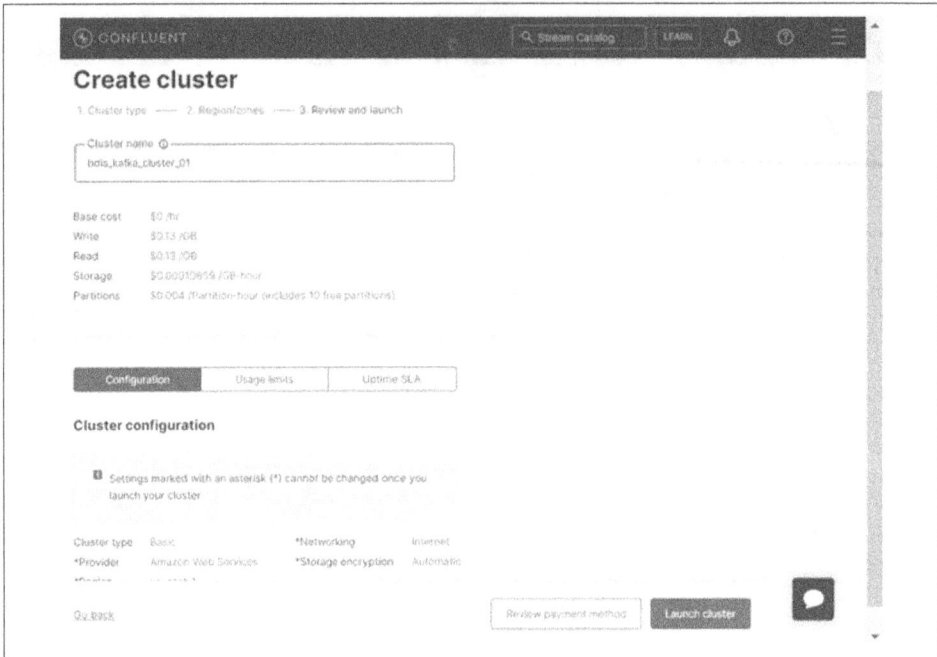

Figure 11-6. Name the cluster

You should now see the cluster overview screen, which should look similar to what's shown in Figure 11-7.

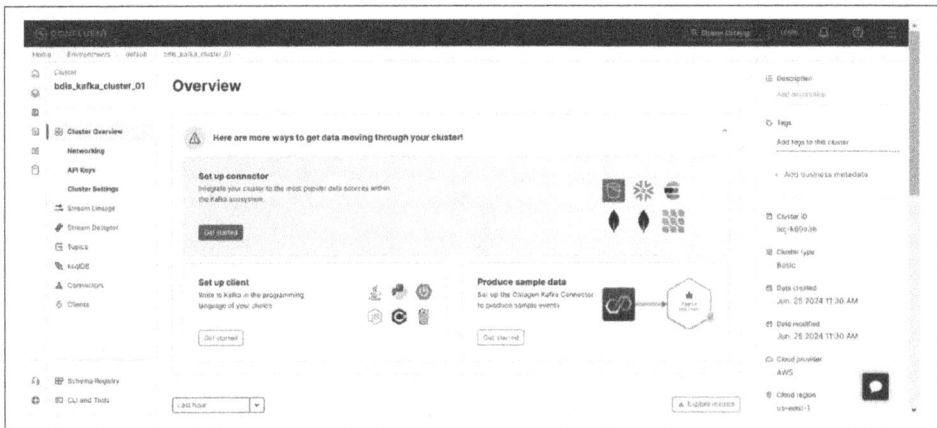

Figure 11-7. Cluster overview screen

Creating a Local Python Environment

In the local Raspberry Pi Ubuntu environment, open a terminal and create a folder in which to keep Python code and configuration files. Here, we create a folder called *dht-sensor-confluent* on the desktop. Then we create a virtual Python environment via virtualenv with the following commands:[1]

```
cd Desktop
mkdir dht-sensor-confluent && cd dht-sensor-confluent
virtualenv env
source env/bin/activate
```

Next, install the confluent-kafka and adafruit_dht Python packages[2] that will be needed later with the following commands:

```
pip install confluent-kafka
pip install adafruit-circuitpython-dht
```

Cluster Settings

Next, back in the Confluent interface, select Cluster Settings from the left menu. You should see something similar to the screen shown in Figure 11-8. Note the bootstrap server. It will also be needed later.

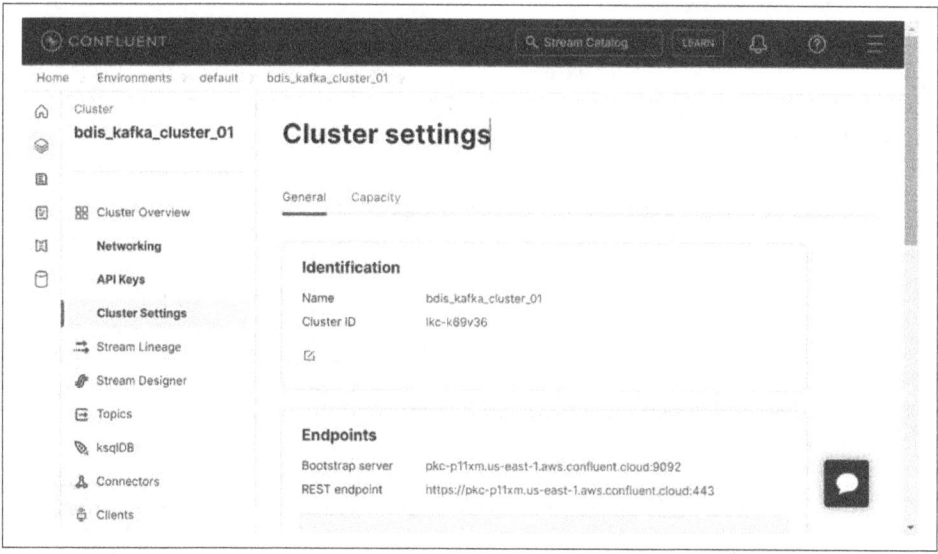

Figure 11-8. Cluster settings

---

1 If not already installed, virtualenv can be installed in Ubuntu via *apt install python3-virtualenv*.

2 This assumes you have *pip* installed.

Next, click on API Keys in the left menu. In the "API keys" window, click the "Create key" button, as shown in Figure 11-9.

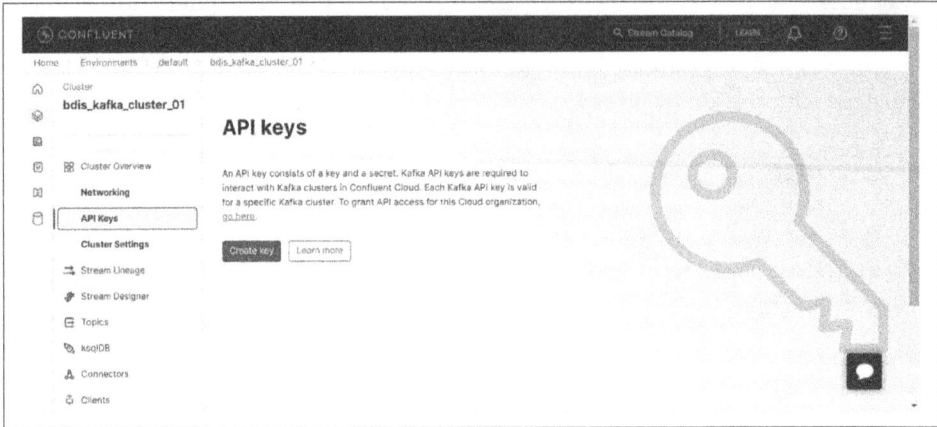

Figure 11-9. API keys

Make sure "My account" is selected and click Next, as shown in Figure 11-10.

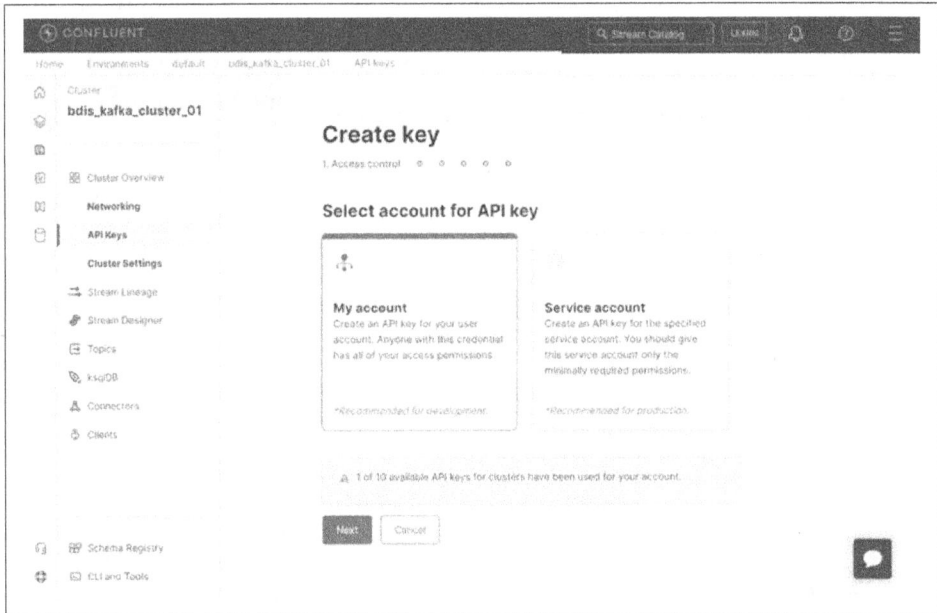

Figure 11-10. Select account for API key

A Key and a Secret should be shown on the next screen, similar to what's shown in Figure 11-11. Click the "Download and continue" button and store the downloaded file in an accessible location (like the *dht-sensor-confluent* folder created previously).

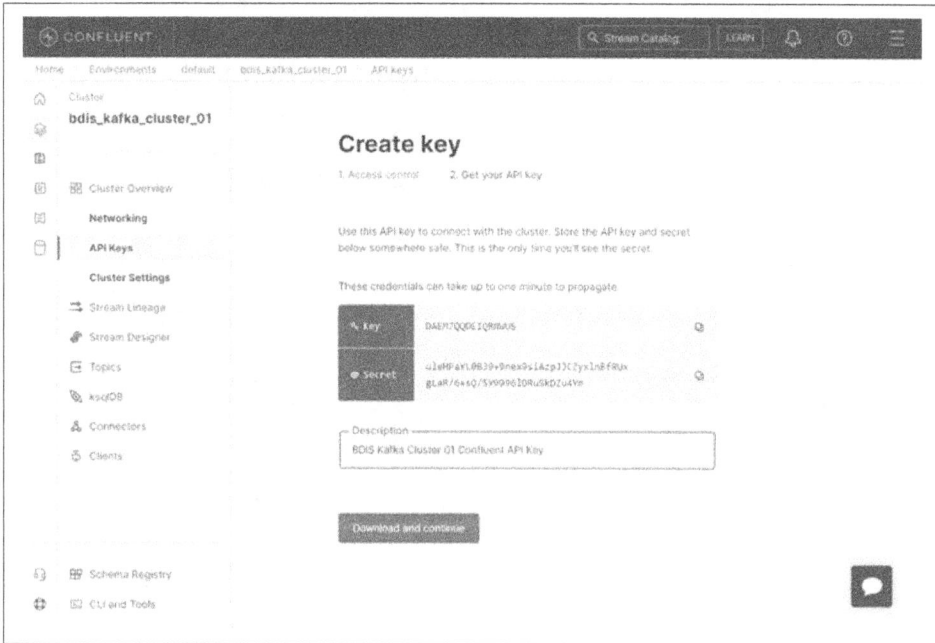

Figure 11-11. Download API key

The next screen, as shown in Figure 11-12, should show the available API keys, including the one that was just created.

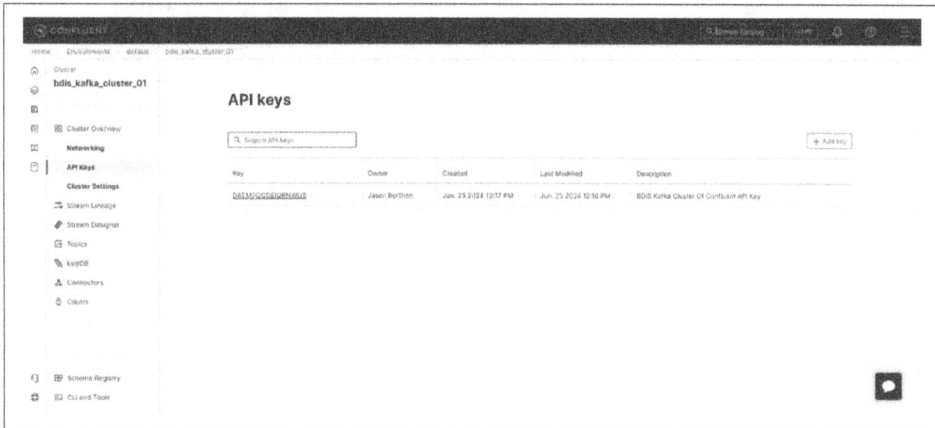

Figure 11-12. Available API keys

Creating a Topic

Confluent defines a topic as "an immutable, append-only log of events." Topics typically comprise similar event types. In our case, the events are humidity and temperature sensor readings.

Navigate to the Topics page via the left menu. Then click "Create topic," as shown in Figure 11-13.

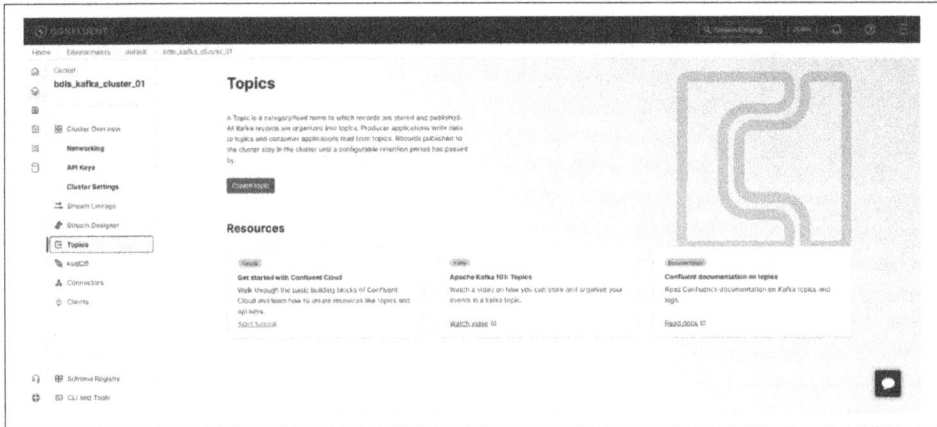

Figure 11-13. Confluent topics

Name the topic and set the number of partitions. As shown in Figure 11-14, we'll use the name *bdis_kafka_cluster_01_topic_01*; for this example, we could use one partition, but we will just use the default number of six in case we want to expand our sensor readings later. A Kafka partition is just a unit of parallelism and scalability within an Apache Kafka topic. Each topic is split into one or more partitions, which are ordered, immutable sequences of messages that are continually appended to.

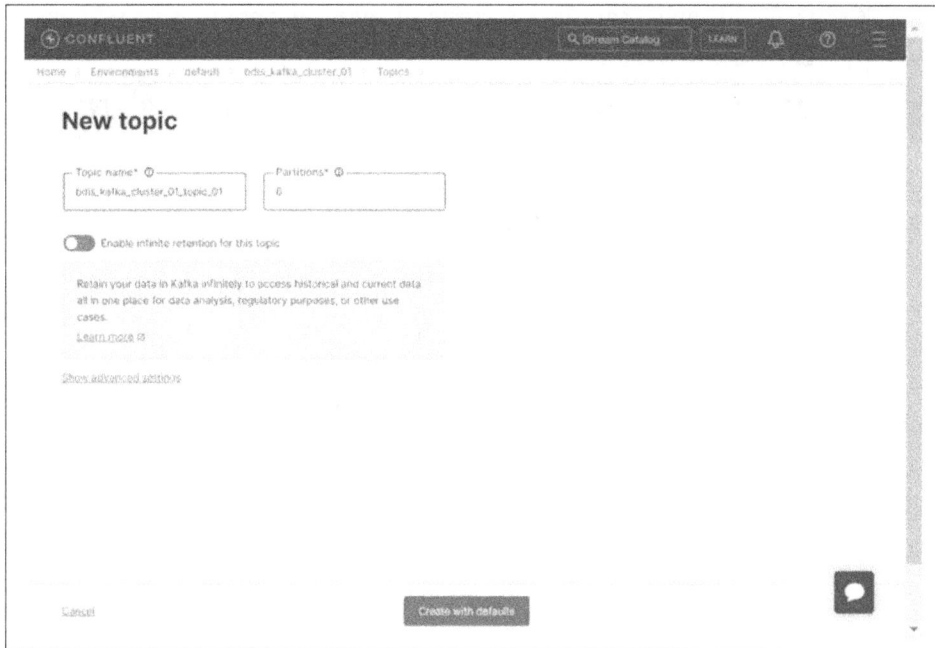

Figure 11-14. New topic

We're going to use default values for the rest of the topic configuration values; however, if desired, you can alter the values by clicking on "Show advanced settings." This will expand out the options to include cleanup policy, retention time, retention size, and message size. The options for cleanup policy include delete and compact. The delete option will discard old segments when their retention time or size limit has been reached, and the compact policy will enable log compaction and will retain only the latest value for each key.

Click "Create with defaults" (or "Save & create" if advanced options were selected, as shown in Figure 11-15).

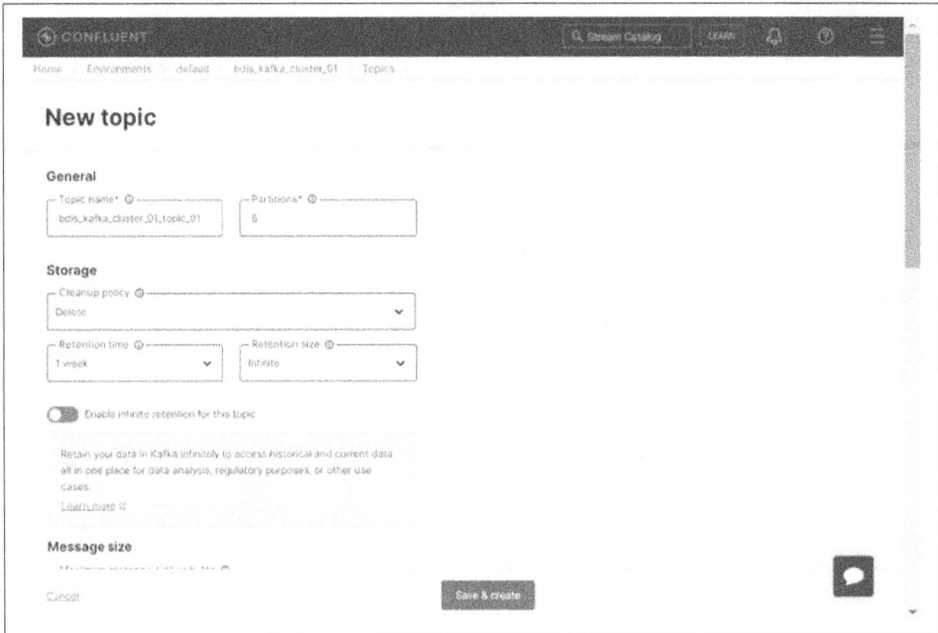

Figure 11-15. Topics and advanced settings

You should now see a message saying that the topic was created successfully, similar to what is shown in Figure 11-16.

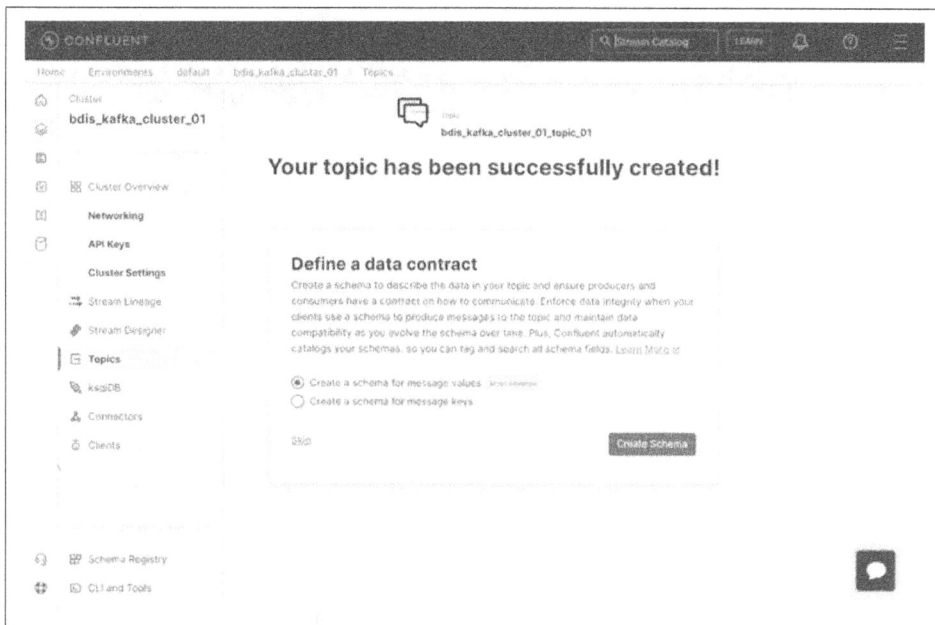

Figure 11-16. Topic successfully created

Configuring a Client

Next, we need to configure Python (i.e., our client). So either select the "Begin setup" button or navigate to the Clients tab in the left menu, as shown in Figure 11-17.

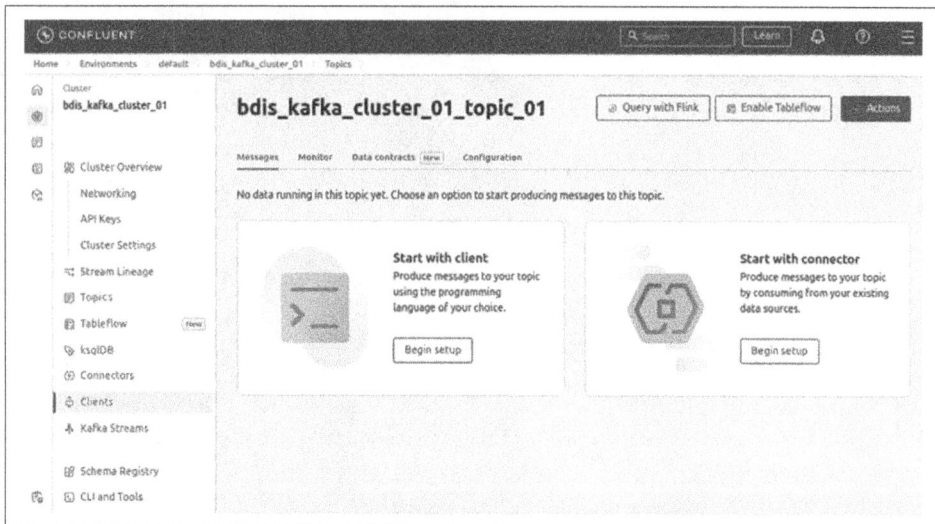

Figure 11-17. Set up the client

In the Clients tab, you should see something similar to what is shown in Figure 11-18.

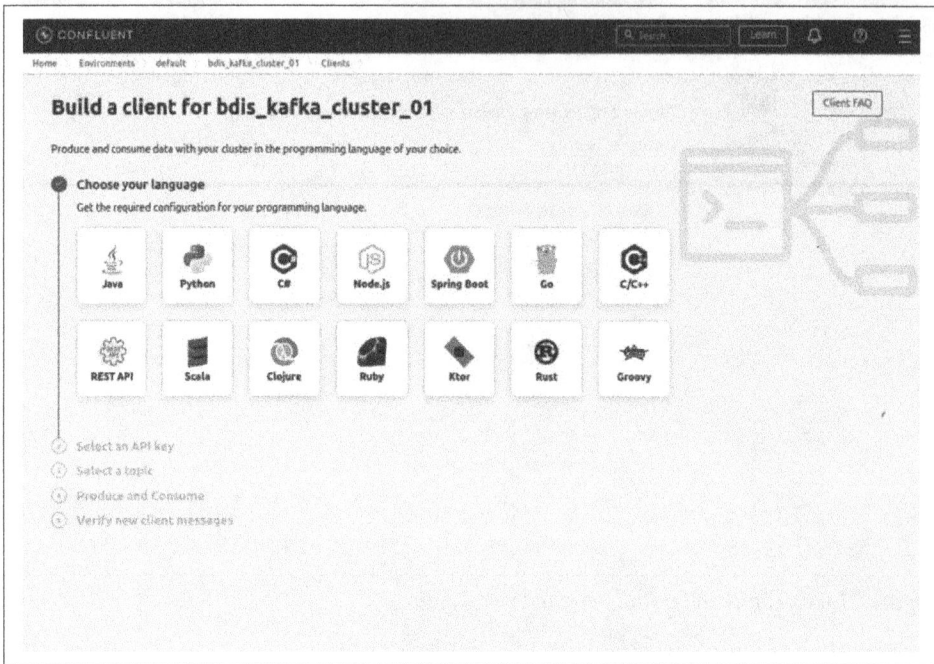

Figure 11-18. Choose your programming language

Select Python. Then select "Use existing API key" as shown in Figure 11-19 and fill in the fields with the appropriate values from the API key created earlier.

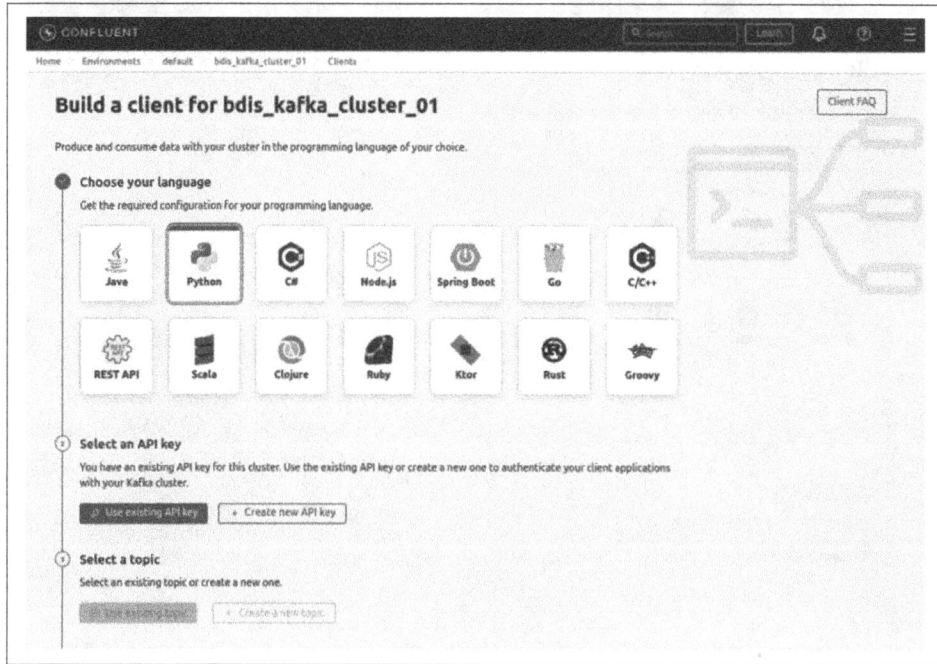

Figure 11-19. Select an API key

Next, select the "Use existing topic" button, as shown in Figure 11-20.

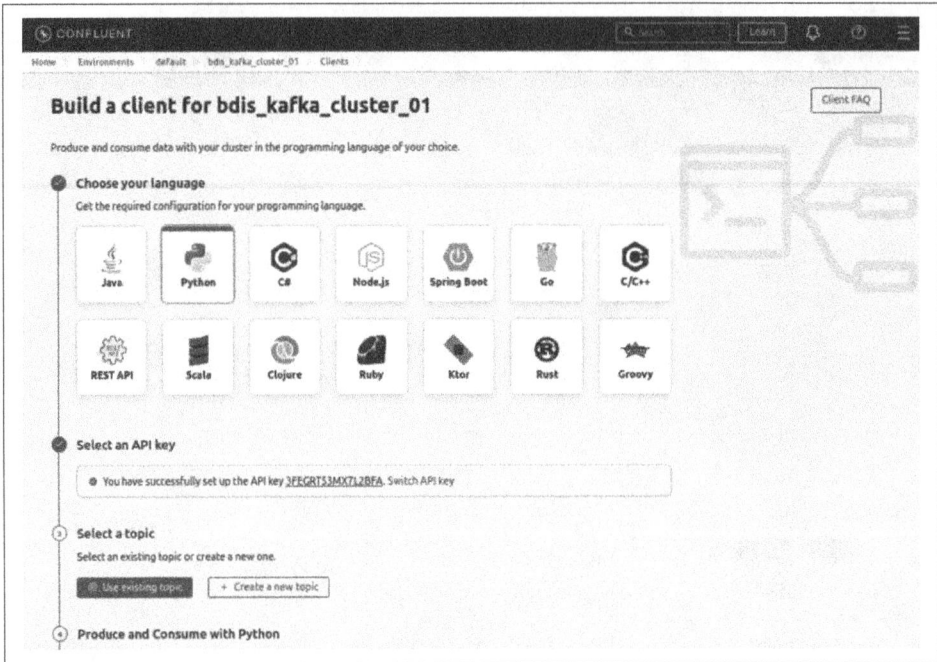

Figure 11-20. Use existing topic

Make sure the topic we created earlier is selected, and then click the Select button, as shown in Figure 11-21.

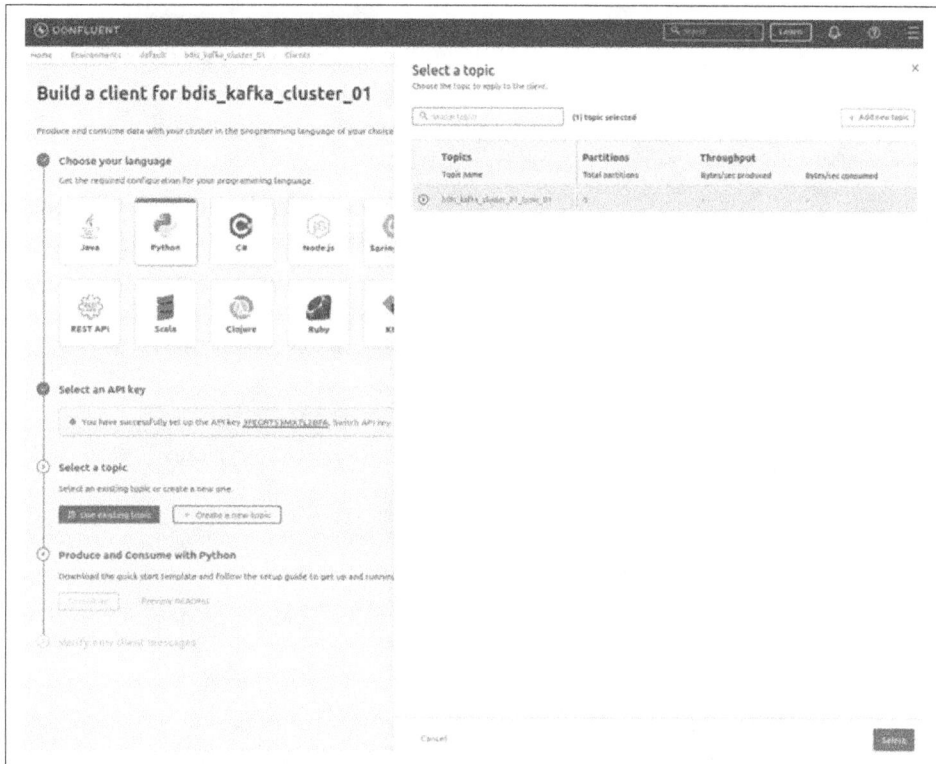

Figure 11-21. Select a topic

Creating the Python Producer and Consumer Applications

Next, create the Python producer application by pasting the code shown in Example 11-1 into a file named *producer.py* and saving the file in the *dht-sensor-confluent* folder that we created in "Creating a Local Python Environment" on page 179. The code first initializes the humidity and temperature sensor and then sets some configuration parameters. When the main function runs, the message producer is created and an error message is displayed if an error occurs.

The values for bootstrap.servers, sasl.username, and sasl.password should all be changed prior to running the code.[3] The bootstrap.servers value should be changed to the corresponding value that was created earlier. The sasl.username and

---

3 The topic name should also be changed in the code if a different name was used.

sasl.password are the API access key and API secret key, respectively, that were also created previously and shown in Figure 11-11.

Example 11-1. Creating the producer application

```python
#!/usr/bin/env python

from random import choice
from confluent_kafka import Producer
import time
import board
import adafruit_dht

# Initialize the dht device
dhtDevice = adafruit_dht.DHT22(board.D4, use_pulseio=False)

# Set configuration parameters
config = {
    'bootstrap.servers': 'pkc-p11xm.us-east-1.aws.confluent.cloud:9092',
    'sasl.username': '3FEGRT53MX7L2BFA',
    'sasl.password': '6PclszbMQOGlGhrPdiu4WL4wJPxzm/KY1+NSzQDL69mZv98Rg8UDjQv4txI2',
    'security.protocol': 'SASL_SSL',
    'sasl.mechanisms': 'PLAIN',
    'acks': 'all'
}

# Optional per-message delivery callback (triggered by poll() or flush())
# when a message has been successfully delivered or permanently
# failed delivery (after retries).
def delivery_callback(err, msg):
    if err:
        print('ERROR: Message failed delivery: {}'.format(err))
    else:
        print("Produced event to topic {topic}: temperature = {key:12},
            humidity = {value:12}".format(topic=msg.topic(),
            key=msg.key().decode('utf-8'), value=msg.value().decode('utf-8')))


def main():
    topic = "bdis_kafka_cluster_01_topic_01"
    # Create Producer instance
    producer = Producer(config)
    while True:
      try:
        producer.produce(topic, str(dhtDevice.humidity), str(dhtDevice.temperature),
            callback=delivery_callback)
        # Block until the messages are sent.
        producer.poll(10000)
        producer.flush()
      except RuntimeError as error:
        print(error.args[0])
```

```
        time.sleep(2.0)
        continue
    except Exception as error:
        dhtDevice.exit()
        raise error
    time.sleep(2.0)


main()
```

Similarly, create the Python consumer application by pasting the code shown in Example 11-2 into a file named *consumer.py* and saving the file in the *dht-sensor-confluent* folder that we created in "Creating a Local Python Environment" on page 179. Unlike the producer script, the sensor does not need to be initialized because we are now consuming the message data; however, some configuration parameters still need to be defined. The consumer is then created and the topic is subscribed to before the message is actually consumed.

Again, the values for bootstrap.servers, sasl.username, and sasl.password should all be changed prior to running the code, and a value for the group.id can be altered to suit (here, we'll use *bdis_kafka*).

Example 11-2. Creating the consumer application

```
#!/usr/bin/env python

from confluent_kafka import Consumer

# Set configuration parameters
config = {
    'bootstrap.servers': 'pkc-p11xm.us-east-1.aws.confluent.cloud:9092',
    'sasl.username': '3FEGRT53MX7L2BFA',
    'sasl.password': '6PclszbMQOGlGhrPdiu4WL4wJPxzm/KY1+NSzQDL69mZv98Rg8UDjQv4txI2',
    'security.protocol': 'SASL_SSL',
    'sasl.mechanisms': 'PLAIN',
    'group.id': 'bdis_kafka',
    'auto.offset.reset': 'earliest'
}

# Create Consumer instance
consumer = Consumer(config)

# Subscribe to topic
topic = "bdis_kafka_cluster_01_topic_01"
consumer.subscribe([topic])

# Poll for new messages from Kafka and print them.
try:
    while True:
        msg = consumer.poll(1.0)
```

```
    if msg is None:
        # Initial message consumption may take up to
        # 'session.timeout.ms' for the consumer group to
        # rebalance and start consuming
        print("Waiting...")
    elif msg.error():
        print("ERROR: %s".format(msg.error()))
    else:
        # Extract the (optional) key and value, and print.
        print("Consumed event from topic {topic}: temperature = {key:12},
            humidity = {value:12}".format(topic=msg.topic(),
            key=msg.key().decode('utf-8'), value=msg.value().decode('utf-8')))
except KeyboardInterrupt:
    pass
finally:
    # Leave group and commit final offsets
    consumer.close()
```

In the Ubuntu terminal, from the *dht-sensor-confluent* directory, run the following shell commands:

```
chmod u+x producer.py
```

```
./producer.py
```

You should see something similar to what is shown in Figure 11-22.

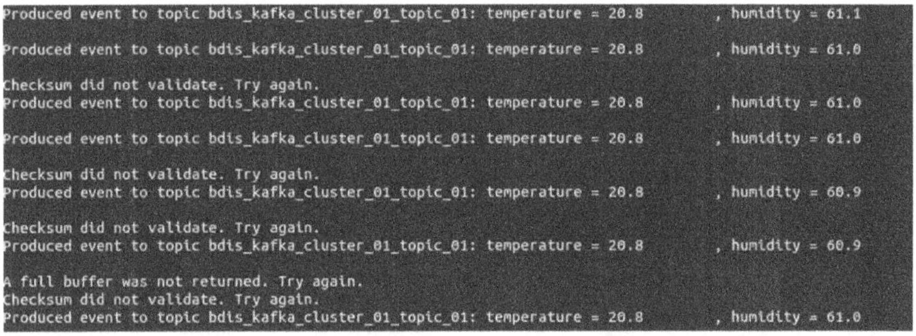

Figure 11-22. Humidity and temperature data being produced

Concurrently, in a separate terminal, but in the same directory, run the following commands:

```
chmod u+x consumer.py
```

```
./consumer.py
```

You should see something similar to what is shown in Figure 11-23.

```
Consumed event from topic bdis_kafka_cluster_01_topic_01: temperature = 20.8       , humidity = 60.8
Consumed event from topic bdis_kafka_cluster_01_topic_01: temperature = 20.8       , humidity = 60.9
Consumed event from topic bdis_kafka_cluster_01_topic_01: temperature = 20.8       , humidity = 60.9
Consumed event from topic bdis_kafka_cluster_01_topic_01: temperature = 20.8       , humidity = 61.1
Consumed event from topic bdis_kafka_cluster_01_topic_01: temperature = 20.8       , humidity = 61.1
Consumed event from topic bdis_kafka_cluster_01_topic_01: temperature = 20.8       , humidity = 61.0
Consumed event from topic bdis_kafka_cluster_01_topic_01: temperature = 20.8       , humidity = 61.0
Consumed event from topic bdis_kafka_cluster_01_topic_01: temperature = 20.8       , humidity = 61.0
Consumed event from topic bdis_kafka_cluster_01_topic_01: temperature = 20.8       , humidity = 60.9
```

Figure 11-23. Consuming humidity and temperature data

Hit CTRL+C in both terminals to stop producing and consuming the sensor data.

Setting Up a Connector

Back in the Cluster Overview window in Confluent Cloud, click on the "Get started" button under "Set up connector," or navigate to the Connectors window via the left menu, as shown in Figure 11-24.

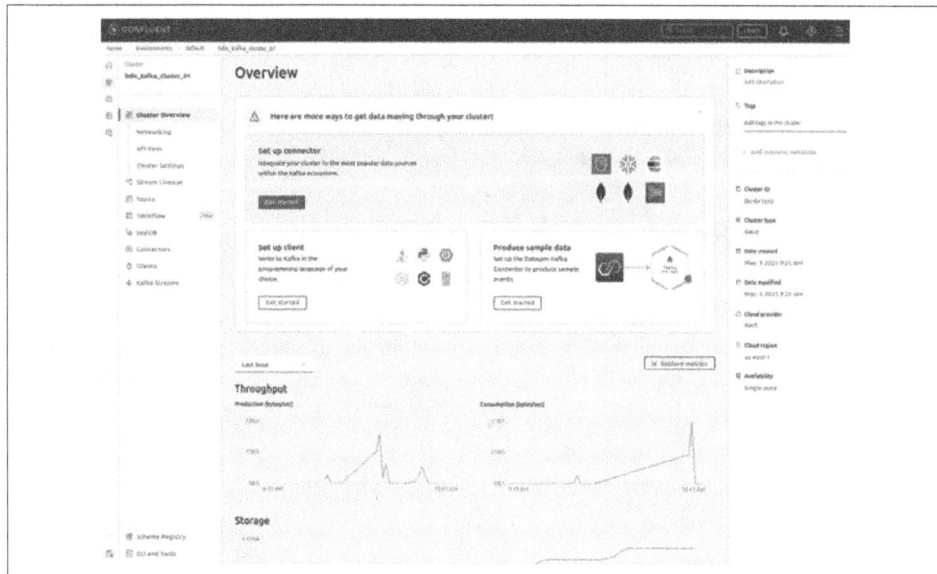

Figure 11-24. Cluster overview

Select the Amazon S3 Sink connector, as shown in Figure 11-25.

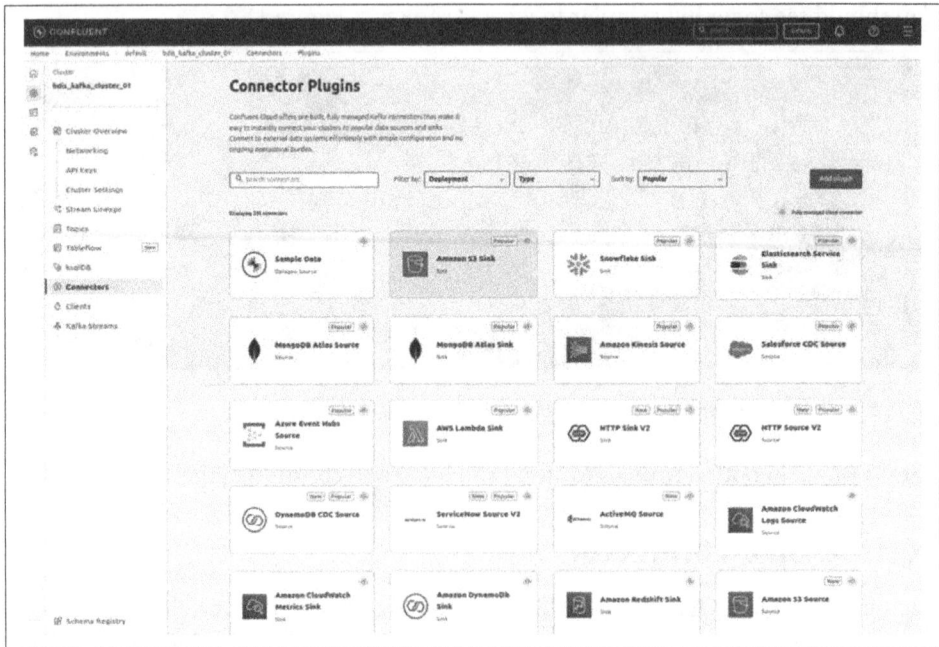

Figure 11-25. Connector plugins

Select the topic we created (i.e., *bdis_kafka_cluster_01_topic_01*) and click the Continue button, as shown in Figure 11-26.

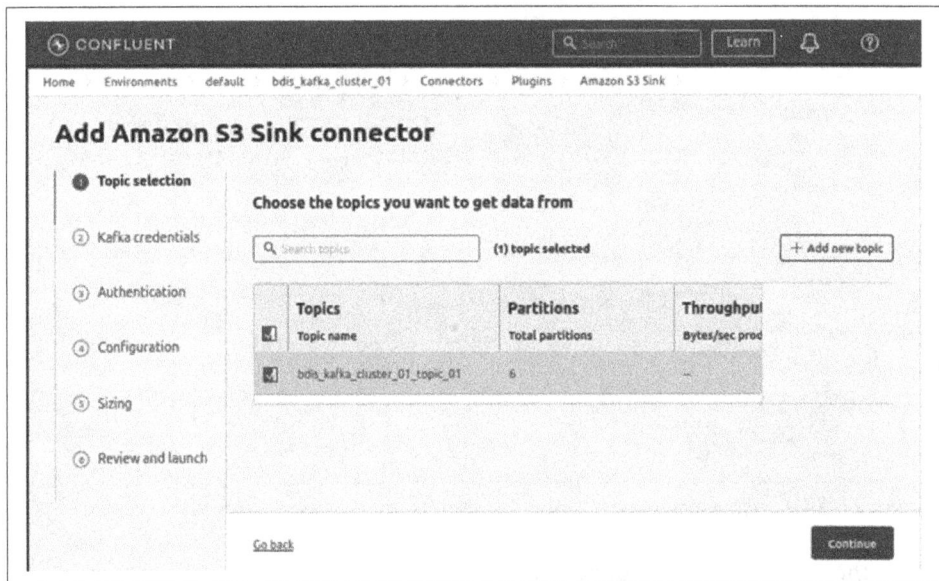

Figure 11-26. Amazon S3 sink connector topic selection

Select "Use an existing API key" and use the key values previously created. Then click Continue, as shown in Figure 11-27.

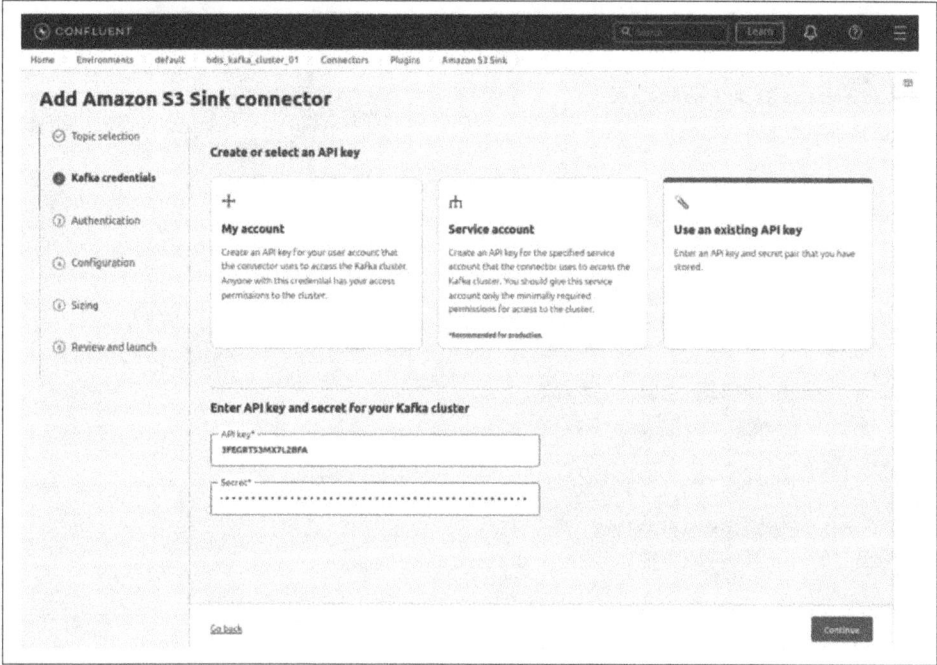

Figure 11-27. Amazon S3 sink connector credentials

Fill in the appropriate values for the Amazon S3 sink location and then click Continue, as shown in Figure 11-28.

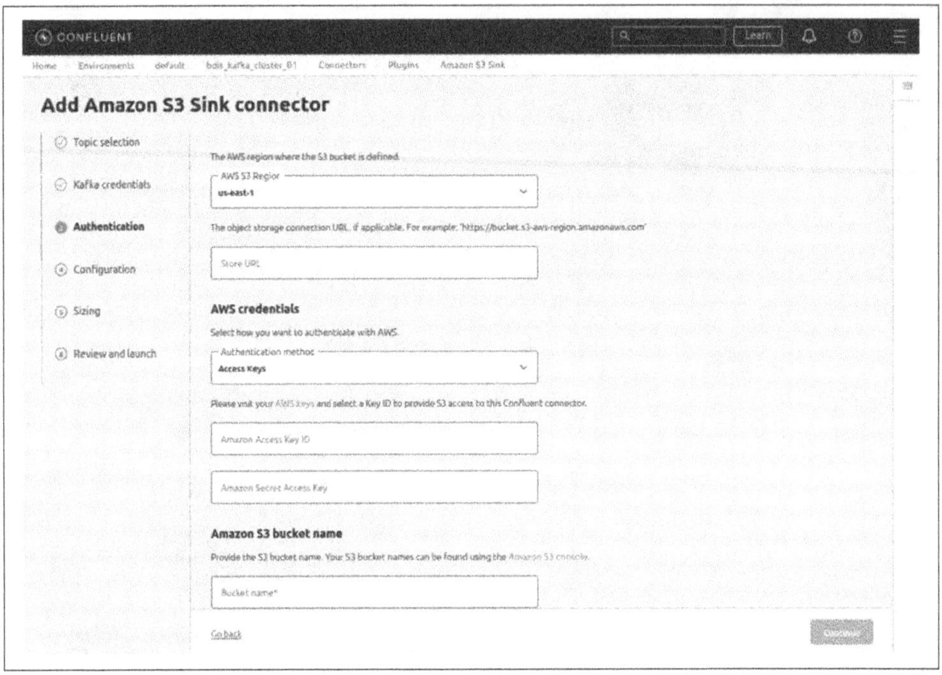

Figure 11-28. Amazon S3 sink connector authentication

Select BYTES for both the "Input Kafka record value format" as well as the "Output message format." Change the "Time interval" to HOURLY, and verify the "Flush size" is 1000. Then click Continue, as shown in Figure 11-29.

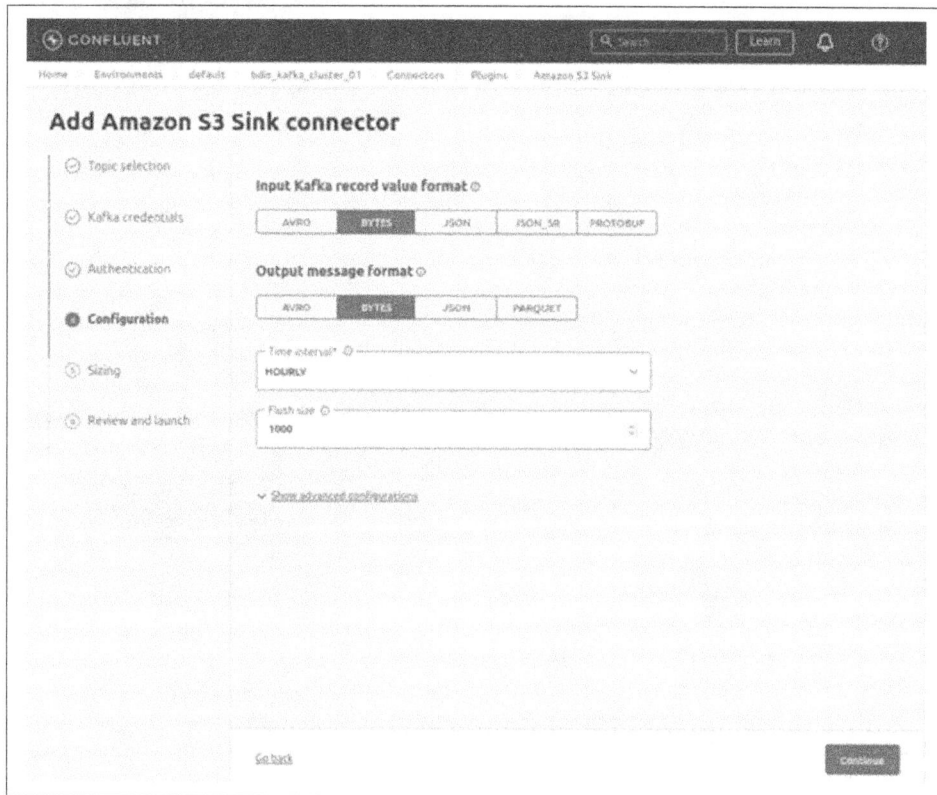

Figure 11-29. Amazon S3 sink connector configuration

On the next screen, you should see something similar to what is shown in Figure 11-30. Verify the Tasks value is 1 and click Continue.

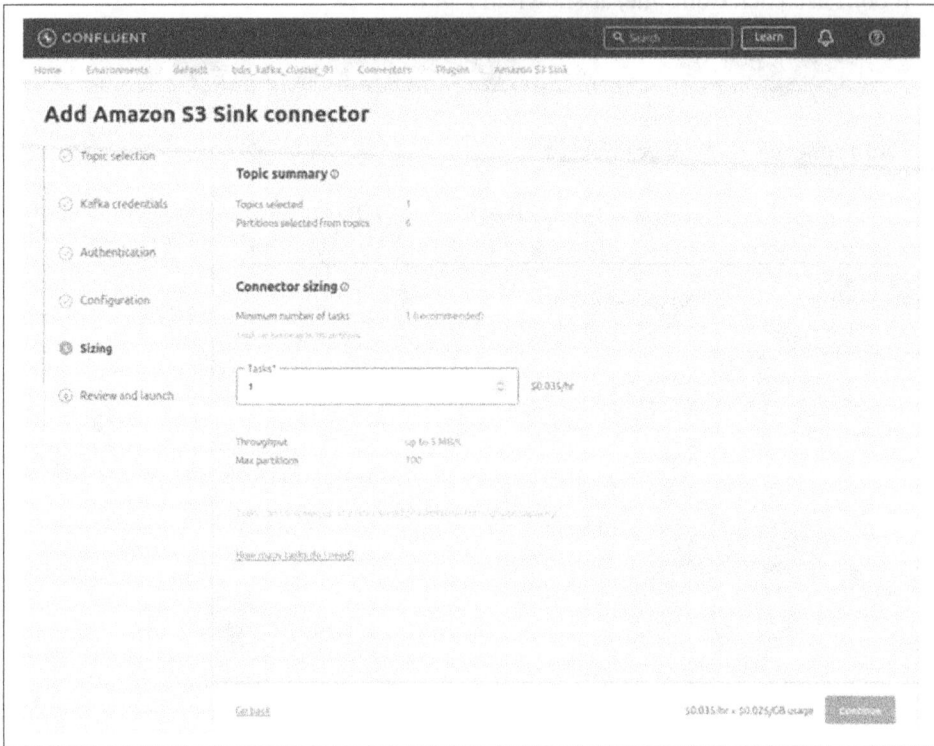

Figure 11-30. Amazon S3 sink connector sizing

MongoDB. n.d. "$group (Aggregation Stage)." MongoDB Database Manual, MongoDB, Inc. Accessed February 2025. *https://www.mongodb.com/docs/manual/reference/operator/aggregation/group.*

MongoDB. n.d. "What Is NoSQL?" MongoDB, Inc. Accessed May 2024. *https://www.mongodb.com/resources/basics/databases/nosql-explained.*

MuleSoft. n.d. MuleSoft from Salesforce (website). Salesforce, Inc. Accessed September 2024. *https://www.mulesoft.com.*

NASA. n.d. GCN Kafka Client for Python. NASA General Coordinates Network GitHub repository. Last modified August 2025. *https://github.com/nasa-gcn/gcn-kafka-python.*

NASA. n.d. NASA General Coordinates Network (website). NASA. Accessed March 2025. *https://gcn.nasa.gov.*

National Security Agency/Central Security Service. 2021. "NSA Releases NiagaraFiles to Open Source Software." National Security Agency/Central Security Service. August 11. Accessed November 2024. *https://www.nsa.gov/Research/Technology-Transfer-Program/Success-Stories/Article/3306190/nsa-releases-niagarafiles-to-open-source-software.*

Neo4j. n.d. Neo4j Graph Database & Analytics (website). Neo4j, Inc. Accessed October 2024. *https://neo4j.com.*

Office of the National Coordinator for Health Information Technology (ONC). 2017. "Benefits of EHRs." Office of the National Coordinator for Health Information Technology (ONC). October 5. Accessed May 2024. *https://www.healthit.gov/topic/health-it-and-health-information-exchange-basics/benefits-ehrs.*

Olesen-Bagneux, Ole. 2023. *The Enterprise Data Catalog.* Sebastopol: O'Reilly.

OpenEI. n.d. Open Energy Data Initiative (OEDI) (website). Accessed February 2024. *https://data.openei.org/submissions/all.*

Oracle. 2022. "FAQs for Autonomous Database." Oracle. Last modified June 10, 2022. Accessed June 2024. *https://www.oracle.com/database/technologies/datawarehouse-bigdata/adb-faqs.html.*

Oracle. 2016. "Oracle GoldenGate Studio 12.2.1.3 Data Sheet." Accessed January 2025. *https://www.oracle.com/technetwork/middleware/goldengate/overview/ds-oraclegoldengatestudio-12211-3073782.pdf.*

Oracle. 2022. "US DoD Accredits Oracle Cloud Infrastructure (OCI) for Top Secret Missions." Februrary 15. Accessed January 2025. *https://www.oracle.com/news/announcement/dod-accredits-oracle-cloud-infrastructure-for-top-secret-missions-2022-02-15.*

Oracle. 2024. "What Is ERP?" Oracle. Accessed May 2024. *https://oracle.com/erp/what-is-erp.*

PAT Research. n.d. "IBM InfoSphere DataStage in 2024." Predictive Analytics Today. Accessed December 2024. *https://www.predictiveanalyticstoday.com/ibm-infosphere-datastage.*

PAT Research. n.d. "Top 13 NewSQL Databases." Predictive Analytics Today. Accessed September 2024. *https://www.predictiveanalyticstoday.com/newsql-databases.*

Penchikala, Srini. 2015. "Fabian Hueske on Apache Flink Framework." *InfoQ.* April 28. Accessed November 2024. *https://www.infoq.com/news/2015/04/hueske-apache-flink.*

Pinecone. n.d. "Hierarchical Navigable Small Worlds (HNSW)." Pinecone Systems, Inc. Accessed July 2024. *https://www.pinecone.io/learn/series/faiss/hnsw.*

Pinecone. 2021. "The Rise of Vector Data." Posted July 8, 2021, by Pinecone. YouTube, 23:49. Accessed September 2024. *https://oreil.ly/WZDfa.*

PostgreSQL.org. n.d. *PSQLODBC Download.* PostgreSQL Global Development Group. Accessed February 2024. *https://www.postgresql.org/ftp/odbc.*

Poudel, Pralabh. n.d. Kaggle World Energy Consumption Dataset. Accessed February 2024. *https://www.kaggle.com/datasets/pralabhpoudel/world-energy-consumption.*

Prayasgupta. 2023. "MultiHop Architecture in Azure Databricks." *Medium.* July 3. Accessed September 2024. *https://medium.com/@prayasgupta13/multihop-architecture-in-azure-databricks-1f9e78bbc872.*

Precedence Research. n.d. Data Integration Market (website). Precedence Research Pvt. Ltd. Accessed May 2024. *https://www.precedenceresearch.com/data-integration-market.*

Qdrant. n.d. Qdrant (website). Qdrant. Accessed October 2024. *https://qdrant.tech.*

Qlik. n.d. Data Integration (website). QlikTech International AB. Accessed May 2024. *https://www.qlik.com/us/data-integration.*

Qlik. n.d. Database Replication (website). QlikTech International AB. Accessed May 2024. *https://www.qlik.com/us/data-replication/database-replication.*

Qlik. n.d. "From QlikView to Qlik Analytics." QlikTech International AB. Accessed November 2024. *https://www.qlik.com/us/products/qlikview.*

Qlik. n.d. "PostgreSQL Source Data Types." QlikTech International AB. Accessed May 2025. *https://help.qlik.com/en-US/replicate/November2021/Content/Replicate/Main/PostgreSQL/postgresql_data_types_source.htm.*

Qlik. 2020. "Qlik Compose for Data Warehouses." Posted December 4, 2020, by Qlik Public Sector. YouTube, 5:06. Accessed January 2025. *https://oreil.ly/7pVys.*

Qlik. n.d. "Qlik Software Requirements." QlikTech International AB. Accessed February 2024. *https://help.qlik.com/en-US/enterprise-manager/May2023/Content/EnterpriseManager/Main/Installation/Software_Requirements.htm.*

Qlik. n.d. "What Is a Data Pipeline? Definition, Types, and Use Cases." QlikTech International AB. Accessed February 2024. *https://www.qlik.com/us/data-integration/data-pipeline.*

Quantexa. 2024. Data Integration Guide (website). Quantexa. Accessed May 2024. *https://www.quantexa.com/resources/data-integration-guide.*

Reis, Joe, and Matt Housley. 2022. *Fundamentals of Data Engineering.* Sebastopol: O'Reilly.

Riak. n.d. "Enterprise NoSQL Database." Riak. Accessed October 2024. *https://riak.com.*

SAP Community Member. 2020. "How to Define Integration Strategy for Your Projects?" Technology Blog Posts by SAP. June 4. Accessed April 2024. *https://oreil.ly/Im2nM.*

Segner, Michael. 2023. "Data Fabric: The Future of Data Architecture." Monte Carlo. Last updated February 21, 2023. Accessed May 2024. *https://montecarlodata.com/blog-data-fabric-the-future-of-data-architecture.*

Sekiyama, Noritaka, Bo Li, Matt Su, Mohit Saxena, Savio Dsouza, Vishal Kajjam, and XiaoRun Yu. 2024. "Introducing Amazon Q Data Integration in AWS Glue." Amazon Web Services, Inc. April 30. Accessed February 2025. *https://aws.amazon.com/blogs/big-data/introducing-amazon-q-data-integration-in-aws-glue.*

SelectHub. 2025. "Oracle Data Integrator Reviews 2025." SelectHub. Accessed January 2025. *https://www.selecthub.com/p/etl-tools/oracle-data-integrator.*

Simsion, Graeme C., and Graham C. Witt. 2005. *Data Modeling Essentials.* 3rd ed. San Francisco: Morgan Kaufmann.

Snowflake. n.d. "Snowpipe." Snowflake, Inc. Accessed October 2024. *https://docs.snowflake.com/en/user-guide/data-load-snowpipe-intro.*

SoftwareAdvice. n.d. "PowerCenter." SoftwareAdvice. Accessed January 2025. *https://www.softwareadvice.de/software/76545/powercenter.*

Stackscale. 2023. "3 Types of Storage: File, Block and Object." Stackscale B.V. June 22. Accessed August 2024. *https://www.stackscale.com/blog/types-of-storage.*

Stitch. n.d. "An Executive's Guide to the Data Integration Process." Talend, Inc. Accessed May 2024. *https://www.stitchdata.com/resources/data-integration-executive-guide.*

Stobierski, Tim. 2021. "8 Steps in the Data Life Cycle." Harvard Business School Online. February 2. Accessed May 2024. *https://online.hbs.edu/blog/post/data-life-cycle.*

StreamSets. n.d. "IBM StreamSets." StreamSets. Accessed May 2024. *https://www.ibm.com/products/streamsets*.

Striim. n.d. "Real-Time Data Integration and Streaming Platform." Striim. Accessed November 2024. *https://www.striim.com*.

Talend. 2016. "Talend Job Design Patterns and Best Practices: Part 4." Talend, Inc. Accessed May 2025. *https://www.talend.com/resources/talend-job-design-patterns-and-best-practices-part-4*.

Talend. n.d. "What Is Reverse ETL? Meaning and Use Cases." Talend, Inc. Accessed May 2024. *https://www.talend.com/resources/reverse-etl*.

Thilakshan, Nipun. 2023. "Data Integration Principles." *Medium.* September 15. Accessed May 2024. *https://medium.com/sysco-labs/data-integration-principles-b13160872507*.

TIBCO. n.d. "What Is a Data Federation?" Cloud Software Group, Inc. Accessed May 2024. *https://www.tibco.com/glossary/what-is-a-data-federation*.

Urquhart, James. 2021. *Flow Architectures.* Sebastopol: O'Reilly.

US Analytics. n.d. "Financial Report Logs Reporting: User Guide for Oracle Data Integrator." US Analytics. Accessed January 2025. *https://www.us-analytics.com/guide-financial-report-logs-reporting-oracle-data-integrator*.

US Department of Defense. 2020. "Executive Summary: DoD Data Strategy." Defense Media Activity. September 30. Accessed May 2024. *https://media.defense.gov/2020/Oct/08/2002514180/-1/-1/0/DOD-DATA-STRATEGY.PDF*.

US Department of Homeland Security. 2018. "Privacy Impact Assessment for the Traveler Verification Service." November 14. Accessed May 2024. *https://www.dhs.gov/sites/default/files/publications/privacy-pia-cbp056-tvs-february2021.pdf*.

US Department of Veterans Affairs. 2024. "VA Technical Reference Model v 25.9: Apache Spark." US Department of Veterans Affairs. October 29. Accessed November 2024. *https://www.oit.va.gov/Services/TRM/ToolPage.aspx?tid=10273*.

US Department of Veterans Affairs. 2024. "VA Technical Reference Model v 25.9: Azure Data Factory (ADF)." US Department of Veterans Affairs. May 6. Accessed January 2025. *https://www.oit.va.gov/Services/TRM/ToolPage.aspx?tid=15933%5E*.

US Internal Revenue Service. 2024. "Internal Revenue Service Data Book, 2024." Accessed October 2025. *https://www.irs.gov/pub/irs-pdf/p55b.pdf*.

VeloDB. n.d. VeloDB (website). VeloDB. Accessed October 2024. *https://www.velodb.io*.

W3Techs. n.d. "Usage of Character Encodings Broken Down by Ranking." Q-Success. Accessed May 2024. *https://w3techs.com/technologies/cross/character_encoding/ranking*.

Warchol, Katarzyna. 2024. "Qlik + Talend—the Future of Data Integration." Inetum Polska. March 14. Accessed November 2024. *https://www.nearshore-it.eu/articles/qlik-talend-the-future-of-data.*

Weaviate. n.d. The AI-Native Database (website). Weaviate, B.V. Accessed October 2024. *https://weaviate.io.*

Wickramasinghe, Shanika. 2023. "Canonical Data Models (CDMs) Explained." February 28. Accessed May 2024. *https://www.splunk.com/en_us/blog/learn/cdm-canonical-data-model.html.*

Zanini, Antonello. 2023. "ER Model, ER Diagram, and Relational Schema: What's the Difference?" DbVisualizer. April 19. Accessed May 2024. *https://www.dbvis.com/thetable/er-diagrams-vs-er-models-vs-relational-schemas.*

Key Terms Glossary

application programming interface

An application programming interface (API) is a set of defined rules and protocols that explain how applications communicate and interact with one another.

arity

The arity of a relation or function indicates how many arguments it requires; e.g., the function f(x, y) = x + y has an arity of 2, which includes x and y.

artificial intelligence

Artificial intelligence (AI) is a wide-ranging branch of computer science concerned with building smart machines capable of performing tasks commonly associated with intelligent beings.

asset

An asset is an economic resource that can be owned or controlled and that holds or produces value.

automation

Automation is any hands-off approach that allows a practitioner to process different types of data.

batch processing

Batch processing involves performing high-volume data tasks that often run without manual intervention. Batch processes are typically scheduled to run as resources permit and are ideal for tasks that are not time sensitive.

big data

Big data is an umbrella term for datasets that cannot easily be handled by traditional computers or tools due to their volume, velocity, or variety.

change data capture

Change data capture (CDC) refers to the tracking of all changes in a data source (a database, a data warehouse, etc.) so they can be captured in destination systems.

cluster computing

Cluster computing, or clustered computing, is the practice of pooling the resources of multiple machines and managing their collective capabilities to complete tasks. Computer clusters require a cluster management layer, which handles communication between the individual nodes and coordinates resources.

content management

Content management is the process of managing data typically stored in unstructured data formats, such as multimedia files.

CSV

A comma-separated values (CSV) file is a delimited text file in which information is typically separated by commas; however, other delimiters are possible, such as semicolons and tab spacing.

data

Data is the raw material of information. Information is a form of data.

data aggregation

Data aggregation is the process of collecting, consolidating, and summarizing datasets from multiple sources. Aggregation typically includes operations such as sums, grouping, and counting.

data analysis

Data analysis is the systematic process of inspecting data and creating models to uncover useful information, draw conclusions, and support decision making.

data analytics

Data analytics is the science of analyzing raw data to develop conclusions; it is one of the three major constituents of data life cycle management.

data architecture

Data architecture is the high-level design and structure of an organization's data assets, data management resources, and data-related policies. It provides a blueprint for how data is collected, stored, integrated, accessed, and governed across systems and processes.

data artifacts

Data artifacts are the tangible outputs or deliverables produced at various stages of the data life cycle. These artifacts document, represent, or facilitate the understanding, movement, processing, and governance of data within a system or organization.

data augmentation

Data augmentation is any technique that artificially increases the amount of model training data without collecting new data.

data capture

Data capture is the process of collecting information and then converting it into data that can be read by a computer.

data catalog

A data catalog is a neatly detailed inventory of all data assets in an organization. It uses metadata to quickly find, access, and evaluate the most appropriate data for organizational purposes.

datacenter (data center)

A datacenter is a large group of networked computer servers typically used by organizations to centralize their shared IT operations.

data cleanroom

A data cleanroom is a secure, protected environment where personally identifiable information (PII) is anonymized, processed, and stored to give teams a secure place to bring data together for joint analysis based on defined guidelines and restrictions.

data cleansing

Data cleansing is the process of preparing data for analysis by amending or removing incorrect, corrupted, improperly formatted, duplicated, irrelevant, or incomplete data within a dataset.

data collaboration

Data collaboration is the coordinated sharing, integration, and use of data among individuals, teams, or organizations to achieve common goals, insights, or outcomes.

data collection

Data collection is the systematic process of gathering data from various sources ultimately to address specific objectives, answer questions, or support decision making.

data contract

A data contract is typically a document that defines the structure, format, semantics, quality, and terms of use for exchanging data between a data provider and its consumers. Data contracts are a communication tool to express a common understanding of how data should be structured and interpreted.

data definition language

Data definition language (DDL) is a subset of SQL. It is a language for describing data and its relationships in a database.

data democratization

Data democratization is the process of making data accessible, understandable, and usable to a wide range of stakeholders, regardless of their technical background.

data engineering

Data engineering refers to managing the source, structure, quality, storage, and accessibility of the data so that it can be queried and analyzed by analysts. Data engineers focus on the infrastructure and architecture to collect, store, and prepare data.

data enrichment

Data enrichment is the process of enhancing, appending, refining, and improving collected data with metadata or relevant third-party data.

data exchange

Data exchange is the process of taking data from one file or database format and transforming it to suit a target schema.

data extensibility

Data extensibility is the capacity to extend and enhance an application with data from external sources such as other applications, databases, and one-off datasets.

data extraction

Data extraction is the process of collecting or retrieving data from a variety of sources for further data processing, storage, or analysis elsewhere.

data fabric

A data fabric is a single environment consisting of a unified architecture with services or technologies running on that architecture to enable frictionless access and sharing of data in a distributed data environment. It is an agile data environment that can track, analyze, and govern data across applications, environments, and users.

data governance

Data governance is the framework of policies, processes, standards, roles, and technologies that ensure the effective and responsible management of an organization's data assets throughout their life cycle. It establishes authority and control over data to ensure quality, security, compliance, and ethical use.

data health

Data health is the state of an organization's data and its ability to support effective organizational objectives.

data hygiene

Data hygiene refers to the processes employed to ensure data is up-to-date, conditioned, and ready to use.

data import

Data import is the process of moving data from external sources into another application or database.

data ingestion

Data ingestion is the process of importing data and often includes transporting data from one or more sources into a centralized database where it can then be accessed and analyzed. This can be done either in a near-real-time stream or in batches.

data integration

Data integration is the process of unifying and organizing data and data infrastructure to provide complete, accurate, and up-to-date information that helps guide organizational decisions.

data integrity

Data integrity is the overall accuracy, consistency, and trustworthiness of data throughout its life cycle.

data intelligence

Data intelligence is the process of analyzing various forms of data to improve an organization's services or investments.

data interoperability

Data interoperability is the ability of different information technology systems and software applications to create, exchange, and consume data in order to use the information that has been exchanged.

data joins

Data joins involve combining multiple data tables based on a common field, or key, between them. There are, generally, six types of joins: inner, left inner, left outer, right inner, right outer, and outer.

data lake

A data lake is a large reservoir or central repository that can store large amounts of raw data in its native format. The term *data lake* is frequently used to refer to the data collected in a big-data system that may be unstructured and that frequently changes.

data lakehouse

A data lakehouse is a data architecture that combines the low-cost storage and flexibility of a data lake with the data management and performance features of a data warehouse in a single platform.

data lineage

Data lineage is the process of understanding, recording, and auditing data as it flows from origin to destination.

data loading

Data loading is the process of transferring data from a source system into a target system, such as a database, data warehouse, or data lake, for storage and analysis.

data management

Data management is the overarching practice of collecting, organizing, protecting, and storing data and involves a broad range of tasks, policies, procedures, and practices.

data manipulation

Data manipulation is the process of adding structure to data or organizing data to make it easier to process.

data manipulation language (DML)

Data manipulation language (DML) represents a collection of programming languages explicitly used to make changes to the database, such as CRUD operations to create, read, update, and delete data.

data mapping

Data mapping is the process of matching data fields from one or multiple source files to a data field in another source.

data marts

Data marts provide data prepared for analysis that is often a subset of warehouse data designed to support particular kinds of analysis or a specific group of data consumers.

data masking

Data masking is a security technique in which a dataset is copied but with sensitive data obfuscated.

data mesh

A data mesh is a highly decentralized data architecture that ensures data is highly available, easily discoverable, secure, and interoperable with the applications that need access to it.

data migration

Data migration is the process of transferring data between different types of file formats, databases, or storage systems.

data mining

Data mining is a broad term for the practice of finding patterns in large sets of data. It is the process of trying to refine a mass of data into a more understandable and cohesive set of information.

data modeling

Data modeling refers to designing, structuring, and representing data within a specific context and specific systems.

data munging

Data munging refers to the preparation process for transforming data and cleansing large datasets prior to analysis.

data onboarding

Data onboarding is the process of bringing conditioned external data into applications and operational systems.

data orchestration

Data orchestration is the automated coordination and management of data movement, transformation, and integration across systems to ensure timely, reliable, and efficient data workflows.

data pipeline

A data pipeline is the series of steps required to perform an action with data, such as moving data from one system (source) to another (destination).

data portability

Data portability is the ability to move data among different applications, programs, computing environments, or cloud services.

data privacy

Data privacy is a branch of data security concerned with the proper handling of data, including consent, notice, and regulatory obligations. It relates to how data should be handled with a focus on compliance with data protection regulations.

data product

A data product is a tool, application, or curated dataset that facilitates an end goal and that typically meets certain governance and quality standards.

data quality

Data quality is a measure of how reliable a dataset is to serve the specific needs of an organization based on factors such as accuracy, completeness, consistency, reliability, and whether it's up-to-date. Data quality is an aspect of a dataset that conveys whether it is fit for its intended uses.

data quality management

Data quality management includes all activities related to managing the quality of data to ensure the data can be used effectively.

data replication

Data replication is the process of storing data in more than one location to improve data availability, reliability, redundancy, and accessibility.

data science

Data science is a multidisciplinary approach to extracting actionable insights from typically large volumes of organizational data. Data science is essentially the union of computer science, applied math and statistics, and domain expertise.

data scientist

A data scientist is a professional who uses technology for collecting, analyzing, and interpreting large amounts of data.

data scrubbing

Data scrubbing is the procedure of modifying or removing data from a database because the data is incomplete, incorrect, inaccurately formatted, repeated, or outdated.

data security

Data security is the practice of protecting data from unauthorized access, theft, or data corruption throughout its entire life cycle. These activities include prevention, auditing, and escalation-mitigating actions.

data silo

A data silo is a collection of information in one part of an organization not easily accessible by other parts of the organization.

data stack

A data stack is a suite of tools used for data loading, data transformation, data analysis, and business intelligence.

data storage

Data storage allows information to be compiled and made accessible to users.

data transfer

Data transfer is the sharing of data between systems or organizations.

data transformation

Data transformation is the process of converting the format, structure, or values of data, often from the format of a source system, into the required format of a destination system.

data upload

Data upload is the transmission of a file from one computer system to another.

data validation

Data validation is the process of ensuring the accuracy and quality of data against defined rules before using, importing, or otherwise processing the data.

data virtualization

Data virtualization is the process of aggregating data across disparate systems to develop a single, logical, and virtual view of information so that it can be accessed by users in near real time.

data warehouse

A data warehouse is a large, structured repository of data that can be used for analysis and reporting. In contrast to a data lake, a data warehouse is composed of data that has been cleaned and integrated with other sources and is generally well ordered.

data workflows

Data workflows are sequences of tasks that must be completed and decisions that must be made to process a set of data.

data wrangling

Data wrangling is the process of restructuring, cleaning, and enriching raw data into a desired format for easy access and analysis.

database

A database is an organized collection of structured data stored electronically in a computer system so that it can be easily accessed, managed, and updated.

database management

Database management involves maintaining databases in support of high-volume, complex-data transactions for specific services or groups of services.

database schema

A database schema is the collection of metadata that describes the relationships between objects and information in a database. In some contexts, it's equated with the term *database*.

data-driven

Being data-driven means not making decisions based on gut feelings or instincts and instead using analytics to gain actionable insight from available data.

dataflow (data flow)

A dataflow (or data flow) represents the path data moves from one part of an information system to another.

DataOps

DataOps is the practice of operationalizing data management used by data teams for developing, improving the quality of, and reducing the cycle time of data analytics.

dataset (data set)

A dataset (or data set) is a collection of individual but related items that can be accessed and processed individually or as a unit.

denormalization

Denormalization is a database optimization technique in which redundant data is added to one or more tables. This can help avoid costly joins in a relational database and is typically performed after normalization.

dummy data

Dummy data is mock data used in a testing environment. Dummy data will have similar content and layout as a real dataset.

eXtensible Markup Language

eXtensible Markup Language (XML) is a simple and flexible markup language designed to store and transport data.

Extensible Stylesheet Language

Extensible Stylesheet Language (ESL) is a language for expressing stylesheets. It is used for transforming and presenting XML documents.

extract, load, transform

Extract, load, transform (ELT) is where data is extracted from a source and loaded into a data store directly without any transformations. Instead of transforming the data before it's written, ELT takes advantage of the target system to do the data transformation.

extract, transform, load

Extract, transform, load (ETL) consists of collecting and processing data from various sources into a single data store so it is easier to analyze. ETL refers to the process of taking raw data and preparing it for a system's use. ETL is traditionally a process associated with data warehouses, but characteristics of this process are also found in the ingestion pipelines of big-data systems.

federated query capability

Federated query capability is the ability to run a single query across multiple disparate data sources and return unified results without moving or duplicating the data.

file transfer protocol

File transfer protocol (FTP) is a standard communication protocol that governs how computers transfer files between systems over the internet.

full load

Full load entails defining all files or tables on the target endpoint, automatically defining the metadata that is required at the target, and populating the tables with data from the source.

graph database

A graph database is a systematic NoSQL collection of data that emphasizes the relationships between the different data entities. It uses mathematical graph theory to show data connections and stores nodes and relationships instead of tables or documents.

information

Information is data in context. Data is a form of information.

in-memory computing

In-memory computing involves moving the working datasets entirely within a cluster's collective memory. Intermediate calculations are not written to disk but are instead held in memory.

JavaScript Object Notation

JavaScript Object Notation (JSON) is a text-based, human-readable data interchange format for storing and transporting data.

machine learning

Machine learning is the study and practice of designing systems that can learn, adjust, and improve based on the data fed to them. This typically involves implementation of predictive and statistical algorithms that can continually zero in on "correct" behavior and insights as more data flows through the system.

MapReduce

MapReduce is a big-data algorithm (and also a Hadoop computation engine) for scheduling work on a computing cluster. The process involves splitting up the problem set, mapping it to different nodes and computing over them to produce intermediate results, shuffling the results to align sets, and then reducing the results by outputting values for each set.

master data management

Master data management (MDM) refers to managing critical data to make sure the data is accessible, accurate, secure, transparent, and trustworthy. It includes the technology, tools, and processes to ensure an organization's data is consistent, uniform, and accurate.

metadata

Metadata is data that describes and provides information about other data.

metadata management

Metadata management involves managing all data that classifies and describes the data. Metadata can be used to make the data understandable, ready for integration, and secure and can ensure the quality of data.

microservice

A microservice is a (relatively) independent service within an application that maps to a single domain, such as order management or customer relationship management.

monolithic architecture

A monolithic architecture refers to a software design in which all components—such as user interface, business logic, and data access—are built as a single, tightly integrated unit. Changes in one part often require rebuilding and redeploying the entire application.

MySQL

Pronounced "My S-Q-L" or "My Sequel," MySQL is an open source relational database management system (RDBMS) that is backed by Oracle. MySQL is named after the daughter of one of the platform's originators.

no-code ETL

No-code ETL is an ETL process performed using software that has automation features and a user-friendly interface with various functionalities that allow the user to create and manage the different dataflows.

NoSQL

NoSQL is a broad term referring to any non-relational database that stores and retrieves data without first needing to define its structure. It is often used as a catchall term for any database model outside of the traditional relational model.

online analytical processing

Online analytical processing (OLAP) is a category of software tools that enables fast, multidimensional analysis of large volumes of data for decision support, reporting, and business intelligence.

operational data mart

An operational data mart (OpDM) is designed to support short-term, tactical decision making. Unlike traditional data marts that pull information from a data warehouse, an OpDM is populated directly from an operational data store, and like that store, it holds up-to-date or near-real-time information. However, the data it contains is usually more volatile and subject to frequent change.

operational data store

An operational data store (ODS) is a central database that provides a snapshot of the latest data from multiple transactional systems for operational reporting.

PostgreSQL

PostgreSQL is a free and open source relational database management system emphasizing extensibility and SQL compliance. It's the fourth most popular database in the world.

program synthesis

Program synthesis is the automated task of constructing a program that provably satisfies a given high-level formal specification.

pushdown

Pushdown is the practice of delegating data processing operations (such as filtering, aggregation, or joins) from an integration or query tool to the underlying database or source system, so the computation occurs closer to the data and reduces data movement.

raw data

Raw data is any set of data that has not been processed, cleaned, or analyzed.

relational database

A relational database (RDB) is a type of database in which data is stored in the form of tables and the tables are connected based on defined relationships.

representational state transfer

Representational state transfer (REST) is an architectural style for designing networked applications and provides a convenient and consistent approach to requesting and modifying data.

stream processing

Stream processing is any technique of ingesting data in which information is analyzed, transformed, and organized as it's generated.

streaming data

Streaming data is the continuous flow of data generated by various sources to a destination to be processed and analyzed in near real time.

structured data

Structured data is data that has been organized and predefined into a formatted repository before being placed in data storage.

tab-separated values

Tab-separated values (TSV) files are used for raw data and commonly used by spreadsheet applications to exchange data between databases.

third-party data

Third-party data is any information collected by a company that does not have a direct relationship with the user on which the data is being collected.

unstructured data

Unstructured data is any data—often large collections of files—that is not formatted in a predetermined data model or schema.

usable data

Usable data is data that is understood and can be employed without additional information.

value

Value is the difference between the cost of a thing and the benefit derived from that thing.

webhook

A webhook is a way for applications and services to submit a web-based notification to other applications that are triggered by specific events. A webhook is also called a web callback or HTTP API.

Acronyms Glossary

3DM
data-driven decision making

3NF
third normal form

AAMM
advanced analytics maturity modeling

ACID
atomicity, consistency, isolation, durability

ACL
access control list

ADC
analog-to-digital converter

ADF
Azure Data Factory

ADLS
Azure Data Lake Storage

ADT
automatic drum transcription

AE
Autoencoder

AGI
artificial general intelligence

AI
artificial intelligence

AIS
Application Interface Services or Azure Integration Services

AMI
Amazon Machine Image

AML
anti-money laundering

AMT
automatic music transcription

ANN
approximate nearest neighbor or artificial neural network

ANOVA
analysis of variance

AOAI
Azure OpenAI

AOF
Append-Only File

AOSD
aspect-oriented software development

API
application programming interface

APM
application performance monitoring

APS
analytics platform system

AQL
annotation query language

ARN
Amazon Resource Name

ARNN
anticipation recurrent neural network

AS
analysis service

ASE
Adaptive Server Enterprise

ASF
Apache Software Foundation

ASM
Automatic Storage Management

AUC
area under curve

AWS
Amazon Web Services

AZ
availability zone

BCAP
boundary cloud access points

BCR
binding corporate rules

BDA
big-data analytics

BDI
big-data integration

BDP
big-data platform

BGP
Border Gateway Protocol

BI
business intelligence

BiLSTM
bidirectional long short-term memory

BLOB
binary large object

BMF
business master file

BPD
business process diagram

BPTT
backpropagation through time

BQML
BigQuery Machine Learning

BRMS
Backup, Recovery, and Media Services

BRNN
bidirectional recurrent neural network

BSR
Buf Schema Registry

BYOD
bring your own device

CAD
computer-aided design

CART
classification and regression trees

cATO
Continuous Authority to Operate

CBOW
continuous bag-of-words

CCA
canonical correlational analysis

CCD
charge-coupled device

CCTV
closed-circuit television

CDBN
convolutional deep belief networks

CDC
change data capture

CDF
change data feed

CDI
customer data integration

CDM
canonical data model

CDN
content delivery network

CDP

continuous data protection or customer data platform

CDS

common data storage or correlated double sampling

CDW

Cloudera Data Warehouse

CEC

constant error carousel

CEP

complex event processing

CFN

CloudFormation

CFPB

Consumer Financial Protection Bureau

CFS

clustered filesystem

CFTC

Commodity Futures Trading Commission

CIA

confidentiality, integrity, availability

CIAM

customer identity and access management

CIDR

Classless Inter-Domain Routing

CIFS

common internet filesystem

CIPM

Certified Information Privacy Manager

CIPP

Certified Information Privacy Professional

CIPT

Certified Information Privacy Technologist

CLI

command-line interface

CLNN

conditionaL neural networks

CLV

customer lifetime value

CMK

Customer Master Key

CMP

Consent Management Platform

CNA

cloud native accelerator

CNN

convolutional neural network

CODASYL

Conference/Committee on Data Systems Languages

CoIP

Communications over Internet Protocol

COIT

consumerization of information technology

ConvNet

convolutional neural network

CORBA

Common Object Request Broker Architecture

CORS

cross-origin resource sharing

COTS

commodity off-the-shelf

CoW

copy on write

CPNI

customer proprietary network information

CPO

chief privacy officer

CQL

Cassandra Query Language or Contextual/Common Query Language or Cypher Query Language

CRBM

Conditional Restricted Boltzmann Machine

CRNN
convolutional recurrent neural network

CRR
cross-region replication

CSS
Cascading Style Sheets

CTL
continuous transformation and loading

CV
cross validation

CVE
Common Vulnerability and Exposure

DAA
Digital Advertising Alliance

DAD
Discover, Access, Distill

DAE
deep autoencoder or denoising autoencoder

DAG
directed acyclic graph

DAMA
Data Management Association

DAS
direct access storage

DASH
Dynamic Adaptive Streaming over HTTP

DAX
DynamoDB Accelerator

Db2
Database 2 (Microsoft)

DBFS
Databricks File System

DBM
Deep Boltzmann Machine

DBMS
database management system

DBN
deep belief network

DDIL
denied, degraded, intermittent, and limited or disrupted, disconnected, intermittent, and low-bandwidth

DDL
data definition language

DeconvNet
deconvolutional neural network

DFD
data flow diagram

DFS
Distributed File System

DGO
Data Governance Office

DHCP
Dynamic Host Configuration Protocol

DHS
Department of Homeland Security

DHSL
distributed Hadoop storage layer

DISN
Defense Information Systems Network

DL
deep learning

DLM
data life cycle management

DLP
data loss prevention

DLT
data load tool or Delta Live Tables

DMA
Data Migration Assistant

DML
data manipulation language

DMM
data maturity model

DMS
database migration service

DNN
deconvolutional neural network or deep neural network

DNS
Domain Name System

DOE
Department of Energy

DOL
Department of Labor

DOT
Department of Transportation

DP
data processing

DPA
data protection authority

DPH
data pipeline hub

DPIA
Data Protection Impact Assessment

DPL
data productivity language

DPO
data protection officer

DPU
data processing unit

DQA
Data Quality Act

DR
disaster recovery

DSAR
data subject access request

DSN
data source name or deep stacking network

DSP
demand-side platform

DSR
data subject request

DSS
data security standard

DTAP
develop, test, acceptance, production

DTD
document type definition

DV
data vault

DWT
discrete wavelet transform

DX
Direct Connect

EAI
enterprise application integration

EBS
Elastic Block Store

EC2
Elastic Compute Cloud

ECE
Elastic Cloud Enterprise

ECL
Enterprise Control Language

ECPA
Electronic Communications Privacy Act

ECS
Elastic Common Schema or Elastic Container Service

EDA
event-driven architecture or exploratory data analysis

EDH
enterprise data hub

EDI
electronic data interchange

EDP
enterprise data platform

EDPB
European Data Protection Board

EDPS
European Data Protection Supervisor

EDR
endpoint detection and response or enterprise data replication

EDW
enterprise data warehouse

EFS
Elastic File System

EHR
electronic health record

EI
enterprise integration

EII
enterprise information integration

EIP
enterprise integration pattern

ELC
enterprise life cycle

ELM
extreme learning machine

ELT
extract, load, transform

EMM
enterprise mobility management

EMR
Elastic MapReduce

EMS
enterprise messaging system

EOD
end of day

ePHI
electronic protected health information

EPM
enterprise process manager

EPN
event processing nodes

EQL
Event Query Language

ER
entity relationship

ERD
entity relationship diagram

ERP
enterprise resource planning

ESB
enterprise service bus

ESP
event stream processing

ETL
extract, transform, load

EULA
end-user license agreement

FACTA
Fair and Accurate Credit Transactions Act

FATCA
Foreign Account Tax Compliance Act

FC
fully connected

FCC
Federal Communications Commission

FCRA
Fair Credit Reporting Act

FDIC
Federal Deposit Insurance Corporation

FERPA
Family Educational Rights and Privacy Act

FI
financial institution

FIFO
First In, First Out

FinCEN
Financial Crimes Enforcement Network

FIP
Fair Information Practice or Fellow of Information Privacy

FIPP
Fair Information Privacy Practice

FIPS
Federal Information Processing Standards

FISA
Foreign Intelligence Surveillance Act

FOIA
Freedom of Information Act

FPCO
Family Policy Compliance Office

FTC
Federal Trade Commission

FUSE
Filesystem in Userspace

GAN
generative adversarial network

GAPP
Generally Accepted Privacy Principles

GBM
gradient boosting machine

GBRCN
gradient-boosting random convolutional network

GCP
Google Cloud Platform

GCS
Google Cloud Storage

GDPR
General Data Protection Regulation (European Union)

GEOFF
graph serialization format

GFNN
gradient frequency neural networks

GLBA
Gramm-Leach-Bliley Act

GLCM
gray level co-occurrence matrix

GLM
generalized linear model

GLRM
generalized low rank models

GPCLK
General Purpose CLocK

GPEN
Global Privacy Enforcement Network

GRU
gated recurrent unit

GSI
global secondary index

GUID
globally unique identifier

HAN
Hierarchical Attention Network

HAR
Hadoop Archive

HCD
Human-centered design

HCI
Hyperconverged infrastructure

HDF
Hierarchical Data Format

HDS
historical data store

HHDS
HipHop Dataset

HHS
Health and Human Services

HIMSS
Healthcare Information and Management Systems Society

HIPAA
Health Information Portability and Accountability Act

HITECH
Health Information Technology for Economic and Clinical Health

HL7
Health Level Seven

HLS
HTTP Live Streaming

HMM
Hidden Markov Model

HMS
Hive Metastore

HNSW
hierarchical navigable small world

HPCC
high-performance computing cluster

HPIL
Hadoop Physical Infrastructure Layer

HSDS
Highly Scalable Data Service

HSM
hardware security module

HTAP
hybrid transactional and analytical processing

HTML
Hypertext Markup Language

HTML5
the most current version of HTML

HTTP
Hypertext Transfer Protocol

HTTPS
Hypertext Transfer Protocol Secure

HUDI
Hadoop upserts, deletes, and incrementals

IAB
Interactive Advertising Bureau

IAM
identity and access management

IAP
internet access point

IAPP
International Association of Privacy Professionals

IBD
integrated business dataset

ICA
independent component analysis

ICDPPC
International Conference of Data Protection and Privacy Commissioners

ICS
intelligent cloud service

ICT
information and communication technology

IDA
initial data analysis

IDFA
identity for advertisers

IDL
Interface Definition Language

IDP
identity provider or intelligent document processing

IDRS
Integrated Data Retrieval System

IDS
Integrated Data Store

IFS
Integrated File System

IICS
Informatica Intelligent Cloud Services

ILM
index life cycle management

IMDB
in-memory database

IMF
Individual Master File

IMS
information management system

IOPS
input/output operations per second

IoT
Internet of Things

IP
Internet Protocol

IPC
inter-process communication

IRAP
Infosec Registered Assessors Program

IS
integration service

ISA
independent supervisory authority

iSCSI
Internet Small Computer Systems Interface

ISMS
information security management system

ISO
International Standards Organization

ISP
internet service provider

IVF
inverted file

IWE
intelligent word embedding

JAQL
JSON query language

JMS
Java Messaging Service or Java Messaging Standard

JSON
JavaScript Object Notation

KCL
Kinesis Client Library or Kinesis Consumer Library

KDF
Kinesis Data Firehose

KDG
Kinesis Data Generator

KDS
Kinesis Data Streams

KFS
Kosmos File System

KMS
key management service or knowledge management system

kNN
k-nearest neighbors

KPI
key performance indicator

KPL
Kinesis Producer Library

LAD
Local Access Database

LB
leader board

LDA
linear discriminant analysis

LLE
locally linear embedding

LOB
large object or line of business

LOOCV
leave-one-out cross-validation

LpO CV
leave-p-out cross-validation

LSA/LSI
latent semantic allocation/indexing

LSI
local secondary index

LSN
log sequence number

LSTM
long short-term memory

LV
logical volume

LVM
logical volume management

LZO
Lempel–Ziv–Oberhumer

MaaS
metal as a service

MAPE
mean absolute percentage error

MCLNN
masked conditional neural networks

MCMC
Markov Chain Monte Carlo

MDE
model-driven engineering

MDM
master data management or metadata management

mDNS
Multicast Domain Name System

MDS
multidimensional scaling

MER
music emotion recognition

MFA
multifactor authentication

MFT
master file transaction

MIS
management information system

ML
machine learning

MLM
music language models

MLP
multilayer perceptron

MOM
message-oriented middleware

MoR
merge on read

MOU
memorandum of understanding

MPI
Message Passing Interface

MPP
massively parallel processing

MQTT
Message Queue Telemetry Transport

MRS
music recommender system

MSDAE
modified sparse denoising autoencoder

MSE
mean squared error

MSK
Managed Streaming for Kafka

MSR
music style recognition

MUK
master user key

MVP
minimum viable product

NAI
Network Advertising Initiative

NAS
network attached storage

NAT
network address translation

NCC
network connectivity configuration

NER
named entity recognition

NFS
Network File System

NIAM
natural language information analysis method or Nijssen Information Analysis Method

NIH
National Institutes of Health

NIST
National Institute of Standards and Technology

NLDR
nonlinear dimensionality reduction

NLP
natural language processing

NMF
non-negative matrix factorization

NN
nearest neighbor or neural network

NNMODFF
neural network–based multi-onset detection function fusion

NRT
near real time

OBA
online behavioral advertising

OBT
one big table

OCI
Oracle Cloud Infrastructure

OCR
optical character recognition

ODBC
Open Database Connectivity

ODBMS
operational database management system

ODF
onset detection function

ODI
Oracle Data Integrator

ODS
operational data store

OEM
original equipment manufacturer

OI&T
Office of Information and Technology

OID
object identifier

OLAP
online analytical processing

OLTP
online transaction processing or online transactional processing

OMB
Office of Management and Budget

OODBMS
object-oriented database management system

OOF
out of fold

OOM
out of memory

OOV
out of vocabulary

OpDM
operational data mart

ORB
object request broker

ORDBMS
> object-relational database management system

ORM
> object-relational mapper or object-relational mapping

OSEM
> object/search engine mapping

OSHA
> Occupational Safety and Health Administration

OSS
> object storage service

OWB
> Oracle Warehouse Builder

PbD
> privacy by design

PCA
> principal component analysis

PCI
> Payment Card Industry

PDO
> pushdown optimization

PET
> privacy enhancing technology

PHI
> protected health information

PI
> personal information

PIA
> privacy impact assessment

PII
> personally identifiable information

PIM
> product information management

PITR
> point-in-time recovery

PKI
> public key infrastructure

pLSA
> probabilistic latent semantic allocation

PMML
> Predictive Model Markup Language

PNN
> probabilistic neural network

POC
> proof of concept

PReLU
> parametric rectified linear unit

PV
> physical volume

PVM
> parallel virtual machine

QA
> quality assurance

QSO
> qualified service organization

RAC
> Real Application Clusters

RAM
> Resource Access Manager

RANSAC
> RANdom SAmple Consensus

RBAC
> role-based access control

RBM
> Restricted Boltzmann Machine

RCF
> record columnar file

RCU
> read capacity unit

RDB
> Redis Database Backup or relational database

RDBMS

relational database management system

RDC

remote desktop connection

RDD

resilient distributed database or resilient distributed dataset

RDF

Resource Description Framework

RDS

Relational Database Service

ReLU

rectified linear unit

RF

random forest

RFE

recursive feature elimination

RFI

request for information

RFID

radio-frequency identification

RFP

request for proposal

RICNN

rotation invariant convolutional neural network

RMSLE

root mean squared logarithmic error

RNN

recurrent neural network

ROC

receiver operating characteristic

RPC

remote procedure call

RS

reporting service

RTO

recovery time objective

RTOS

real-time operating system

RTRL

real-time recurrent learning

RTSP

Real-Time Streaming Protocol

S3

Simple Storage Service

S4

Simple Scalable Streaming System

SaaS

software as a service

SAE

stacked autoencoder

SAM

Serverless Application Model

SAML

Security Assertion Markup Language

SAR

subject access request

SASL

Simple Authentication and Security Layer

SCA

Stored Communications Act

SCC

standard contractual clause

SCCA

Secure Cloud Computing Architecture

SCD

slowly changing dimension

SCRAM

Salted Challenge Response Authentication Mechanism

SCT

Schema Conversion Tool

SDA

software-defined architecture

SDAE
stacked denoising autoencoder

SDLC
software development life cycle or systems development life cycle

SDS
software-defined storage

SEC
Securities and Exchange Commission

SGD
stochastic gradient descent

SIEM
security information and event management

SLA
service-level agreement

SLO
service-level objective

SMB
Server Message Block

SMOTE
Synthetic Minority Over-Sampling Technique

SMT
single message transformation

SNA
shared-nothing architecture

SNS
Simple Notification Service

SOA
service-oriented architecture

SOR
system of record

SOX
Sarbanes-Oxley

SP
service provider

SPL
Streams Processing Language

SPOG
Single pane of glass

SQL
Structured Query Language

SQS
Simple Queue Service

SRR
Same Region Replication

SSADM
structured systems analysis and design method

SSAS
SQL Server Analysis Service

SSD
solid-state drive

SSDP
Simple Service Discovery Protocol

SSDT
SQL Server Data Tools

SSE
server-side encryption

SSL
Secure Sockets Layer

SSMS
SQL Server Management Studio

SSN
Social Security number

SSO
single sign-on

SSP
supply-side platform

STS
Security Token Service

SVD
singing voice detection

SVM
support vector machine

SVS
singing voice separation

TC
transaction code

TCF
Transparency and Consent Framework

TCP
Transmission Control Protocol

TCPA
Telephone Consumer Protection Act

TDA
topological data analysis

TDD
test-driven design

TDE
Transparent Data Encryption

TFA
two-factor authentication

tf-idf
term frequency-inverse document frequency

TLD
top-level domain

TLS
Transport Layer Security

TPS
transactions per second

t-SNE
t-distributed stochastic neighbor embedding

TTL
time to live

UAI
uniform access integration

UDAF
user-defined aggregate function

UDAP
unfair and deceptive acts and practices

UDP
User Datagram Protocol

UDTF
user-defined table-generating function

UIMA
Unstructured Information Management Architecture

UML
Unified Modeling Language

UP
unified platform

URL
uniform resource locator

USCDI
US Core Data for Interoperability

US-CERT
US Computer Emergency Readiness Team

UUID
universally unique identifier

V&V
verification and validation

VAD
voice activity detection

VAE
variational autoencoder

VAN
value-added network

VC
Vapnik-Chervonenkis

VG
volume group

VID
Version Identifier

VMS
video management system

VoIP
voice over IP

VPC
virtual private cloud

VPN
virtual private network

VPNN
vector product neural network

VSM
value stream management

W3C
World Wide Web Consortium

WAF
web application firewall

WAN
wide area network

WCU
write capacity unit

WLM
workload management

WORM
write once read many

WPE
weighted prediction error

XDR
eXternal Data Representation

XML
eXtensible Markup Language

YARN
Yet Another Resource Manager

ZFS
Zettabyte File System

ZTRA
Zero Trust Reference Architecture

Index

physical data integration models, 60
MongoDB, 95
MSSQL, 89-90
MuleSoft, 130
multicloud storage, 34
multimodel databases, 32
MySQL, 90

N

natural language processing (NLP), character
    encoding, 17
navigational metadata, 15
Neo4j, 97
network filesystems, remote-access storage, 23
New Technology File System (NTFS), 23
NiFi, 116-117
NLP (natural language processing), character
    encoding, 17
no-code platforms, compared to programming
    languages, 79-80
non-relational databases, 28
NoSQL, 27, 93-96
NTFS (New Technology File System), 23

O

object storage, 24
    compared to file and block storage, 25
    relational databases, 28
object storage services, 107-111
object-oriented databases, 31
ODI (Oracle Data Integrator), 131
on-premises infrastructure, advantages and
    challenges, 81-82
open source tools, 77-78
    advantages, 78
OpenTelemetry, gRPC protobuf, 21
operating system, example streaming solution,
    174
operational data, context, 22
operational metadata, 15
optimized row columnar (ORC) files, 21
Oracle Cloud Platform, 83
Oracle Data Integrator (ODI), 131
Oracle Database, 91
Oracle GoldenGate, 131
ORC (optimized row columnar) files, 21

P

packet flow, pipelines, 42
Parquet, 19
patterns, 66-72
PCI DSS (Payment Card Industry Data Security
    Standard), 85
Pentaho, 131
performance optimization, virtual storage, 26
personality conflicts, challenges caused by, 50
personnel, challenges caused by, 50-51
physical data integration models, 60
Pinecone, 100
pipelines, 42-44
platforms, compared to tools, 77
point-to-point architecture, 62
policies, challenges caused by, 49-50
PostgreSQL, 92
    example batch solution, database creation,
        211-217
PowerCenter, 129-130
Privacy Act of 1974, 85
project scoping, conceptual data integration
    models, 59
Protocol Buffers, 20-21
PuTTY Security Alert, 211
Python, example streaming solution
    client configuration, 185-189
    consumer code, 191-192
    environment, 179
    producer code, 189-191

Q

Qlik, 131-133
    Basic System hardware configuration, 141
Qlik Replicate
    downloading, 148-149
    endpoint connection setup, 152-156
    installation requirements, 148
    installing, 150
    registering, 150-152
    Windows Server EC2 Instance setup,
        141-147
Qlik Sense, 133
Qlik Stitch, 133
Qlik Talend, 132-133
quality assurance, 5

T

tax administration case study, 10
terminology, consistency considerations, 57-58
text analytics, character encoding, 17
thin provisioning, virtual storage, 26
throughput, data pipelines, 43
TIBCO BusinessWorks, 133
TIBCO Cloud Integration, 133
TigerGraph, 98
tools
    commercial, 77-78
        advantages, 78-79
    compared to platforms, 77
    open source, 77-78
        advantages, 78
    selection considerations, 77
topics (Confluent), creating (example streaming solution), 182-184
transactional CDC, 45
transactional data, context, 22
transformation
    compared to conditioning, 44
    rules, conceptual models, 59

U

Ubuntu
    example batch solution, AWS EC2 setup, 203-211

example streaming solution, 174
unethical behavior, challenges caused by, 51
uniform access data integration, 65
unstructured data, 14
US government, data centricity, 6
use cases
    Apache Kafka, 120
    Confluent, 120
    data integration, 8
    object storage, 24
UTF-8, character encoding, 16

V

vector databases, 31-32, 98-101
vector embeddings, 99
virtual storage, 26-27

W

Weaviate, 101
web service connectors, 35
web services, 7
wide-column data stores, 29
wide-column databases, 101-103
Windows Server EC2 Instance setup, 141-147
Windows, checking IPv6 status, 209
workflow design, conceptual models, 59
wrangling data, 67
    (see also data transformation)

About the Author

Jay Borthen is the head of data science and engineering at Swish Data. After graduate school, he migrated from engineering into data science–specific roles and has since worked with clients including the IRS, the FDA, the US Navy, the US Department of State, and a handful of commercial enterprises. Jay has almost 20 years of experience analyzing complex systems, leading tech teams, and leveraging technologies, such as AWS, Databricks, Kafka/Confluent, Qlik, and Snowflake. He has an undergraduate degree in engineering from Virginia Tech and a master's degree in mathematics and statistics from Georgetown University.

Colophon

The animal on the cover of *Building Data Integration Solutions* is a bohor reedbuck (*Redunca redunca*), a medium-sized antelope species native to sub-Saharan Africa and commonly found near water sources in moist grasslands, floodplains, and savannas. Its range extends from Senegal and Gambia in West Africa across to Ethiopia and down to northwestern Tanzania. The species requires tall grasses for cover and typically avoids forested or arid regions. Their dependence on water-rich habitats makes them indicators of healthy wetland ecosystems.

Bohor reedbucks have a distinctive appearance, with males displaying forward-curving, ridged horns that can reach up to 14 inches in length, while females lack horns. Both sexes have a yellowish-brown coat with a white underbelly and a characteristic white patch under the tail, often raised as a warning signal. Adults weigh between 88 and 154 pounds, with males generally larger than females. These antelopes are mainly grazers and feed on grasses, preferring tender, green shoots. Bohor reedbucks are typically solitary or form small family groups, although males may maintain territories and use scent-marking to deter rivals and attract females during mating season. The gestation period lasts 7–8 months, after which females give birth to a single calf.

Many of the animals on O'Reilly covers are endangered; all of them are important to the world.

The cover illustration is by José Marzan Jr., based on a black-and-white engraving from *Brehms Thierleben*. The series design is by Edie Freedman, Ellie Volckhausen, and Karen Montgomery. The cover fonts are Gilroy Semibold and Guardian Sans. The text font is Adobe Minion Pro; the heading font is Adobe Myriad Condensed; and the code font is Dalton Maag's Ubuntu Mono.

O'REILLY®

Learn from experts.
Become one yourself.

60,000+ titles | Live events with experts | Role-based courses
Interactive learning | Certification preparation

**Try the O'Reilly learning platform
free for 10 days.**

www.ingramcontent.com/pod-product-compliance
Lightning Source LLC
Chambersburg PA
CBHW061349210326
41598CB00035B/5928